OpenVMS

J. Ranade DEC Series

0-07-056402-7	Shah	*VAX C Programmer's Guide*
0-07-053675-5	Shah	*VAX/VMS: Concepts and Facilities*
0-07-056384-5	Shah	*VAXClusters: Architecture, Programming, and Management*
0-07-039822-4	Malamud	*The Book of DEC Networks and Architectures*
0-07-707220-0	Chernatony	*A User's Guide to the VAX/VMS Operating System*

OpenVMS

**Architecture, Use,
and Migration**

Raj Bhargava

McGraw-Hill, Inc.

New York   San Francisco   Washington, D.C.   Auckland   Bogotá
Caracas   Lisbon   London   Madrid   Mexico City   Milan
Montreal   New Delhi   San Juan   Singapore
Sydney   Tokyo   Toronto

Library of Congress Cataloging-in-Publication Data

Bhargava, Raj.
   OpenVMS : architecture, use, and migration / Raj Bhargava.
     p.   cm. — (J. Ranade DEC series)
   Includes bibliographical references and index.
   ISBN 0-07-005157-7
   1. Operating systems (Computers) 2. OpenVMS. I. Title.
  II. Series.
  QA76.76.063B48 1995
  005.4'469—dc20   94-41493
                                             CIP

1 2 3 4 5 6 7 8 9 0   DOC/DOC   9 0 9 8 7 6 5 4

ISBN 0-07-005157-7

The sponsoring editor for this book was Jerry Papke, the editing supervisor was Joseph Bertuna, and the production supervisor was Pamela Pelton. It was set in Century Schoolbook by North Market Street Graphics' composition unit.

Printed and bound by R. R. Donnelley & Sons Company.

McGraw-Hill books are available at special quantity discounts to use as premiums and sales promotions or for use in corporate training programs. For more information, please write to the Director of Special Sales, McGraw-Hill, Inc., 11 West 19th Street, New York, NY 10011; or contact your local bookstore.

To Vishnu

Contents

Preface   xiii

Part 1   OpenVMS Usage and Application Development

Chapter 1. OpenVMS Architectural Overview   3

    1.1   OpenVMS Organization   4
    1.2   Login Procedure   5
    1.3   User Accounts   6
    1.4   Virtual Address Space   7
          1.4.1   Hardware and Software Contexts   7
    1.5   Process Types   8
    1.6   Priorities   9
    1.7   Paging and Swapping   10

Chapter 2. Entry to OpenVMS   13

    2.1   Logging in   13
    2.2   OpenVMS Commands   15
    2.3   Some Frequently Used DCL Commands   17
    2.4   Error Messages   19
    2.5   Devices   20
    2.6   Other Information via SHOW Commands   22
    2.7   SET Command   23
    2.8   File Protection   24
    2.9   CREATE Command   24
    2.10 Command Line Editing   25
    2.11 Summary   28

Chapter 3. Extensible VAX Editor   29

    3.1   Introduction   29
    3.2   Buffer   33

3.3   Windows   36
         3.3.1   TWO WINDOWS Command   36
         3.3.2   Place Markers   37
         3.3.3   LEARN Command   37
3.4   Procedures   38
3.5   Help   39
3.6   Other Functions   41
3.7   Summary   43

Chapter 4. DCL Programming   45

4.1   Introduction   45
4.2   If-Then-Else Block Structures   48
4.3   Subroutines and Subprocedures   49
4.4   CASE-like Structures in DCL   49
4.5   Input/Output Using Files   51
         4.5.1   OPEN Command   53
         4.5.2   OPEN/READ Command   54
         4.5.3   OPEN/WRITE Command   54
         4.5.4   OPEN/APPEND Command   56
         4.5.5   Opening a File for Reading and Writing   56
         4.5.6   Sharing the File Input/Output   56
         4.5.7   READ Command   56
         4.5.8   WRITE Command   57
         4.5.9   Updating Records   58
         4.5.10 Creating a New Output File Upon Update   59
         4.5.11 Appending Records to a File   60
         4.5.12 Handling File I/O Errors   60
4.6   Error Handling   61
         4.6.1   ON Commands   61
4.7 $STATUS Global Symbol   62
4.8   Handling CTRL/Y Interrupts   63
4.9   Iterations and Recursions   64
4.10 Summary   65

Chapter 5. Logical Names and Lexical Functions   67

5.1   Logical Names   67
         5.1.1   Process Logical Name Table   67
         5.1.2   Job Logical Name Table   68
         5.1.3   Group Logical Name Table   68
         5.1.4   System Logical Name Table   68
         5.1.5   Using the Logical Name Tables   68
5.2   Lexical Functions   73
         5.2.1   Getting File and Directory Information   74
         5.2.2   Getting Information About a Process   74
         5.2.3   Getting the System Information Using Lexical Functions 75
         5.2.4   Lexical Functions for Manipulating Strings   76
5.3   Summary   77

Chapter 6. Application Development Using OpenVMS   79

6.1   Introduction   79
6.2   Compilation   80

6.3   Linking   83
6.4   RUN Command   88
6.5   System Services and Run-Time Libraries   90
6.6   Summary   92

Chapter 7. Command Definition Utility   93

7.1   Introduction   93
7.2   DEFINE VERB Command   94
7.3   DEFINE SYNTAX Clause   96
7.4   DISALLOW Clause   98
7.5   Summary   99

Chapter 8. OpenVMS Symbolic Debugger   101

8.1   Modes of the Debugger   101
8.2   Stepping Through the Code   103
8.3   Breakpoints and Watchpoints   104
8.4   Accessing Program Variables   106
8.5   Optimizer   107
8.6   Initializing   108
8.7   SHOW and SET Commands   109
8.8   Display Control   111
8.9   Keypad Input   113
8.10 Spawning DCL Commands   113
8.11 Control Structures   113
8.12 Run-Time Symbol Table   114
8.13 Examining Arrays   115
8.14 Resolving References   116
8.15 Summary   116

Chapter 9. OpenVMS Record Management Services   117

9.1   Introduction   117
9.2   RMS Data Structures and Functions   119
9.3   Disk Cluster   122
9.4   Bucket   123
9.5   Spanning and Nonspanning Records   124
9.6   Indexed Files   125
9.7   RMS Utilities   126
      9.7.1   FDL   126
      9.7.2   CONVERT Utility   128
9.8   Summary   128

Chapter 10. Utilities   129

10.1 MAIL Utility   129
      10.1.1   Sending Mail   131
      10.1.2   Responding to Messages   131
      10.1.3   Mail Characteristics   131
      10.1.4   Folders   133

10.2   PHONE Utility   134
10.3   SORT and MERGE Utilities   135
10.4   DIFFERENCE Utility   136
10.5   DUMP Utility   136
10.6   SEARCH Utility   137
10.7   NOTES Utility   138
10.8   Summary   139

Part 2   OpenVMS Architecture

Chapter 11. A Process in OpenVMS   143

11.1   Introduction   143
11.2   Process Communications   145
        11.2.1   Lock Management System Services   146
        11.2.2   Mailboxes   146
        11.2.3   Logical Names   146
        11.2.4   Global Sections   147
        11.2.5   Event Flags   147
11.3   Input/Output   150
        11.3.1   I/O System Services   152
        11.3.2   I/O Processing   153
11.4   Mailboxes   154
11.5   Timer Support   155
        11.5.1   Timer Support in OpenVMS AXP   156
        11.5.2   TImekeeping in OpenVMS   156
11.6   Summary   157

Chapter 12. Executive   159

12.1   System Services   159
12.2   Process Control   160
12.3   Asynchronous System Traps (ASTs)   161
12.4   Synchronization Techniques   163
12.5   Memory Barriers   164
12.6   Spinlock   164
12.7   Mutual Exclusion Semaphores (Mutexes)   165
12.8   Modularities in the Executive Organization   165
12.9   Summary   168

Chapter 13. Memory Management   169

13.1   Introduction   169
13.2   Memory Management in Alpha AXP and OpenVMS AXP   170
        13.2.1   Alpha Virtual Addresses   171
        13.2.2   Translation Buffer (TB)   171
        13.2.3   Granularity Hint Regions   172
        13.2.4   Virtual Address Space in OpenVMS VAX   172
13.3   Management of Physical Memory   173
        13.3.1   Page Fault Wait State   174
        13.3.2   Free Page Wait State   175

	13.3.3	Working Set Dynamics	175
	13.3.4	The Working Set List	176
13.4	Summary		176

Chapter 14. Scheduling in OpenVMS   177

14.1	Introduction	177
14.2	Process Priority	178
14.3	Capability and Affinity	184
14.4	Scheduling Dynamics	184
14.5	Quantum Expiration	185
14.6	Event Reporting	185
14.7	PIXSCAN Priority Boosts	185
14.8	Rescheduling Interrupt	185
14.9	Condition Handling	186
14.10	Software Conditions	188
14.11	Interrupts	189
	14.11.1 Comparison of Exceptions and Interrupts	190
	14.11.2 Software Interrupts	191
14.12	Summary	193

Chapter 15. OpenVMS System Management   195

15.1	Introduction	195
15.2	User Accounts	195
15.3	Security of User Accounts	196
15.4	VMSINSTAL Utility	198
15.5	Software Licenses	199
15.6	Volume Recovery	199
15.7	SYSMAN Utility	199
15.8	Booting the Operating System	200
15.9	Queues	200
15.10	Shutdown	201
15.11	Memory Management Files	202
15.12	BACKUP Utility	202
15.13	SYSBOOT and SYSGEN Utilities	203
15.14	AUTOGEN Utility	203
15.15	Error Handling	204
15.16	MONITOR Utility	205
15.17	Summary	205

Part 3   Migration from OpenVMS VAX to OpenVMS AXP

Chapter 16. Alpha AXP Architecture   209

16.1	Introduction	209
16.2	Alpha AXP Data Structures and Processor State	211
16.3	Alpha Instructions	214
	16.3.1 Load/Store Instructions	216
	16.3.2 Operate Instructions	217

16.3.3   Branching Instructions   218
16.3.4   PALcode Library   220
16.4   Summary   225

Chapter 17. Binary Translator   227

17.1   VEST: VAX Image Translator   227
        17.1.1   Code Generation   229
        17.1.2   Translated Images   230
17.2   Translated Image Environment (TIE)   230
17.3   Performance of VEST   233
17.4   Untranslatable Images   233
17.5   Instruction Atomicity   234
17.6   VAX Exceptions   235
17.7   OpenVMS Differences   235
17.8   Summary   236

Chapter 18. VAX-to-AXP Migration   239

18.1   Introduction   239
18.2   Synchronization Problems   240
18.3   Atomicity of Instruction   241
18.4   Memory Granularity   242
18.5   Data Alignment   244
18.6   Read-Write Ordering   245
18.7   MACRO-32 Assembly Language   249
18.8   Important Architectural Differences in the OpenVMS Kernel   250
18.9   Translation Buffer and Granularity Hint   251
18.10   Summary   254

Glossary   255
Bibliography   261
Index   263

Preface

VAX and Alpha AXP computer systems are from Digital Equipment Corporation (DEC). VAX is a 32-bit complex instruction set computer (CISC) architecture, and Alpha AXP is a more recent 64-bit reduced instruction set computer (RISC) architecture. DEC, known for its prominent presence in the computer manufacturing industry, has carefully considered future implications when developing the new, high-speed Alpha architecture. DEC has made every attempt to develop compatible AXP systems so that transition from existing VAX systems to AXP systems is as quick and as smooth as possible. The following key issues formed a basis for Alpha architecture:

- High performance
- Longevity
- Run OpenVMS AXP and DEC OSF/1 AXP (Unix) operating systems
- Smooth migration from VAX and MIPS architecture

This book deals with OpenVMS—the operating system for the VAX (OpenVMS VAX) and AXP (OpenVMS AXP) systems.

I have attempted to provide a novice cum semi-advanced treatment of OpenVMS, hoping that it will be appealing to students, novices, and application programmers alike. In this book, the complexity of the topics discussed is cautiously and gradually advanced as we go from Chap. 1 to Chap. 18. Contents for the initial chapters are carefully chosen to discuss some basic tools required for using OpenVMS and to develop application programs. The second part of the book deals with some advanced concepts of OpenVMS like scheduling, etc. The advanced discussions will be useful to students of operating systems and also to system programmers who may often need to be familiar with some system management issues.

Broadly, this book is intended to help in:

- introducing the usage and application development on OpenVMS
- giving cursory treatment of the concepts used in the internals of OpenVMS
- providing some technical hints that may be observed when migrating applications from VAX to AXP systems

Accordingly, the book is divided into three parts corresponding to use, OpenVMS architecture, and migration (from VAX systems to AXP systems). The first part deals with some basic issues like login procedures. Then it discusses some necessary tools used in developing applications on OpenVMS. Especially the separate chapter on the debugger may be beneficial to application developers.

The second part deals with the OpenVMS concepts of a process, OpenVMS executive, the scheduler, and the memory management. An understanding of the topics discussed in the beginning chapters in this part may be essential to achieve an optimal system management. The last chapter in this part deals with system management of OpenVMS.

The issues concerned with VAX-to-AXP migration are discussed in two chapters of Part 3: one on the binary translator and the other on some tips and cautions to be observed when migrating from VAX to AXP systems.

A chapter briefly discussing Alpha architecture forms the first chapter in Part 3 as a prelude to subsequent discussions on VAX–AXP migration.

A list of references is provided at the end of the book. These reference books and articles can form a useful supplement to your library of DEC manuals and guides on OpenVMS and its tools. This book on OpenVMS is to be used as reference material in addition to the DEC manuals.

The glossary provided in the book briefly explains some new terminologies, especially in connection with Alpha architecture.

Acknowledgments

Many people are directly or indirectly involved in writing this book. I am grateful to Jayanthi Ramachandran, who introduced me to several operating systems including RSX-11M and VMS at Raman Research Institute (RRI), Bangalore, India. I wish to thank Prof. S. Krishna of the Indian Institute of Management, Bangalore, India, and Prof. V. Radhakrishnan, Prof. K. R. Anantharamaiah, and P. A. Johnson of RRI who helped me to expand my horizons of experience in computer technology.

I would like to thank Rachel Ross, John McCrosson, Bob Collier, and Mike Ciaccio—all of Digital Equipment Corporation—for teaching me many of the advanced techniques in OpenVMS when I was working as a consultant to DEC.

I wish to acknowledge the hospitality and guidance of Prof. Harold Abelson, Prof. Philip Morrison, and Prof. R. V. Ramnath, all of the Massachusetts Institute of Technology, during my visits to Cambridge, where I developed some ideas to write a book on OpenVMS.

My special thanks are due to Jay Shaw for his critical reading of the manuscript and for making valuable comments.

I am thankful to Sini Pandit of Tech-Source who helped me with his computer systems for typesetting the initial and final drafts of the manuscript.

I thank K. Horuntoor, President of Grace Binary Corporation, for allowing me to use their computer laboratory while developing the final draft of the manuscript.

The Murthys and their family, especially Divya, Putti, and Luke, deserve my special thanks for their kind hospitality in their New Jersey home where I prepared the final draft of the manuscript.

My sincere thanks to Jay Ranade, Jerry Papke, and other staff members of McGraw-Hill for their advice and cooperation.

Raj Bhargava

OpenVMS Usage and Application Development

1

OpenVMS
Architectural
Overview

OpenVMS symbolizes the refinement of an operating system over the years to emerge as a primary operating system supporting as well as advocating the age of "open-ness" in the computer industry today. The evolution of OpenVMS spans the age of PDP through the age of Alpha AXP. The RSX-11M operating system that supported PDP-11s represented the implementation of early concepts of an operating system for DEC's minicomputers. These concepts were eventually evolved and implemented as the VMS operating system for DEC's mini and super-mini computers.

Two important requirements—namely, the need for supporting high-speed computing that resulted in the birth of 64-bit Alpha AXP processors and the need for open computing that supports operability of software applications on multiple platforms—made it necessary for the VMS operating system to undergo another cycle of revolution to smooth VAX to AXP migration that seems to be somewhat similar to the era of PDP to VAX transition. Alpha AXP architecture provided a reasonable compromise between the support for high-speed computing and the backward compatibility with VAX architecture. The new hardware architecture features eliminated a total rewriting of an operating system resulting in a timely delivery of OpenVMS as soon as AXP systems were announced. This is probably the single reason that enabled modifying the existing VMS instead of designing and rewriting an operating system for Alpha AXP that would have taken an appreciable amount of time. What resulted from the modifications to VMS was

OpenVMS VAX and OpenVMS AXP operating systems—to support VAX and Alpha platforms, respectively.

Transportability of programs written in VMS for VAX platforms to OpenVMS on Alpha AXP-based platforms, user-friendliness, and abundant availability of reliable tools for software development are some of the major strengths of OpenVMS.

This book attempts to cover three aspects of OpenVMS. First, some necessary tools required for using and developing applications on OpenVMS. Second, a little more advanced discussion on the main components of OpenVMS including the OpenVMS Executive, Scheduler, and System Management. Third, the last three chapters discuss the Alpha architecture and the issues related to migrating applications from VAX to AXP systems. Accordingly, the chapters are grouped into three parts.

This chapter is first in this part dealing with usage and application development using OpenVMS. In particular, Part 1 deals with the login procedures, command level programming, editors, logical names, lexical functions, and application development sequences.

1.1   OPENVMS ORGANIZATION

OpenVMS is organized into four layers called Kernel, Executive, Supervisor, and User level. These layers follow the well-known onion layer structure: the Kernel representing the core and the User level representing the outermost layer (Fig. 1.1).

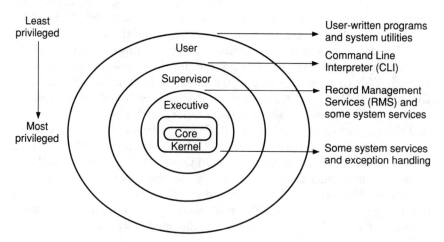

Figure 1.1   Access modes in OpenVMS.

Various types of errors, warnings, and fatal bugs generated by either user programs or system programs are known as *exceptions* or *conditions*. The actions taken by OpenVMS to handle these conditions are known as *condition handling*. Kernel has, at its core, the OpenVMS executive programs, many system service programs, and the condition-handling mechanism.

In OpenVMS, the file structures and the corresponding input/output mechanisms are handled by the Record Management Services (RMS). The Supervisor layer consists of Record Management Service programs and many system service programs.

The OpenVMS command line interpreter analyzes the user input commands; it decodes user input and encodes the system output for display into a file or onto a device. The user inputs commands using a command language called *Digital Command Language* (DCL). One can write fairly complicated programs using DCL (Chap. 4 will discuss how procedures can be written using DCL). The supervisor mainly contains command tables, command language interpreter, and several lexical functions.

The user level contains the programs developed by users and numerous OpenVMS utilities like MAIL, PHONE, etc. The program development cycle consists of coding the program using one of several editors (chiefly EDT or EVE), compiling the program using a compiler for the specific programming language used in the program like C, Pascal, or Fortran. Then the file is linked with system programs and, if necessary, with user programs to create an executable image. The program is then debugged to remove any execution time errors. The application development cycles, the debugger, the libraries, and frequently used OpenVMS utilities are discussed in later chapters.

The OpenVMS concept of a privilege is with respect to objects like data structures, files, memory, and devices and other system resources like hardware registers, cache, etc. There are many privilege classes like read, write, delete, and execute. The kernel mode is the most privileged and the user level is the least privileged in terms of accessing system data structures and hardware registers.

1.2 LOGIN PROCEDURE

When the user logs in to OpenVMS using an interactive terminal, many system functions play their role to create an environment called a *process*. The process can execute one or more program images either as a detached process or a spawned subprocess sharing the quotas and privileges. The login procedure involves the following sequences:

1. The system program LOGINOUT.EXE that runs when the 'Enter' key is pressed is capable of sensing the user input at the 'Username:' prompt.

2. After receiving a valid string of ASCII characters for the username, the system prompts for user password.

3. The user input goes through a validation check procedure by comparing the input with the entries in the user authorization file SYSUAF.DAT in a system area.

4. If the validation test is passed, a welcome message is displayed on the screen indicating a successful login. Otherwise, the message "User authorization failure" is displayed on the screen.

5. Commands from a system command file (SYSLOGIN.COM) are executed.

6. Any DCL procedures, commands, or definitions specified in the LOGIN.COM file in the user's root directory are executed next automatically.

A process is the basic scheduling entity on OpenVMS. The process creation involves creating the necessary data structures for the user to access various system functions like input/output, etc. The process information is contained in a unit of memory called Process Control Block (PCB). (See Fig. 1.2.)

1.3 USER ACCOUNTS

A user account is usually referred to by the username. Internally, OpenVMS refers to account numbers in terms of a set of two numbers. The first number indicates the user account and the second number indicates the group with which the account is associated. Several users may be associated with the same group. For example, [500,256] and [600,256] are two user account numbers where user accounts indicated by the user identification numbers 500 and 600 belong to the same group that is indicated by the user group identification number 256.

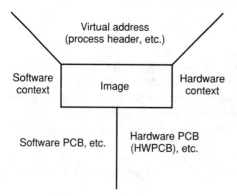

Figure 1.2 The environment of a process in OpenVMS.

1.4   VIRTUAL ADDRESS SPACE

A process has several components, mainly the program code and data. In addition, the process makes use of some system programs and data structures. The operating system uses the *virtual address space* (see Fig. 1.3) to distinguish between user data structures and system data structures.

A region called P0 in the virtual address space is used as the *program region*. It contains the user's program code and data. Another region called P1 is used as the *process control region*. It contains command tables and other necessary data structures.

The region known as S0 is used by the OpenVMS Executive for its many services like swapping, paging, Record Management Services, etc. The region known as S1 is not used.

1.4.1   Hardware and software contexts

There are two OpenVMS contexts that can be identified for each process: the software context and the hardware context. The software context contains information on

Privileges—indicated by mnemonic words. They imply access to resources, data structures, files, directories, etc. GRPPRV is an example; it implies that the process can share the resources used by accounts in the same user group.

Priority—For all normal processes priority is a number ranging between 0 and 15. Normally, priority 4 is assigned to an active process (see Fig. 1.4).

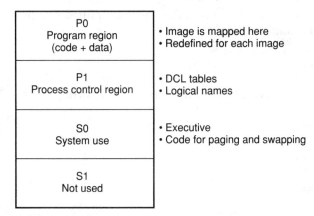

Figure 1.3 Virtual address space in OpenVMS.

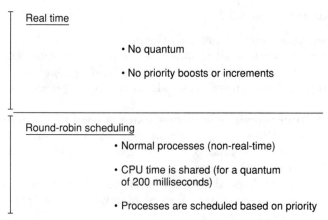

Figure 1.4 The concept of priority in OpenVMS.

Quotas—These are numbers that indicate the allowed usage of memory, etc. An example is the page file quota which sets a limit on the size of program that can reside in memory.

Limits—These indicate things like how many processes or subprocesses are allowed to be executed per user.

The software context is the one in which you can access the system resources for which you have privileges.

The hardware context contains the data structures used in rescheduling the system tasks. It saves information from the 16 general purpose registers R0 through R15. The hardware context also contains the context of the code at the time it is being scheduled out. This context essentially reflects what you are doing at a given time in the operating system.

Essentially, the virtual address space is the range of memory addresses potentially known to an image. An *image* is defined as a program executing in the context of a process.

1.5 PROCESS TYPES

The processes in OpenVMS can be classified into the following types:

- Interactive processes
- Batch processes
- Network processes
- Detached processes
- Subprocesses

An interactive process always communicates to the operating system via a terminal. Usually, the terminals used in the VAX or Alpha AXP environments are capable of providing some intelligent features like split screen, different sizes of character displays, and different ways of rendering the text, like blinking. These facilities are specially used by editors, debuggers, MAIL, NOTES, and a host of other OpenVMS utilities. It is the interactive mode in which you can use most of the features of OpenVMS. The X-window terminals used in the workstations provide an advanced user interface to use the interactive mode much more effectively.

Batch processes are treated as off-line processes. No terminal is attached to such processes. Mainly, a batch process makes use of other system resources like memory, disk, tape, and printer, and of course the CPU. Typically, a batch process is CPU-intensive and does not normally require user intervention until the process is completed. A well-tested program or routine tasks are submitted as batch jobs for overnight processing.

A network process could be either an interactive process or a batch process. The main aspect of a network process is that it is capable of cross-utilizing the applications like MAIL, NOTES, etc., from any of the nodes in a network of VAX or AXP computers.

Essentially, all the utilities in the cluster are shareable by a network process. Programs may address other nodes also; for example, a program can write output data to files on a disk belonging to a node other than the one from where the batch process was initiated.

A detached process is a derived process from an interactive process. It does not make use of the terminal. It behaves more like a batch process.

A subprocess is like a child process initiated by any one of the processes mentioned above. A subprocess that is spawned by a parent process shares quotas, privileges, and other attributes of the parent process.

1.6 PRIORITIES

The current versions of OpenVMS have 32 priority levels (see Fig. 1.4). The low-priority range 0 through 15 is reserved for all normal processes. In this range, low-priority processes are scheduled in a round-robin way, each process getting a quantum of CPU time. A *quantum* is a unit of time that determines the period at which CPU allocates its time to a process at some priority levels, in a round-robin scheduling. Processes at a higher-priority level are scheduled before low-priority processes. Priorities can be boosted up or decremented after certain WAIT states.

The higher-priority range of 16 through 31 is reserved for time-critical processes like real-time programs. There is no concept of quantum used in these priority levels, which means that the CPU time can be totally dedicated to the process. There are also no boosts or decrements of priorities in these priority levels.

1.7 PAGING AND SWAPPING

A *page* is a unit memory. Its size is 512 bytes (note that a *block* is also of the same size, but in reference to storage unit on disk).

The concept of *paging* in OpenVMS is fundamental to proper memory management. With paging a program is not limited to the available physical memory. Ideally, the address space for a process is 2^n-1 where n is address length. In Alpha AXP it is 64 bits. So, $2^{64}-1$ addressable memory is available in principle, but so much memory is not technologically realizable. The physical memory could at most be a few hundred megabytes. Paging takes care of bringing only the required portions of the process into the physical memory. Whenever a different portion of the process is required in the memory, paging fetches the new portion of the program and replaces a portion of the memory with it. This situation is known as *page fault*.

The memory management module handles this situation. Because the physical memory is also shared, only a part of the physical memory can be allocated per process. The amount of physical memory a process can have is known as *working set*. Therefore, as and when other portions of the program are required, they are paged into the process's working set.

Swapping	Paging
Entire processes are moved in and out of physical memory.	Process working sets are moved in and out of memory.
Swapper is an independent process that OpenVMS wakes up from its hibernating state as and when there is a need for swapping.	Paging is performed as a subroutine action by a page fault handling exception procedure in the context of the process incurring page fault.
The unit of swapping is the set of pages of the inswapped process so that it can fit into the working set of the process.	A page is the unit of paging. Typically more than one page is read by the page fault handler.
A SYSGEN parameter (SWP_PRIO) determines the queuing of the swapper I/O requests.	The base priority of the process incurring the page fault determines the queuing of page read requests.
Concurrently active processes compete for swapping into memory.	Pages of a process with large address space compete for paging.

Figure 1.5 Swapping and paging compared.

Swapping is similar to paging but it operates at the level of processes and not programs. It is a scheme that allows OpenVMS to be working with only the necessary processes in memory at any given time.

The differences between paging and swapping are shown in Fig. 1.5. Some concepts of memory management are discussed in Part 2.

The rest of the chapters in Part 1 on the OpenVMS usage discuss some tools required for using and developing applications on OpenVMS.

2

Entry to OpenVMS

In this chapter on the use of OpenVMS we will not distinguish between OpenVMS VAX and OpenVMS AXP, because at the entry level both the operating systems seem to behave identically. Any differences and their impact on the behavior of user application will be discussed in Part 3 on migration.

2.1 LOGGING IN

The first requirement to enter and use OpenVMS is that you must have a *user account*. This is created by the system manager for you. Initially, your account defines the characteristics of the minimal environment that you will be privileged to use, privileges you can use, and an area on the disk. A *password* is generated for you initially, which you should know in order to enter OpenVMS. You are also advised to change this password upon first login to secure your account.

First, the terminal should be prompting: Username: If not, just press the <RETURN> key at the terminal. Input your username as specified in your account. Then you will receive the Password: prompt.

```
Username: RAJ
Password:
```

Logging in could also be qualified with certain allowed parameters. For example, if you have more than one area spread over two different disk units, you could direct your default working directory to be one of those disks by qualifying your username input at the time of logging in.

```
Username: RAJ/DISK=AXP_DISK
```

If you are logging in for the first time, the first thing you would normally do is to change the password.

```
$ set password
```

And you would change the password again only if you wish to change the password or if you receive a message from the system on the terminal indicating that your password would be expired soon. You can also ask the system to generate a password by qualifying the set password command. Use help to see more details on this.

Once you become a regular user of OpenVMS, you would be normally familiar with such frequently used utilities like MAIL, PHONE, etc. If there are mail messages for you, this is indicated soon after your login by the system after it displays welcome messages.

If you are using the operating system from a remote terminal, the communicating software would display the prompt Local> at the terminal. You can then enter the command connect with a string parameter for the node name of the system to log into. The Username: prompt should be displayed. Enter your username followed by the Return key.

On successful login you will see a $ prompt. The prompt indicates that the module interfacing you to the operating system called Digital Command Language (DCL) is active. DCL commands can now be issued. All DCL commands are terminated with the Return key. Here is a sample of connecting to a node on a VAXcluster using a terminal server.

```
Local> Connect HUGO
        Welcome to OpenVMS AXP V1.0
Username: ALBERT
Password:
        :
        :
        (Welcome messages are displayed)
```

You can monitor the status of a command execution by using <control/t>. Entering <control/t> will display a one-line status of the execution. Execution will not be interrupted. The status line displays the CPU time and Input/Output performed. These should keep increasing every time <control/t> is entered. A command execution can be aborted by issuing the <control/y> sequence. If <control/y> is entered by mistake, execution can usually be resumed by entering the CONTINUE command. Here is an example response to the <control/t> function:

```
<control/t>:
HUGO::ALBERT 14:03:45 VMSHELP CPU=00:01:12.54
PF=3278 IO=425 MEM=106
```

The parameters displayed are node name, process name, time, image name, CPU time used by the process, page faults, I/O count, and working set size.

2.2   OPENVMS COMMANDS

Digital Command Language is the name of the command interpreter in OpenVMS. DCL processes the commands. The line commands of DCL can be interactively executed at the '$' prompt. DCL can also be programmed. To know more about DCL programming see Chap. 8. Some special keys from the terminal keyboard help to edit the command inputs (see Fig. 2.1).

The general syntax for any command in OpenVMS is:

```
$ command/qualifiers parameters/qualifiers !comment
```

For example, the SHOW command has /FULL as one of the qualifiers. To make qualifiers apply for only a single parameter out of a list of parameters, you would specify the qualifier after the parameter, as in

```
$ directory [.next]*.*,[.previous]*.*/full
```

Here, the /FULL qualifier is applicable to the files in directory [.previous] only. Whereas, the command:

```
$ directory/full [.next]*.*,[.previous]*.*
```

applies the /FULL qualifier to files from both [.next], [.previous] directories.

After logging in, you may be interested in either inputting a code for a program, word processing, or in learning a new tool. In most of these cases you would use one of the editors available in OpenVMS. The

Key	Function
DELETE	A single character on the left side of the cursor is deleted.
CTRL/A	Switch between overstrike and insert modes.
Left Arrow	The cursor moves one column to the left.
CTRL/E	The cursor moves to the end of the command line.
Right Arrow	The cursor moves one column to the right.
F12, CTRL/H, or BS	The cursor moves to the beginning of the line.
F13 or CTRL/J	The word to the left of the cursor is deleted.
CTRL/U	All characters to the left of the cursor are deleted.

Figure 2.1 Keys for editing the command line.

Extensible VAX Editor (EVE) is discussed in Chap. 3. The outcome of these editors is a file, either a new file you have just created or a modified file you just modified.

A file in OpenVMS has several attributes to uniquely define it, as well as to provide the characteristic properties of the file. The file structure will be discussed later in this chapter. The files reside in the directories. When an account was created for you, you would normally have a single directory. A directory has the syntax:

device_name:[your_directory_name]

For example, DISK$1A:[HARRY] could be a directory, where DISK$1A is the disk on which an area called HARRY is designated.

You can view the file existence and other details using the DIRECTORY command:

```
$ directory *.*
```

Here * is called a *wildcard*. The above command fetches the directory of *all* files. This command tells OpenVMS to list all files in the current directory. Note that if you do not specify a device name, the device for the default directory is used.

You can view the files you create using the DIRECTORY command.

```
$ directory [my_dir]testfile.txt
Directory DUA0:[MY_DIR]
TESTFILE.TXT;1
Total of 1 file.
$
```

Some important attributes associated with a file are the number of blocks used, the number of blocks allocated, date of creation, date of last backup, file protection, file format, and date revised. All this information can be viewed with the same DIRECTORY command with a /FULL qualifier:

```
$ directory/full testfile.txt
Directory DUA0:[MY_DIR]
TESTFILE.TXT;1            File ID:        (142, 1,0)
Size:       3/5           Owner:     [YOUR_NAME]
Created:    11-NOV-1993   14:13:17.32
Revised:    11-NOV-1993   14:18:12.03 (1)
Expires:    <None specified>
Backup:     <No backup specified>
File organization: Sequential
File attributes: Allocation:  3,     Extend: 0,
```

```
Global buffer count:   0  No version limit
Record format:       Variable length, maximum 78 bytes
Record attributes:   Carriage return carriage control
RMS attributes:      None
Journaling enable:   None
File protection:     System: RWED, Owner: RWED,
Group:     RWED, World: RE
Access Control List:     None
Total of 1 file, 3/5 blocks
$
```

2.3 SOME FREQUENTLY USED DCL COMMANDS

The COPY command copies files on a specified device and directory to another or the same directory and device with a specified name. For example, to copy the file MY_TEXT.TXT to the directory [YOU] with a new name YOUR_TEXT.TXT, the command is:

```
$ copy MY_TEXT.TXT [YOU]YOUR_TEXT.TXT
```

The RENAME command is used to change the names of existing files on disk. For example, to rename MY_TEXT.TXT to OUR_DOC.TXT, the command is:

```
$ RENAME MY_TEXT.TXT OUR_DOC.TXT
```

This command is useful to move a file from one directory to another— that is, to place the file in the new directory and remove it from the original directory. For example,

```
$ RENAME [VICTOR]A_TEXT.TXT [ALBERT]B_TEXT.TXT
```

A_TEXT.TXT is removed from the directory [VICTOR] and placed in the directory [ALBERT]. In fact, this feature can be used to move a complete directory and its subdirectories. For example, suppose the directory [PETER] is under the directory [HUGO] and now it is to be removed from [HUGO] and placed under the directory [YOU.NOVICE]. The command is:

```
$ RENAME [HUGO]PETER.DIR [YOU.NOVICE]PETER.DIR
```

Now the directories and files which were under [HUGO.PETER] are accessed through the directory [YOU.NOVICE]. Files cannot be moved from one disk to another using this command. The COPY command, followed by the DELETE command, will have to be used.

The DELETE command is used to delete files. For example, the next command deletes version 5 of the file A_TEST.DOC.

```
$ DELETE A_TEST.DOC;5
```

When a file is edited, a new version of the file is created, but the old version still exists. For example, editing A_TEXT.TXT;1 creates a new file A_TEXT.TXT;2, with the same name and extension but a higher version number. If older versions are not deleted, many versions of files will exist on disk. Older versions should be periodically deleted to reduce the pileup of files and to conserve space on disk. The DELETE command can be used to delete files, but the PURGE command specifically deletes older versions of files. For example, to delete all versions except the latest version of file A_TEST.TXT, the command is:

```
$ PURGE A_TEST.TXT
```

Note that no version field is specified in this command.

The /KEEP:n qualifier is useful to retain the last n versions of a file. To delete all but the latest two versions of A_TEST.TXT the command is:

```
$ PURGE/KEEP:2 A_TEST.TXT
```

or

```
$ PURGE A_TEST.TXT/KEEP:2
```

If you have OPER and LOG_IO privileges, you can use the SET command to set the date and time. The format for this is:

```
$ SET TIME=12-NOV-1993:12:04:00:12.54
$ SET TIME=12-NOV-1993
$ SET TIME=9:04
```

The PRINT command is used to queue files for printing. To print the file A_TEST.TXT and B_TEST.DOC, the command is:

```
$ PRINT A_TEST.TXT, B_TEST.TXT
```

The command has a number of qualifiers:

/COPIES   number of printed copies of the file.
/DELETE   delete the file after printing.
/FLAG   print a banner page before printing the file.

/FORM	use a specified form (paper type) to print the file. The list of forms can be seen by SHOW QUEUE/FORM.
/HEADER	print a header line on every page of output. The header contains the file name and page number.
/PAGE	print specified pages of the file. For example, to print pages 3 through 18, the qualifier is /PAGE:(3,18).
/QUEUE	queue the file to a specified queue. Typically, each printer on the system will have one associated queue. To see the queues on the system the command is SHOW QUEUE. If this qualifier is not specified, the file is sent to the queue SYS$PRINT.

For example,

```
$ PRINT A_TEST.TXT/COPIES=2/DELETE/FORM=PORTRAIT -
$_                  /QUEUE=HP03$PRINT
```

2.4   ERROR MESSAGES

OpenVMS error messages follow a standard in providing information related to the error message. The operating system, compilers, utilities, and most other software display error messages in a uniform format. Here is an example of an error message when the COPY command is entered wrongly:

```
$ COPI A_TEST.TXT
%DCL-W-IVVERB, unrecognized command verb - check validity and
spelling
\COPI\
```

The syntax for error messages is:

```
%FACILITY-L_IDENT, text
```

The fields are

FACILITY	The name of the program issuing the message.
L	Severity level of the message:
	S—success
	I—informational
	W—warning
	E—error
	F—fatal or severe error
IDENT	Abbreviated description.
text	Description of the error.

2.5 DEVICES

The naming standard for devices in OpenVMS assigns a two letter mnemonic identifying the type of device. An example of a device name is DUA0:. The general format for device specification is:

```
PPCxxx
```

where *PP* is the generic peripheral name (sometimes this has 3 characters).

C is the controller designated.

xxx is the specific device on the controller.

Figure 2.2 shows some devices and the mnemonic names used to identify them.

Note that in OpenVMS, logical names are normally used to address a device and directory, in order to make the references to devices consistent. See Chap. 5 on logical names for more details.

The system also supports *software devices*. These are device drivers in the operating system but there is no hardware corresponding to them. An example is the mailbox device MB, which is used for sending data from one process to another.

Device names on VAXcluster systems are preceded by the name of the computer on which the device resides and a $ sign. For example,

```
HUGO$DUA3: ! device name DUA3: on VAXcluster HUGO.
```

Type	Name	Some Examples of Device Types
Console floppy	CS	RX02 floppy drive
Disks	DJ	RA60 removable disks
Disks	DU	RA90 fixed disk
Line printer	LI	LP25 300-lines-per-minute line printer
Line printer	LP	LP29 2000-lines-per-minute line printer
LAT ethernet devices	LT	VT320 terminal or LN03 laser printer
Tape drives	MU	TA78 125 inches per second tape drive
Tape drives	MS	TU81-PLUS streaming tape drive
Tape drives	MT	TE16 tape drives
Mailbox	MB	A software mailbox virtual device
Network device	NET	A software communication device
Operator console	OP	A software device for system operations
Terminals	TT	VT320 terminal
Terminals	TX	VT320 terminal
Virtual terminals	VT	A software device like VTA1:

Figure 2.2 Some device types and their mnemonics.

The general format for file specification is

```
nodename::device:[directory]filename.filetype;version
```

Fields not specified assume default values. Default values depend on the command used to operate on the file. Generally, if version number is not specified, then the latest version is assumed. Node name is the computer on which the file resides. If it is not specified, the node is assumed to be the local VAX or AXP system you are currently using.

Each process has a default device and directory. These are specified by the system manager in the user authorization file. When specifying file names, if the device and directory are not specified, the default values are assumed. To see the default device and directory, use SHOW DEFAULT. To change the defaults, use SET DEFAULT. For example,

```
$ SET DEFAULT DUA2:[TEST.PROGRAMS]
```

The concept of version numbers for files in OpenVMS facilitates a kind of backup feature. Unlike many other operating systems, instead of retaining a single copy of the file corresponding to the last editing, in OpenVMS virtually any number of editions of the same file can be retained. Version numbers start at 1 and can go up to 32,767. When not specified, it is assumed to be the latest version number. The latest version of the file can also be referenced as version 0. Versions can be specified going backward, starting at the latest version, by using a minus sign before the version. For example, if a file has 4 versions, then −1 is the same as version 3.

The information about the process or the session to which you are logged in can be obtained using the SHOW PROCESS command. It displays full information about the process with the /FULL qualifier. The SHOW MEMORY command displays a summary on system memory usage.

The *balance set* indicates the number of processes which can be in memory. If more processes than the maximum are created, some processes will be swapped out onto disk. Processes may also be swapped out if there is not enough physical memory to accommodate all the processes. The fixed-size pool area contains fixed-size slots of memory which are used when quick allocation and deallocation of pagelets of memory is required. Dynamic memory is where the processes and most of the operating system reside. Only a part of the operating system resides in static memory. The paging files are used for swapped-out processes and pages. These files must be created using the SYSGEN procedure and they must be large enough to accommodate any swapping and paging space requirements of the operating system.

The SHOW DEVICES command displays a summary of devices on the system. It is useful to find out which devices are mounted, free space on disks, which devices are allocated to processes, and the number of device malfunction errors on devices.

The error count gives the number of errors encountered while accessing the device. Error details can be displayed by creating an error report using the command ANALYZE/ERROR. Devices having the 'alloc' status are for exclusive use of the process which has issued the ALLOCATE command for the device. The devices are grouped by disks, tapes, terminals, printers, and others. Further details on devices, like total space on a disk, can be displayed by using the /FULL qualifier.

2.6 OTHER INFORMATION VIA SHOW COMMANDS

Information on many characteristics of OpenVMS, like terminal settings for your terminal, your default directory, your disk quota, and names of users logged on in your system, is available for you to display using the SHOW commands. For a summary of available SHOW commands see Fig. 2.3. For example, you can see user accounts logged into your system in addition to your account:

```
$ show users
  OpenVMS VAX Interactive Users
  11-Nov-1993 10:12:11.43
  Total number of interactive users = 3
```

$ SHOW DEFAULT	Displays the default directory and device that are being currently set. Use the SET DEFAULT command to change the default directory and/or device.
$ SHOW MEMORY	The statistics of memory usage are displayed.
$ SHOW NETWORK	Names and node numbers of computers in the network are displayed.
$ SHOW PROCESS	All process information, like quota, privileges, etc., is displayed.
$ SHOW SYSTEM	Names of the processes currently running and their id's are displayed.
$ SHOW TIME	System data and time are displayed.
$ SHOW USERS	Interactive users' information, like username, terminal, etc., are displayed.

Figure 2.3 Frequently used SHOW commands in DCL.

```
Username    Process Name    PID         Terminal
SAKATA      DEJAVU          00001345    TXA3:
FERMAT      CASTLE          000054CF    TXB1:
NEEDHAM     THING           0000452E    TXA5:
```

You can see the characteristics of your terminal using the SHOW TERMINAL command:

```
$ show terminal
Terminal: _TXB6    Device_Type: VT100    Owner: Your_username

Input: 1200     LFfill: 0     Width: 80     Parity: none
Output: 1200    CRfill: 0     Page: 24      :
  :               :             :             :
  :               :             :             :
  :               :             :             :
```

This command shows all information, like baud rate, terminal name, etc.

All SHOW commands have many qualifiers associated with them, as do most of the OpenVMS commands. For details see the online help facility.

2.7 SET COMMAND

You can alter certain settings made by the system for you, like terminal settings, default directory, etc. For example, the terminal is normally set to display 80 characters per line. If you wish to see more characters per line, another permissible setting is 132 characters per line. This you can do by executing the SET command:

```
$ set terminal/width=132
```

The terminal clears what is on the screen and puts its cursor at the top left corner, which is its "home" position.

Normally, the system prompt is '$'. You can change this to whatever character or character string you like. For example,

```
$ set prompt = "MAPLE"

MAPLE>
```

Just executing set prompt without any qualifier will return the setting to the default prompt '$'. Some frequently used SET commands are shown in Fig. 2.4.

Command	Action
SET PASSWORD	The user password is changed to a newly specified password.
SET PROMPT	OpenVMS prompt "$" is changed to a specified string. If no string is specified, "$" prompt is restored.
SET PROCESS	The attributes related to the execution of a process are defined.
SET TERMINAL	Attributes of the interactive terminal are defined.

Figure 2.4 Frequently used SET commands.

To see more details on the usage of the SET commands, use help set or help set command.

The `logout` command makes you exit out of OpenVMS. It has many qualifiers. The one that is most widely used is the /FULL qualifier, which gives a summary of the session being logged out with accounting information.

2.8 FILE PROTECTION

The security of the files created by you in your area will have default security set up by the system. The security of files is viewed in terms of four classes of users: First, you as owner of the file, second the group to which you belong, third the system, and fourth the world, anyone other than the first three classes of users. There are four classes of protections envisaged for files and directories in OpenVMS. These are read, write, execute, and delete. Each class of users can be assigned with any combination of these protections by you. You would do this using the SET PROTECTION command. For example,

```
$ set protection = (owner:rwed, system:rwed, group:rwe,
world:r)
$_*.*
```

will enable read, write, execute, and deletion privileges for all of your files for both yourself and the system; the group members can only read, write, and execute all of your files while all others can only read the files.

2.9 CREATE COMMAND

Simple files can be created using the CREATE command. It needs the filename as input:

```
$ create sample.txt
```

would create a file called sample.txt and prompt you to input text from the keyboard. The prompting is indicated by the absence of a '$' at the beginning of the line. Type Control and z together to close the file. You should see the '$' prompt now, which indicates that the file is closed.

```
$ create sample.txt
This is a sample text
<control/z>
|Exit|
$
```

Note that the commands, the parameters, or the file-naming convention is case-independent in OpenVMS. It means the same whether you type lowercase or uppercase. The commonly used commands on a typical interactive session are listed in Fig. 2.5.

2.10 COMMAND LINE EDITING

When you input a command, especially a long one, you may commit typographical mistakes. You may like to move the cursor back and forth to edit the command line. The command line interpreter of OpenVMS provides a set of control key commands to assist you in this. <control/a> acts as a toggle switch between insert and overwrite modes of inputting. If the characters are getting overwritten on the command

Command	Action
CREATE	A new file is created with the specified filename.
DELETE	The specified file is deleted.
DIRECTORY	Displays a list of files.
EDIT	Edits the specified file. If the file is not an existing one, a new file is created with the specified name.
HELP	On-line help about OpenVMS commands is displayed.
LOGOUT	The logged in interactive session is terminated.
MAIL	The OpenVMS utility MAIL is activated. MAIL is used to send and receive messages.
PHONE	The PHONE utility that enables phone-like conversation between users is activated.
PURGE	All versions of the specified file/s except the last version are deleted.
RENAME	Renames a file to a new name.
SET	Defines or modifies the files and device characteristics.
SHOW	Various information about the system and user activity, like quota, memory usage, etc., are displayed.
TYPE	Lists the contents of a file.

Figure 2.5 Frequently used DCL commands.

line and you want the text to move to the right as you input, use <control/a> and resume inputting. <control/h> puts the cursor at the beginning of the line and <control/e> puts the cursor at the end of the line. Use <left arrow> and <right arrow> to move back and forth on the command line. <control/j> deletes the previous word from the command line. If you wanted to clear the entire command line, position the cursor at the end of the line and type <control/u>. In fact, <control/u> deletes the part of the command line that is on the left side of the cursor. See Fig. 2.1 for a summary of keys used for command line editing.

The OpenVMS supervisor maintains a recall buffer for each process that is logged in. This buffer stores by default the last 20 commands entered on the screen. You can call the commands from this buffer and execute, thus avoiding retyping of the command. The RECALL/ALL command displays a list of up to 20 commands you last entered. Associated with each command is a serial number displayed on the screen. The recall buffer behaves like a stack with the most recently entered command appearing first in the buffer, i.e., having number 1 associated with it. So, to execute the most recently entered command you would enter $ RECALL 1. For example,

```
$ RECALL/ALL
1 SET PROTECTION = (OW:RWED, SY:RWED, GROUP:RWE, WORLD:R)
2 SHOW PROCESS
3 TYPE MYFILE.TXT
  :
  :
```

In this example, if you wanted to type the file myfile.txt again, you can type:

```
$ RECALL 3
$ type myfile.txt
```

To scan the recall buffer you can use the <UP ARROW> and <DOWN ARROW> keys.

When the terminal is engaged in outputting something on the screen, you will still be able to input commands. This is made possible by a *type-ahead buffer* that the command interpreter maintains for your process. The input is kept in this buffer until the terminal output activity is complete. Once the outputting is complete, the buffered input command is echoed and executed. You can clear the contents of the type-ahead buffer by typing <control/x> after inputting the command. The size of the type-ahead buffer depends on the setting used when the system was installed.

You can organize your program development area in terms of subdirectories. These subdirectories usually follow a tree structure, with your main directory that was assigned when your account was created acting like a root directory. You create a subdirectory using $ CREATE/DIR command.

```
$ create/directory [.my_sub_dir_1]
```

The " indicates that it is a branch of the current directory. A subdirectory is created by creating a file with the subdirectory name as the filename and 'DIR' as an extension in the current directory. You can default to work in the subdirectory by using the command:

```
$ set default [.my_sub_dir_1]
```

Initially, this directory will be empty. You can create new files, copy files from other areas, and so on.

You can abbreviate almost all commands to reduce typing. For example, 'directory' command can be shortened to 'dir'. Also, you can assign special keys like PF1, etc., from the keyboard to commands to reduce typing for periodically used commands and string parameters. Use the DEFINE/KEY command to do this. You will then be able to use single keystrokes to execute a command. The syntax for this is:

```
$ define/key name_of_the_key "string"
```

For example, you can define 'directory' to be the command to execute when you press PF1. You can do this by:

```
$ define/key PF1 "directory"
DEFAULT key PF4 has been defined
%DCL-W-DEFKEY
```

When you press PF1 now, the command

```
$ directory
```

is displayed. To execute the command you have to press the <return> key. If you want the key definition to take care of this <return> also, then you can use the /TERMINATE qualifier with the DEFINE/KEY command. Not all keys can be defined this way. Only certain keys from the application keypad can be defined this way. For details, you can consult the DCL manuals. You can display a list of all defined keys using the command 'show key/all':

```
$ show key/all
DEFAULT key definitions:
PF1 = "directory"
PF2 = "show process"
```

or you can ask for definition of a single key:

```
$ show key PF1
DEFAULT key definitions:
PF1 = "directory"
```

The commands you want to regularly execute, or make various definitions available for the entire session, can be input in a file and executed using the command:

```
$ @command_file.com
```

Such a file is called a command procedure. Details of command programming are discussed in the chapter on advanced DCL programming. A particular file called LOGIN.COM (the extension COM indicates that it is a command procedure file) is of special importance. The commands, definitions, and procedures from this file are automatically executed when you log in to OpenVMS.

Although you can use the 'create' command to create a command file, it is not possible to edit the file while the file is being created. The editing has to be done by an OpenVMS editor. Two widely used editors on OpenVMS are EDT and EVE. EVE is discussed in Chap. 3.

2.11 SUMMARY

The logging-in sequences, familiarity with the keyboard, usage of on-line help, and the knowledge of frequently used OpenVMS commands discussed in this chapter are necessary to use the operating system interactively.

Extensible VAX Editor

3.1 INTRODUCTION

OpenVMS provides two popular editors, EDT and EVE. Extensible VAX Editor (EVE) is more advanced than EDT and provides a user-interface that is easy to use. Capabilities like learning commands and multiple window editing, in addition to programmability to suit special editing requirements, are some of the important features of EVE.

EVE is written in VAXTPU, a high-performance, programmable, text-processing utility. The EVE editor can be activated on X-Window terminals and ANSI standard terminals like the VT100 or VT200.

With keypad mode, you can easily manipulate text using simple keystrokes. Using the keys on the numeric keypad on VT100 or the auxiliary keypad of VT200, you can work with characters as well as with larger portions of text. Cursor position determines how text will be affected by the EVE commands, and you can move the cursor through the file in a variety of ways. In keypad mode, EVE keypad commands make it possible to delete, find, insert, substitute, and move text in a file with a single keystroke.

The line commands allow you to manipulate a range of one or more lines of text using any of the EVE line commands. The command line is activated with the DO keypad command. You type simple commands after the "Command:" prompt on the command line, which is located at the bottom of your screen.

In addition, EVE provides the following features to make your editing easier:

- An on-line Help facility, which you can use at any time during editing without disrupting the editing session.

- Searching the text in various ways.

- Various cursor movement key functions.

- Journaling, to secure the editing session and to restore in case the file is lost due to a system failure.

- Multiple windowing: You can split the window to accommodate more than one file for editing in a single session and also to accommodate DCL command interaction and spawning.

Once you have entered the EDIT command with the /TPU qualifier and the file name, you have activated EVE. EVE goes directly into keypad mode, and legend information showing the file name and a blank screen appears if the file is being newly created. This blank screen shows that it is in insert mode. If the file already exists, the first 21 lines of the file are displayed on the screen. The status line, containing the legend information about the editing session and the filename, is located at the bottom of the screen. It shows buffer name, editing mode, i.e., whether "insert" or "overstrike," and the direction of editing, whether forward or backward.

Many EVE editing commands are assigned to the numeric keypad on the VT100 keyboard. On the VT200 keyboard, the auxiliary keypad, i.e., the eight-key keypad with four arrow keys, and the function keys <F10> through <F14> are assigned with many EVE editing commands. The VT200's numeric keypad is used by EVE only for numerical entries. See Figs. 3.1 and 3.2 for the keypad diagrams for the VT100 and VT200 terminals.

The *screen mode* is the default in the EVE editor. However, *line mode,* which is another way to communicate with EVE, is implicitly used by the DO commands as well as several single key operations.

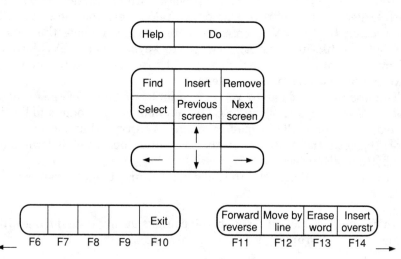

Figure 3.1 Editing keypad used by EVE on VT200 terminals.

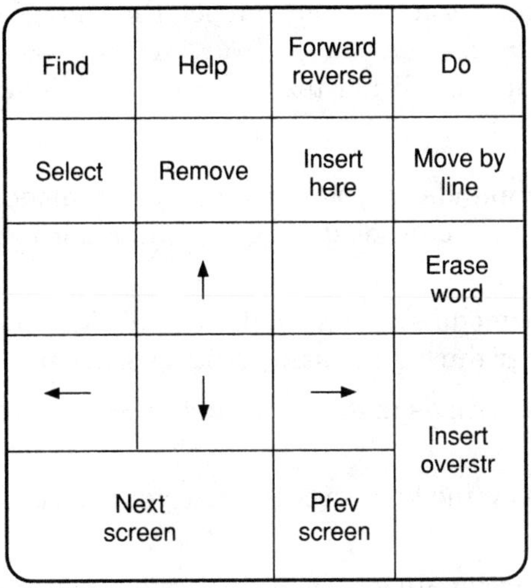

Find	Help	Forward reverse	Do
Select	Remove	Insert here	Move by line
	↑		Erase word
←	↓	→	Insert overstr
Next screen		Prev screen	

Figure 3.2 Application keypad of VT100 used by EVE.

You access the command line with the DO command, which is issued by pressing the <DO> key on the auxiliary keypad on the VT200 or the <PF4> key on the VT100 numeric keypad. After you press the <DO> key, EVE places the cursor on the line below the status line and prompts you for the command, by displaying

```
Command:
```

Once you give the command and any parameters that the command may require, the editor executes it on the screen or gives a failure message on the status line. If you do not give additional parameters for the command when required, EVE prompts for these parameters on the command line.

The line commands are *case insensitive*. That is, you can type either 'TOP WINDOW' or 'top window'; both mean the same for the command to interpret. But it is not so with the text. By default, when you search for text the EVE is *case sensitive*. If you wanted to search for a string "SYSTEM DESIGN" and you enter "system design" as a parameter for the search command, EVE comes up with a failure message. But, this case sensitivity can be controlled by setting one of the flags. Help facility can be used to find details regarding this. You can abbreviate the DO commands; for example, TOP WINDOW can be abbreviated as TOP WIN.

EVE is one of the most versatile editors available on OpenVMS. You can use it for editing many kinds of text and program files. With EVE you can create new files, insert text into them, and edit and manipulate text in existing files. EVE is interactive; you can see the changes you make to a file as they take place.

EVE offers many features to make editing text easy and efficient. These features include the following:

- Two ways to enter editing commands: keypad mode and line mode. You can move from one mode to the other during the same editing session.

- Two ways to enter text: insert mode and overstrike mode. You can move from one mode to the other during the same editing session.

- Files and buffers: You can work with as many files and buffers as you need during your EVE session.

- Key definition facility: You can define keys to customize your keypad editing functions.

- VAXTPU procedures: You can automate your editing sessions by programming.

EVE was originally designed for use on either the VT200- or VT100-series terminals. However, this chapter emphasizes the use of the VT200-series terminals. Whenever a specific key is mentioned without reference to the screen or the terminal series, you can assume that key is on the VT200 keyboard.

To invoke EVE you have to specify a file name of a file which is to be either created newly or modified. EVE is invoked with the following format:

```
$ EDIT/TPU filename.ext
```

The editor enters into the screen mode by default. You can use the DO key to issue various line commands once you are in the editor. Some of the important commands you can execute within EVE using the DO key are:

```
-SPAWN
-ATTACH
-TWO WINDOWS
-INCLUDE FILE
-BUFFER
-WRITE
-DCL
-LEARN
```

For a list of other line commands that can be executed using the DO command, refer to Fig. 3.3.

Command	Description
BOTTOM	Moves the cursor to the end of a file.
END OF LINE	Moves the cursor to the end of the current line.
ERASE CHARACTER	Erases the character on which the cursor is blinking.
ERASE LINE	Erases the remainder of the line from the current cursor position to the end of the line.
FILL PARAGRAPH	Reformats a paragraph within current margins.
GET FILE	Gets the contents of a specified file, stores it in an editing buffer, and displays it on the screen.
HELP	Provides on-line help for the EVE command line interface.
MOVE BY WORD	Moves the cursor to the beginning of the next word.
ONE WINDOW	Deletes a second window.
OTHER WINDOW	When more than one window is active, this command switches the cursor to make one of the other windows active.
QUIT	Exits EVE without saving your current editing work in a new file.
REPLACE	Replaces the next occurrence of the current search string with a new string.
RESTORE	Restores the text last erased.

Figure 3.3 Some line commands of EVE.

The most frequently used editing functions are associated with the key belonging to the application keypad (see Fig. 3.4). These commands can edit the text, change the editing environment, or provide information about the current editing session. You can edit a command while entering it, using the EVE keypad commands.

3.2 BUFFER

The storage areas that EVE occupies in the computer are called buffers. Buffers contain text during an EVE session. EVE buffers exist only for the duration of your editing session. When the session ends the buffers are discarded.

When you start to edit an existing file, EVE copies the text into an empty buffer. This empty buffer is given the same name as the file you are editing. If, for example, you want to edit the file POKER.LIS, EVE places a copy of this file in an empty buffer, and names the buffer POKER.LIS. The original file still exists in your directory. EVE always

Command	Description	VT200 Key	VT100 Key
DO	Activates the command mode.	DO	PF4
ERASE WORD	Deletes the current word.	F13	COMMA
EXIT	Exits EVE after saving the file.	<control/z> or F10	<control/z>
FIND	Locates a search string.	FIND	PF1
FORWARD/ REVERSE	Switches the editing direction.	F11	PF3
HELP	On-line help for the editor keys is displayed.	HELP	PF2
INSERT HERE	Inserts the contents of the Insert buffer to the left of the cursor.	INSERT HERE	9
INSERT/ OVERSTRIKE	Switches the editing mode to insert or overstrike.	F14	ENTER
MOVE BY LINE	Moves the cursor to the end of lines.	F12	MINUS
NEXT SCREEN	A screenful of the text is vertically scrolled towards the end of file.	NEXT SCREEN	0
PREV SCREEN	A screenful of the text is vertically scrolled towards the beginning of file.	PREV SCREEN	<Period>
REMOVE	Deletes the selected range of text and places it in the Insert buffer.	REMOVE	8
RETURN	Inserts a Carriage Return.	RETURN	RETURN
SELECT	Marks the text for selection range.		

Figure 3.4 Frequently used keypad functions of EVE.

works only on the copy. If you look at the status line you will see that the name of the buffer corresponds to the name of the file. When you invoke EVE without providing a filename, the first thing the editor does is to set aside an empty buffer called MAIN. No new file actually exists until you end your EVE session, at which time EVE prompts you for a filename for the contents of the buffer.

When you work with EVE, you use the commands assigned to the keypad to modify and manipulate the text. Some of the commands are used to move the cursor to particular places in the text. You can also use the arrow keys to move the cursor.

Initially, when EVE is invoked, the cursor is placed at the beginning of the file, which is indicated by its position at the top left corner of the screen. You can move the cursor in any direction through the file using the arrow keys. The cursor movement keys <RIGHT ARROW> and <LEFT ARROW> move the cursor one character to the right and left, respectively. The <UP ARROW> and <DOWN ARROW> keys move the cursor up and down one line.

There is also a quick way to move to the next line of text, the MOVE BY LINE command, which is the <F12> key on the VT200 and the

<MINUS> key on the VT100 numeric pad. You can use the START OF LINE command to move to the beginning of the current line and the END OF LINE command to move to the end of the current line. In addition, you can use the MOVE BY WORD line command to move one word at a time.

Those users who are familiar with EDT can simulate the EDT keypad mode on EVE by setting the keypad. You do this by executing the following DO command:

```
SET KEYPAD EDT
```

In this case, the numeric keypad keys get defined to behave like an EDT editor. For example, the '0' key on the numeric keypad moves the cursor by one space, <PF4> deletes the line, <PF1> <PF4> undelete the line, etc. So, you will not be losing your EDT experience when working with EVE. This is made possible by means of a set of procedures supplied along with EVE. We will discuss the procedure writing in EVE later in this chapter.

If required, text can be added to a file by positioning the cursor where the text should be added and typing the text. The cursor and any text following it will be moved to the right as you type each character. You can insert a single character on many lines of text. The characters are always inserted to the left of the cursor. Use <RETURN> when you want to start a new line. To break a line of text, position the cursor on the character that will be the first character of the new line and press <RETURN>.

When you use the EXIT command to finish your editing session, EVE copies the contents of the current buffer into a new file. EVE deletes all the buffers created during your session, and returns the storage space they occupied to the operating system for other uses. When you do not want to save a copy of the current buffer, end your session with the QUIT command instead of EXIT. If you use the EXIT command, the buffer is not written to the same file, but to a new file with the same filename and extension, and with a version number one more than that of the existing file.

At the start of your session, EVE also sets up another buffer called INSERT HERE. EVE uses the INSERT HERE buffer for SELECT REMOVE and INSERT HERE functions. The INSERT HERE buffers are a part of your EVE session. You can erase the contents of these buffers during your editing session, but you cannot remove the buffers themselves until you end the session.

EVE also provides a HELP buffer. You can access HELP through the HELP key on the keyboard, or by entering HELP on the command line.

If you want to edit several different files in one EVE session, EVE makes it easy. Each file is placed in a separate buffer. You can create additional buffers to store portions of text or other material that you might want to look at during your editing session. Various line commands enable you to create new buffers. The status line always displays the name of the current buffer.

Buffer names can contain any printing characters (letters, punctuation marks, and digits). There are no restrictions on name size, except that you must type this name at least once, so you will find short names easier to use.

The SHOW command displays information about the buffers that you have created during your editing session. EVE creates other special-purpose buffers which are not normally displayed by the SHOW command. These buffers include the INSERT HERE and HELP buffers, as well as the COMMANDS, MESSAGES, SHOW, DCL, CHOICES, and PROMPT buffers.

3.3 WINDOWS

A window is a section of the screen of your terminal. A window displays the contents of a buffer. The EVE editing environment has more than one window: the main window, which is mapped or assigned to the current buffer, and the message and command windows, which are below the status line. EVE allows you to create two text windows, each mapped to a different buffer. This ability to split the screen allows you to compare two files during the same editing session.

EVE places the cursor in the main window at the beginning of an editing session. Notice that the bottom boundary of the window is the highlighted status line. The top boundary is the first line on the screen.

EVE automatically scrolls or moves the text in the current window (the window the cursor is in) for you. For example, when you have entered enough text to fill up the window, EVE scrolls the text up line by line so that you continue to see what you are typing. When text is scrolled, the top part of your document moves up beyond the top of the window, temporarily out of view. EVE also provides some keypad and line commands to allow you to scroll through text.

When you want to see different parts of a long document at the same time, you can split the one window into two windows. The window splits horizontally, creating two windows, each having its own status line.

3.3.1 TWO WINDOWS command

The TWO WINDOWS command creates sections on the screen, making it possible to view different parts of one file, or two different files. Before creating two windows, invoke EVE and the desired file. The file is displayed in a single window. Use the TWO WINDOWS command to display the file in two windows.

3.3.2 Place markers

The current text position can be marked by the MARKER command, which takes marker name as a parameter. Marker name is a string of ASCII characters. Different places can be marked by using different marker names for each position. Later, to go to any marked position, use the GO TO command, which also takes the marker name as its parameter.

3.3.3 LEARN command

EVE editor has a built-in feature to learn the commands. You can use the LEARN command to do this. Most of the nonprintable keys, like the control and function keys, can be defined as a sequence of other keys by the LEARN command. To define a key, follow the steps below:

Press the DO key

Enter the command LEARN

Enter any sequence of keys except <control/r>

Enter <control/r>

Enter the key to be defined

Any particular line from the buffer contents can be displayed using the line command, which takes the line number to be displayed as the parameter. You can import and execute any OpenVMS utility into your EVE environment without disrupting the editing session. For this, you can use the DCL command. For example,

```
Command: DCL DIR *.TXT
```

will first split the screen to make room for the DCL output, and then on that screen display all TXT files. The screen contents of this split screen are inserted in a buffer called DCL, which is displayed in the legend information below the screen.

The SPAWN command can be used to create a subprocess in which a set of DCL commands can be executed. You may prefer to do this when you wish to use the entire screen area for interactive use of DCL commands. After having completed the spawned process, you can resume your editing session with EVE by typing LOGOUT at the '$' prompt that is displayed by the spawned process.

3.4 PROCEDURES

You can enhance the editing capabilities using some advanced features of EVE. EVE is written in a text processing package on OpenVMS called VAXTPU (VAX Text Processing Utility). TPU by itself is a self-contained programming language used for text processing. A TPU file has a default extension of .TPU and an output file with a file extension .TPU$SECTION. You can use the /SECTION qualifier on the $EDIT/TPU command line. If you do not specify an output file by default, the section file is created on the SYS$LIBRARY area with filename EVE$SECTION.TPU$SESSION. Many programs that EVE uses, as well as many example programs showing the EVE programming techniques, are written in TPU and available in the area called SYS$EXAMPLES.

You may wish to make EVE available for your customized use. For this you can extend EVE features by programming it. A typical sequence for EVE programming includes the following steps:

1. Create a .TPU program file for processing by EVE. This file contains procedures, branches, etc., coded in TPU language.

2. Create MASTER and VERSION files. These are required to make the extensions to TPU.

3. The file SYS$EXAMPLES:EVE$BUILD.TPU is available to build EVE programs. Use this filename as an input parameter in the EDIT/TPU command to create a specified section file (with .TPU$SECTION extension). The original EVE functions as well as the new functionalities specified in this section file are available when you use EVE next time.

To implement your additions to EVE functionality, execute the following command:

```
$ EDIT/TPU/COMMAND=SYS$EXAMPLES:EVE$BUILD.TPU/NODISPLAY/-
NOINITIALIZATION/OUTPUT=output_file_name TPU_input_file_name.
```

For details of EVE programming please refer to DEC manuals on EVE and VAXTPU.

Deleting text in EVE is a simple operation handled by a single keystroke or command. You can delete text by the character, the word, or the line. To delete characters, use the <x] key on the VT200 or <DELETE> on the VT100. This deletes the characters located to the left of the cursor. You can also define any other key to be an ERASE CHARACTER command and use that key for deleting. In this case, the character located to the right of the cursor is deleted.

To delete a word, position the cursor on the word and use the ERASE WORD command or the <F13> key on the VT200 or the <COMMA> key on the numeric pad of the VT100. To delete a line of text, position the cursor at the beginning of the line and use the ERASE LINE command.

The deleted text is stored by EVE in a workspace called the Delete buffer. This buffer contains the most recently deleted character, word, or line. You can use the contents of the buffer to restore the most recent text that you have deleted.

To restore the deleted text that is stored in the Delete buffer, use the RESTORE line command. This is sometimes used as a cut and paste function. If you wanted to move a string of text in the file from one place to another, you can delete that word or line and restore the same at the required position on the screen. But it is safer to use the range selection mechanism of EVE.

3.5   HELP

EVE's on-line Help facility allows you to obtain help on a specific EVE key or command during your editing session.

While in the keypad mode, you can use the HELP command, i.e., the <HELP> key on the VT200 or <PF2> on the VT100 to help with keypad commands. A help screen appears; you can then press any key to obtain help with that key.

To get help from the command line, type HELP at the 'Command:' prompt and Press <Return>. A help screen appears. You can then type HELP and the name of a command to obtain help with that command.

Among the many available keypad functions for editing a file, changing the editing direction, searching for text strings, and cutting and pasting portions of text are frequently used.

When you begin an EVE editing session, the cursor movement through the text in a file is forward, or toward the end of the buffer. This is the default editing direction. For example, when you use the MOVE BY LINE command, the cursor moves to the end of lines, or when you use the FIND command to search for a text string, the search advances from the cursor toward the end of the line.

In addition to moving the cursor by one character, word, or line at a time, EVE provides ways to move the cursor in larger increments. For example, the TOP and BOTTOM line commands move the cursor to the beginning or the end of the file quickly. These commands are particularly useful when you are working with large files.

You can also move the cursor through the file a screenful of text at a time using the PREV SCREEN command, i.e., <PREV SCREEN> on the VT200 and <PERIOD> on the VT100 numeric keypad, or the NEXT SCREEN command, i.e., <NEXT SCREEN> key on the VT200 or <0>

key on the numeric keypad of the VT100. This brings the previous page or next page of the file content onto the display.

Moving the cursor a character or a word at a time in a small file can be time-consuming but acceptable. However, using this method on large files can be tedious. EVE provides a simpler method of locating text with the FIND command, i.e., the <FIND> key on the VT200 or the <PF1> key on the VT100. FIND searches through the current file for a previously specified word, character, or any string. It locates an item quickly, thus minimizing the time to scan the text. FIND can also be used with the wildcard specification.

When the FIND command is activated, it searches for the specified item in the current editing direction. EVE prompts you for the text string to search for, or the search string. You type the search string and press <Return>, and EVE searches for the string. EVE moves the cursor to the first occurrence of the search string that it encounters.

EVE accepts either lowercase or uppercase letters. If the word is typed in all lowercase letters, EVE finds the word whether it is in lowercase, uppercase, or a combination of the two. If the word is typed in all uppercase letters, EVE finds the word only if it is in all uppercase letters. If the word is typed in a combination of lowercase and uppercase, EVE finds only those occurrences that have the same combination of lowercase and uppercase letters.

If you want to find the next occurrence of the search string, you can press the <FIND> key twice and EVE will search for the previously entered search string.

This method of locating text can save a considerable amount of time when editing a big file. The search string must be made unique in order to confine the search if you want to get it quickly. If the string cannot be found, EVE comes up with a message indicating that either the string was not found or the string exists, but located in the opposite direction. In the latter case, the editor will ask you whether to find the string in the other direction by displaying a question string on the command line.

Grouping large amounts of text using the SELECT RANGE command is another useful feature of EVE. The SELECT command, i.e., the <SELECT> key on the VT200 or the <7> key on the VT100 numeric keypad, can be used to select a section or range of text. The section of text can be made up of one or more words of one or more lines of text. On the screen a highlight identifies the selected text.

To select a range of text, move the cursor to the beginning of the text to be manipulated, press <SELECT> or <7>, then use any of the cursor movement keys to highlight the text, either a word, line, or pages of it. Portions of text can be excluded from a selected range by moving the cursor back until the unwanted text is no longer highlighted. You can cancel any selection by pressing the <SELECT> key a second time.

The REMOVE command, i.e., the <REMOVE> key on the VT200 or the <8> key on the numeric keypad of the VT100, allows you to delete the text in a selected range. This method allows you to remove larger portions of text with a single keystroke. The REMOVE command erases the text that was highlighted using the SELECT command from the screen and arranges the text suitably to make the displays contiguous. All the text thus removed is stored in the Insert buffer. The text remains in this buffer until it is replaced by other text or until the editing session is completed. If you select another range of text and remove it, the Insert buffer replaces the old range of text with the new range of text. It is to be noted that when selecting a portion of text for removal, you should move the cursor one space beyond the last character you want to remove. The character or space the cursor is on is not included in the removed text.

The removed text available in the Insert buffer can be placed anywhere on the screen, i.e., on the editing buffer. This can be done by positioning the cursor at the position you wish and invoking the INSERT HERE command, i.e., the <INSERT HERE> command on the VT200 or the <9> key on the numeric keypad of the VT100. All the text to the right of the cursor is moved to the right to accommodate the insertion of text.

The EVE editor by default is in the insertion mode. As you key-in text to the editor, the characters from the existing display move to the right of the cursor to accommodate the new text. You can change this mode to the overstrike mode, in which case the characters are overwritten. No text is inserted in this mode, and you do not see any movement of existing text. The INSERT/OVERSTRIKE is a toggle-like function invoked by the <F14> key on the VT200 and the <ENTER> key on the VT100. The status line will show whether you are in INSERT mode or OVERSTRIKE mode.

3.6 OTHER FUNCTIONS

Suppose you make changes in a paragraph which results in extending one of the lines beyond the right margin. In this case, you may wish to reformat the text so that it appears aligned according to the original page setting. You can use the FILL PARAGRAPH command to do this. After making changes in the paragraph you can place the cursor anywhere on the paragraph and execute this command. Note that there is no single key function for this command, but you can define one using the DEFINE KEY command. If you have more than one paragraph requiring reformatting, then you can use the 'SELECT RANGE' technique discussed earlier to highlight the necessary part of the text. If you execute the FILL PARAGRAPH command now, the entire highlighted text gets reformatted.

On many occasions, you may like to compare text between two or more files. Or you may like to extract a part of the text from one file and include it in another file. If you are involved in a medium- to large-scale software development project, the chances are that you need to access more than two files for comparison, extraction, pruning, and so on. You can use the GET FILE line command to get another file other than the one being edited. The editor places the file gotten using GET FILE in a separate edit buffer identified by the filename, and the status line changes accordingly. The display area now acts like toggle space, initially showing the new buffer. Using the NEXT BUFFER command you can get the contents of the buffer corresponding to the originally edited buffer.

When you want to work with two files simultaneously, it is preferable to have the view of text from both the files on a single display instead of toggling between. You can do this using the TWO WINDOWS command. This command splits the screen into two halves, each having its own status line. When you split the screen like this, initially the status lines on the two screens show identical information and the text displayed on the two screens is also identical, being from the same file. Now, if you had already executed the GET FILE command, the text being displayed is from that newly obtained file. To get the contents of the original buffer, issue the PREVIOUS BUFFER command (or even NEXT BUFFER command, because you have only two files at this stage). Then the text from the original file is displayed on one of the two windows with the status line properly changed.

If you have not executed the GET FILE command after issuing the TWO WINDOWS command, the text from the same file is available for editing on two windows. Whatever changes you make in one of the windows is reflected in the other window, too. You cannot attempt to produce two versions of the same file at the same time. The only way is probably to make a copy of the file using the DCL command and then execute GET FILE to get the new file. This is because the edit buffer is identified by the filename alone; also, the file gets written with the name once you save the edited text.

During editing, it is likely to get messages corresponding to MAIL utility, system messages, broadcast messages from other users, or PHONE messages. This alters the arrangement of the text on the window. You can use <control/w> to clear the screen and redraw the file contents in this case. This command will refresh the screen and display the text as it existed before any message.

All editing sequences of EVE are saved as a journal file by default. Therefore, you can resume an interrupted editing session. The likely causes of interruption are system failure, power failure, or <control/y> mistakenly entered by the user. No contents of the edited text is lost in such cases. You can resume editing using the /RECOVER qualifier when you invoke EVE next time for this file. Be cautious, though, not to invoke EDT without this qualifier. If you do so, and by mistake you exit from EVE in a normal way, i.e., by using the EXIT command, then the file gets written as a new version and the contents of the journal for the original file will be lost. So, you have to use the /RECOVER qualifier if you want to save your edits for particular files. The filename of the journal file is the same as the edited file, but the file extension is .TJL. When you resume an edit session involving such a recovery, you can actually see the entire editing like a motion picture, the cursor moving here and there and making deletions, additions, and so on. You need to wait until the cursor comes to a flicker-free, stationary position before you can start your editing. Another caution you need to observe is that you must use the same type of terminal when you resume editing. If you edited using VT200 you have to use a VT200-type terminal; you cannot use a VT100-type terminal and vice versa.

If you exceed your disk quota while you are saving an edited file using EVE, you will get the following message:

```
Output file could not be created
Filename: DISK:[USER]A_FILE.TXT
ACP file create failed
Disk quota exceeded
Press Return to continue
```

Now, in order not to lose the editing, you have to come out of EVE by using <control/y>. You will get back to '$' prompt. Although your file could not be saved, by interrupting thus you will save the journal file. When you resolve the disk quota problem by deleting unwanted files, purging files, or requesting the system manager for more quota, you can resume the EVE editing session using the /RECOVER qualifier to recapture the editing session and save the edited file.

If you had already exceeded disk quota when you invoked EVE, you will get a message similar to the following:

```
Error opening DISK:[USER]B_TEXT.TXT as output
ACP file extend failed
Disk quota exceeded
```

In this case, you can resolve the disk quota problem first and simply reinvoke EVE.

3.7 SUMMARY

Flexibility, ease of learning because of a detailed on-line help feature, learning capabilities, and key definability make the Extensible VAX Editor a reliable and most frequently used editing tool on OpenVMS.

DCL Programming

4.1 INTRODUCTION

The Digital Command Language, DCL, has become one of the most friendly command-level interfaces. Over the years it has matured to become a major command programming language also. In the current version of OpenVMS, DCL can provide the user with block-structured programming, advanced string manipulations, and fairly advanced file and other input/output handling. In conjunction with system services called lexical functions, DCL can be programmed to view and change various system-related, executive-related, and process-related information. Thus it provides an efficient supervisory tool to interact safely with kernel and executive levels of OpenVMS.

The main goal of this chapter is to illustrate advanced capabilities of DCL programming. This chapter is punctuated with several examples to prepare the reader to write DCL codes for routine jobs, housekeeping, and other special procedures. The techniques discussed here in association with the lexical functions discussed in the previous chapter can be used to write such advanced procedures as installation kits for simple and complex software products.

In this chapter we will study IF-THEN-ELSE structuring, string handling, error handling, interrupt handling, and input/output, including files, iteration, and recursion capabilities of EVE.

We will quickly recall some important DCL definitions and usage.

The dollar sign "$" is the DCL prompt by default. Command procedures are usually files containing DCL commands. The exclamation sign "!" is used to provide comments in these procedures.

A symbol is any alphanumeric string which can be assigned with a string expression or an integer expression. A string is assigned to a symbol by placing the string in between double quotations.

Symbol substitution is the mechanism that the DCL command interpreter performs to interpret the symbol. The single quote character " ' " is used variously to tell the interpreter that the symbol substitution needs to be performed. Suppose a symbol called NEBULA is defined as CRAB:

```
$ NEBULA := CRAB
```

Then an example for symbol substitution is:

```
$ WRITE SYS$OUTPUT "Determining if ''NEBULA' has a Pulsar"
```

Then the above statement will display the following string on the screen:

```
Determining if CRAB has a Pulsar
```

And

```
$ CC/LIS 'NEBULA.C
```

will input a C program called CRAB.C to the C compiler.

Figure 4.1 shows a summary of DCL command interpreter functionality. Examples in Figs. 4.2 and 4.3 demonstrate DCL programming for substring overlays and binary overlays.

DCL command level can be treated as level 0. Usually command procedures execute at level 0. Other command procedures and subroutines can be invoked using the @ command and CALL command, respectively, from within a command procedure in which case the called procedure executes at one level higher than the level of the calling procedure. Such nestings can go up to 32 levels.

A local symbol is defined within a level. It is not available outside the level. Local symbols can be assigned as follows (Note the special uses of assignment symbol ":="):

Phases of Command Interpretation in DCL

Command Input search or Lexical Analysis of input (Locating symbols at the beginning of string—bypass translation if "=" or ":" encountered, locating symbols ended with apostrophes, perform symbol substitution from left to right, if nothing found equate null string.)

Parsing: Interpreter checks the form, function, and syntactical relationship of each part. Symbols preceded by & substituted, null string if not found.

Execution: Replaces symbols not translated until execution time—IF, WRITE, and symbols in lexicals. If not defined, ERROR.

Figure 4.1 The command interpretation by DCL.

```
$ NAME = "MICKEY MOUSE"
$ DEGREE = "Ph. D in Gastronomy"
$ DISNEY_MEMBER[0, 15] := 'NAME'
$ DISNEY_MEMBER[20, 15] := 'DEGREE'
     OR
$ DISNEY_MEMBER[F$LENGTH(NAME)+2, 15] := 'TYPE'
$ SHOW SYMBOL DISNEY_MEMBER
Can create blanks:
$LINE [0,80] := "" !Previous 79 are automatically blanks.
```

Figure 4.2 Substring overlays in DCL.

```
$ PEGASUS = "A mythical Horse. Here, a DCL String example"
$ STALLION := Another Horse ! No quotes needed with ":="
$ FERMAT = 17     !An Integer assignment
```

You can define symbols as global symbols so that they are available throughout the process. (Recall that a process is either an interactive session to which you are logged in or a batch job which is submitted using the SUBMIT command.) Hence they can be used to pass data across procedures as they maintain unique values for the entire session. Global symbols can be defined like this:

```
$ GLOBEX == "A Global SYMBOL"
$ RUN_MY_JOB :== RUN MY_DISK:[MY_AREA]MY_PROGRAM
$ DEV_STATUS == %x10000000    ! A hexadecimal status value
```

The SHOW SYMBOL command displays the string or arithmetic value assigned to the symbol:

```
$ SHOW SYMBOL PEGASUS
$ PEGASUS = "A mythical Horse -- But here, a DCL String example"
```

Multiple lines of the command need to be separated by a hyphen ("-") on each line as follows:

```
$ This_is_a_long_symbol = "This is too long a string to be -
$_contained in a single line"
```

```
Binary overlays:
$ A = 1 ! 0001
$ A [1, 3] = 3  ! 0111
$ SHOW SYMBOL A ! 7
```

Figure 4.3 Binary overlays in DCL.

Labels are names generally starting a section of the procedure, sub-procedure, or subroutine. Labels are referred to by the GOTO, GOSUB, and CALL commands.

Command qualifiers for a task can be specified in a separate procedure and invoked. Suppose the CC_SWITCH.COM file has the following line:

```
$ /LIST/NOOPT/DEBUG
```

Then you could compile your file as CC filename@CC_SWITCH.

The procedures and subroutines can receive up to 8 passed parameters in variables named P1, P2, etc. Parameters must be enclosed in quotes if the string has spaces or if the string is lowercase; otherwise, the interpreter converts lowercase to uppercase and uses spaces as delimiters. Also, if the first parameter begins with /, enclose it in quotes and if the parameter contains literal quotation marks, use a double set of quotation marks like:

```
$ CALL FUGUE "A string within a ""STRING"" "
```

If passing a symbol as a parameter, use it with apostrophes. For example, to call a subroutine named SUB2 passing the values in a symbol called ENTIRE_GROUP, you would do the following:

```
$ CALL SUB2 'ENTIRE_GROUP'
```

You can verify (debug) the execution of a command procedure using the SET VERIFY command. You can turn off the verification mode with the SET NOVERIFY command. This setting is global to the process. Setting it anywhere in any command procedure or DCL command level will result in it being set for all procedures including level 0.

4.2   IF-THEN-ELSE BLOCK STRUCTURES

IF-THEN-ELSE-ENDIF structures are supported in DCL for OpenVMS VAX version 5.0 onwards and OpenVMS AXP version 1.0 onwards. It provides a Pascal-like programming tool as demonstrated in the example shown in Fig. 4.4.

Note that IF—THEN—ENDIF or IF—THEN—ELSE—ENDIF nesting can go up to 16 levels. The symbol-substituting apostrophe character is not required for symbols specified with the IF command; the symbol substitution is automatic in this case.

Notice the usage of lexical functions in this example. The symbol substitution is automatic for symbols specified as arguments for lexical functions.

```
$!------------------------------------------------------------------
$!  An example to demonstrate If-Then-Else block structure in DCL
$!  Finds the Architecture of the system you are logged in.
$!------------------------------------------------------------------
$ Vax_or_Axp := "Vax" ! Assume that the architecture is VAX
$ If (F$getsyi("CPU") .eq. 128)      ! If not Vax.......
$ Then
$    Vax_or_Axp := F$getsyi("ARCH_NAME")
$    If (Vax_or_Axp .nes. "Alpha")
$      Then
$          If (f$locate("ALPHA", f$edit(Vax_or_Axp,"UPCASE")) -
$                          .lt. f$length(Vax_or_Axp))
$          Then
$               Vax_or_Axp := "Alpha" ! ......Alpha AXP
$          Else
$               Write sys$output "Unknown hardware architecture "Vax_or_Axp""
$               Exit
$          Endif ! Unknown
$      Endif ! Not "Alpha"
$ Endif ! Not VAX
$!
$ Write Sys$output "Your system architecture is: "Vax_or_Axp""
$ exit
```

Figure 4.4   An example of If-then-else block structure in DCL.

4.3   SUBROUTINES AND SUBPROCEDURES

Subroutines in DCL are executed at a separate level than the main procedure which calls the subroutine. Thus, subroutines maintain their own parameters P1...P8. This is in contrast to subprocedures which are executed at the same level as the main procedure. Hence subprocedures inherit the same parameter list P1...P8 as that of the main procedure. The example in Fig. 4.5 illustrates the use and syntax of subroutines.

The example in Fig. 4.6 illustrates the use of subprocedures.

4.4   CASE-LIKE STRUCTURES IN DCL

1. Assign to a symbol the list of options.

2. Get the option.

3. Use lexicals F$LOCATE and F$LENGTH to verify if the option is valid by searching the list of options, or use F$ELEMENT to see if the user's choice is one of the valid commands.

4. Use the GOTO statement to direct control to the appropriate action module.

An example using the lexical function F$ELEMENT is shown in Fig. 4.7.

```
$!-------------------------------------------------------------------------------
$! An example of a subroutine in DCL. Input to this program is a list of
$! up to 8 C program files to be linked together. The files are assumed to
$! have extension C.
$! This module conditionally calls one of the two subroutines, one for
$! building images and another for building debug images
$!-------------------------------------------------------------------------------
$!
$! Define Symbol "Say"
$!
$ Say := Write Sys$output
$!
$! Ask for program files in the order to be linked together
$!
$ Say ""
$ Say "Input C program filenames (no extensions) in the order to be linked."
$ Say "Separate the filenames with commas (maximum 8 files)
$ Say ""
$ Inquire File_list "Filenames> "
$ Inquire Debug "Do you want to build Debug Version. Y,N [N]"
$ If Debug .eqs. "Y"
$   then Call Build_with_debug 'File_list
$ Else
$   Call Build 'File_list
$ Exit
$!
$! Subroutine to build image
$!
$ Build: Subroutine
$!
$! Extract filenames one by one
$!
$ File_count = 1
$ Define Sys$error Build.rep          ! Log errors to a file
$ On warning then goto compile_error
$ Compile:
$    CC_File = F$element(File_count-1, ",", P1)'
$    If CC_File .eqs. "," then goto Link
$    Say ""
$    Say " Compiling file "CC_File'......."
$    Say ""
$    Define Sys$output NI: ! Discard compile and link messages
$    CC/LIS 'CC_File
$    Success = $Status
$    Deassign Sys$output
$    If Success
$    then
$       File_count = File_count + 1
$       Goto Compile
$    Else
$       Deassign Sys$error
$       Say " "
$       Say " Error compiling file "CC_File'. Image "
$       Say " cannot be created. Errors logged into file: Build.rep"
$       Say " "
$       Return
$    endif
$ Link:
$ On warning then goto link_error
```

Figure 4.5 A subroutine in DCL.

```
$    Say ""
$    Say " Linking files......."
$    Say ""
$    Define Sys$output NI:  ! Discard compile and link messages
$    Link 'P1
$    Success = $status
$    Deassign Sys$output
$    If Success
$       then
$            Say " "
$            Say " Image "F$element(0, ",", p1)' built successfully"
$            Say " "
$       Else
$            Say " "
$            Say " Image "F$element(0, ",", p1)' could not be built."
$            Say " Error during link. Errors logged into file: Build.rep"
$            Say " "
$    endif
$    Deassign Sys$error
$    Return
$ Exit
$ Compile_error:
$    Deassign Sys$output
$    Deassign Sys$error
$    Say " "
$    Say " Error during compile time. Errors logged into file: Build.rep"
$    Say " "
$ Return
$ Exit
$ Link_error:
$    Deassign Sys$output
$    Deassign Sys$error
$    Say " "
$    Say " Error during link time. Errors logged into file: Build.rep"
$    Say " "
$ Return
$ Exit
$ Endsubroutine
```

Figure 4.5 (*Continued*) A subroutine in DCL.

Another example for a conditional code using F$LOCATE and F$LENGTH is given in Fig. 4.8.

A third example shown in Fig. 4.9 for building and using CASE structures in DCL involves a special usage of local and global symbols. This example uses two global symbols—INPUT to hold user input and CASE_STATUS to hold the status of the case condition test in the subroutine. This example also illustrates how data can be returned in global symbols.

4.5 INPUT/OUTPUT USING FILES

DCL provides input/output commands for files. Even indexed sequential files can be accessed using KEY and INDEX qualifiers. The general strategy for file I/O in DCL is:

```
$! Routine to demonstrate Subprocedures. Note the usage of parameter
$!  FILE_TYPE.
$! This routine displays the disk usage on a sub-directory basis
$!  (one level)
$! for file types that are requested
$!-----
$! Inquire for what kind of files, the disk space statistics is
$!  required.
$!
$ Say := Write Sys$output
$ Set Def Sys$login
$ Inquire file_type "Input the file extension (Ex: COM, FOR, C, DOC, OBJ)"
$! Get the sub-directories one by one
$ Say ""
$ Say "The disk space statistics for "file_type' files is:"
$ Say ""
$ Loop:
$ Sub_dir = F$SEARCH("*.DIR", 1)
$ If Sub_dir .eqs. "" then Exit
$ Gosub Get_stat
$ Goto Loop
$ Exit
$!
$! Beginning of sub-procedure Getstat. Notice the usage of parameter
$!  "file_type"
$! which is local to both the main procedure and this sub-procedure.
$!
$ Get_stat:
$ Sub_dir = "[." + F$parse(Sub_dir,,,"name") + "]"
$ Void = F$search(""sub_dir"*."file_type"")
$ If Void .eqs. ""
$ Then
$ Say "No "file_type" files in "Sub_dir""
$ Return
$ Endif
$ Directory/total/siz 'Sub_dir
$ Return
$ Exit
```

Figure 4.6 A subprocedure example in DCL.

- Use OPEN to open a file, be it a new or old file.
- Use READ and WRITE.
- Use CLOSE to close the file after performing the input/output on the file.

When you log in, OpenVMS opens four files for you automatically. These are SYS$OUTPUT, SYS$INPUT, SYS$COMMAND, and SYS$ERROR. These are, by default, assigned to the terminal for interactive sessions and to the root directory for batch jobs.

```
$!
$! An example of CASE like structure in DCL
$! This procedure mimics some Unix Shell commands
$!
$ Supported = "Is/who/whoami/quit/exit"
$ Ask_command:
$ Inquire/Nopunctuation Command "Vunix>"
$ Command = F$edit(Command, "lowercase")
$ If command .eqs. "quit" .OR. command .eqs. "exit" then exit
$ list_marker = 0
$ Search_list:
$ Unix = F$element(list_marker,"/",Supported)
$ list_marker = list_marker + 1
$ If Unix .eqs. "/"
$       then
$           Goto invalid_command
$       Else
$          If Unix .nes. command
$             then goto Search_list
$          endif
$ endif
$ Goto 'command
$ Exit
$ Is:
$ Dir/br
$ Goto Ask_command
$ Exit
$ who:
$ sho users
$ Goto Ask_command
$ Exit
$ whoami:
$ show process
$ Goto Ask_command
$ Exit
$ Invalid_command:
$ Write sys$output ""
$ Write
$ Write Sys$output " Command error"
$ Write sys$output ""
$ Goto Ask_command
$ Exit
```

Figure 4.7 A conditional code in DCL using the lexical function F$ELEMENT.

4.5.1 OPEN command

The OPEN command assigns a logical name; READ, WRITE, and CLOSE commands refer to this logical name. You don't have to open SYS$INPUT, SYS$OUTPUT, SYS$COMMAND, and SYS$ERROR. The files opened using OPEN are process-permanent unless closed, and the usage of these files is subjected to RMS restrictions. The syntax for the OPEN command is:

```
$ Debug_build_list = "list/run/build"
$ Get_command:
$    Inquire File "Enter the source program name (Press RETURN to
exit)"
$    If File .eqs. "" then Exit
$    Inquire Command -
$    "Enter command (List, Run, Build)"
$    Command = F$edit (Command, "lowercase")
$    IF F$Locate(Command+"/", Debug_build_list) .eq. -
$    F$Length(Debug_build_list) then goto error
$    Goto 'Command'
$ !
$ List:
$ Type 'File'
$ Exit
$ Run:
$ Run 'File'
$ Exit
$ Build:
$ CC/LIS/NOOPT/DEBUG 'File'
$ LINK 'File'
$ Exit
$ Error:
$ Write Sys$output "Invalid option"
$ Goto Get_command
$ Exit
```

Figure 4.8 Another conditional code in DCL using lexical functions F$LOCATE and F$LENGTH.

```
$ OPEN/<READ or WRITE or SHARE or APPEND or ERROR>
a_symbol_$_a_file
```

where "a_symbol" indicates the symbol receiving the logical name assignment corresponding to the file "a_file".

4.5.2 OPEN/READ command

The OPEN/READ command opens a file for read only; no write can be done on the file. This command places the file pointer at the beginning of the file. Upon a read, the file pointer moves to the next record.

An example of using this command is:

```
$ OPEN/READ INFILE RRI_DISK:[RAJ]BOOK.DOC
```

4.5.3 OPEN/WRITE command

The OPEN/WRITE command creates a new file. The file will be a sequential file in print file format. The record format for the file is variable with fixed control (VFC), with a two-byte record header. If the file already

```
$! A Case like structure in DCL. Processes Unix like commands on
OpenVMS
$! Commands supported: Is, who, whoami etc.
$!
$ case := call case_string
$ break := if case_status then goto ask
$ esac := goto ask
$ default := "write sys$output ""? -- command not defined"""
$ process := if case_status then
$ input == ""
$ ask:
$ case_status == 1
$ inquire/nopunctuation input "Vunix> "
$ case Is
$     process dir
$     break
$ case who
$     process show users
$     break
$ case whoami
$     process show process
$     break
$ case quit
$     process exit
$     break
$ case verify
$     process set ver
$     break
$ case noverify
$     process set nover
$     break
$ default
$     break
$ esac
$ exit
$ case_string: subroutine
$ case_status == 0
$ if input .eqs. p1 then case_status == 1 $ return
$ endsubroutine
$ exit
```

Figure 4.9 A CASE structure using global and local symbols in DCL.

exists, this command creates a file with the same name and extension, but with the version number one greater than the existing file.

Here's an example of OPEN/WRITE:

```
$ OPEN/WRITE OUTFILE DEC_DISK:[RAJ]BOOK_THIS_BOOK.TXT
```

By keeping the WRITE command in a loop you could write records one by one until the end of the file or until some other condition is met. An example:

```
$ Open/write output rri_disk:[raj]book.doc
$ Update:
$ Inquire a_record "Input a string of characters (Press
RETURN $_ to quit)"
$ Write output a_record
    $ If output .eqs. ""then goto Finish
    $ Goto Update
    $ Finish:
    $ Close output
    $ Exit
```

4.5.4   OPEN/APPEND command

You can open a file by adding records to it. Use the /APPEND qualifier. This does not create a new version of the file being opened. It allows adding records to a file by positioning the file pointer at the end of the file. An example of using this qualifier is given:

```
$ Open/Append Output Rri_Disk:[Raj]Test.Dat
$ Inquire A_Record "Enter Text......One Line At A Time"
$ Write Output A_Record
$ :
$ :
$ Close Output
$
```

4.5.5   Opening a file for reading and writing

You would use an OPEN/READ/WRITE command to open a file for both input and output. In this situation, the record pointer is placed at the beginning of the file. You can only replace the record that is most recently read. Also, the revised record must be exactly the same size as the record being replaced. The syntax for this command is indicated in the following example:

```
$ open/read/write file rri_disk:[raj]nebulae.dat
```

4.5.6   Sharing the file input/output

To open files for shared input/output, use the /SHARE qualifier. Others may read or write to the file. Use /SHARE=READ to allow other users to read the file and /SHARE=WRITE to allow other users to write to the file and access the file with the TYPE or SEARCH command.

4.5.7   READ command

To read and get contents into a symbol from a file, you would first open the file:

```
$ open/read input_file rri_disk:[raj]tensor.lsp
```

From here on, the input/output with the file TENSOR.LSP takes place with reference to the local symbol INPUT_FILE. This symbol refers to the channel associated with the file. You would read until the end of the file as follows:

```
$ read/end_of_file=eof_process input_file record
    :
    :
$ eof_process:
$ close input_file
$ exit
```

The symbol RECORD gets redefined for each read as in

```
$ start:
$ read/end_of_file=eof_detected input_file record
    :
    :
$ goto start
    :
    :
$ eof_detected:
$ close input_file
$ exit
```

It is a good practice to include the END_OF_FILE control action routine whenever a file is read. Otherwise OpenVMS RMS performs error detection returning error status %RMS-E-EOF. This results in procedure exiting unless you include your own error handling as shown above.

Reading records randomly from indexed sequential files. Use /INDEX and /KEY with READ to read a record associated with the given key in the index. The default primary index is 0. After reading randomly, the remainder of the file can be sequentially read without the /KEY or /INDEX qualifiers. You can also use /DELETE to delete records with the /KEY and /INDEX qualifiers.

4.5.8   WRITE command

You can write a character string or a list of expressions using the WRITE command. First, you should have opened the file for writing.

```
$ open/write output airy_disk:[huygen]optics.vis
$ write output "non-linearity and solitons"
    :
$ close output
```

Note in the WRITE command that substitution for symbols and lexical functions is automatic. You can intersperse symbols and strings as in this example:

```
$ write output "the record is ",record1,"and", record2
```

or

```
$ write output "the record is ''record'."
```

Here is an example showing symbol and lexical substitution in the WRITE command:

```
$ write output "Record ''record' is from the file named",
f$parse(file,,,"name")
```

Note that you do not need to force symbol substitution for lexical functions in WRITE commands as in the IF command.

For WRITE commands, the record pointer is positioned after the record just written. You can write a record that is up to 2048 bytes long. If you are writing a record that is longer than 1024 bytes, or any expression in the WRITE command is longer than 255 bytes, you have to use the /SYMBOL qualifier. Use /UPDATE to modify a record. The file must have been opened for read and write.

4.5.9   Updating records

For updating the records from a file, you would first open the file with READ and WRITE qualifiers:

```
$ open/read/write
```

When opened like this, no new version of the input file is created. For sequential files, the updating record and the record to be replaced must be of the same size. There is no such restriction for indexed sequential files.

Use READ to get records for modification. In sequential records, if the record is shorter, then you have to pad it with spaces. If the record is longer this method of updating will not work.

Use WRITE/UPDATE to write the modified record back to the file. Continue updating like this until you are finished updating. Use CLOSE to close the file.

The above scheme is employed in the following example template for updating a file:

```
$ Open/Read/Write File Rri_Disk:[Raj]Viola.Txt
$ Begin:
$ Read/End_Of_File=Eof File Record
$ Tell := Write Sys$Output
$ Inquire/Nopunct Change "Modify? Y Or N"
$  If Change .Eqs. "N" Then Goto Begin
$  Inquire Modified_Record "New Text"
$  Old_Len = F$Length(Record)
$  New_Length = F$Length(New_Record)
$  If Old_Len .Lt. Then Goto Error
$  If Old_Len .Eq. New_Len Then Goto Write_Record
$  Spaces = "
$  Pad = F$Extract(0,Old_Len-New_Len, Spaces)
$  New_Record = New_Record + Pad
$ Write_Record:
$  Write/Update File New_Record
$  Goto Begin_Loop
$ Error:
$  Tell "Error -- New Record Is Too Long"
$  Goto Prompt
$ End_Loop:
$  Close File
$  Exit
```

4.5.10 Creating a new output file upon update

You may prefer to write the updated records into a new file. In this case you can open the input file and a new output file separately. If you use the same name as the input filename for the output file, then a new version of the file is created.

```
$ Open/Read Infile Rri_Disk:[Raj]Input.Dat
$ Open/Write Outfile Rri_Disk:[Raj]Output.Dat
$ Tell := Write Sys$Output
$ Begin:
$ Read/End_Of_File=End_Loop Infile Record
$ Tell Record
        Inquire/Nopunctuation Ok "Change? Y Or N "
        If Ok .Eqs. "N" Then Goto Write_Record
$  Inquire Record "New Record"
$ Write_Record:
$ Write Outfile Record
$ Goto Begin
$ End_Loop:
$ Close Infile
$ Close Outfile
$ Exit
```

4.5.11   Appending records to a file

An example of updating a file by appending records to it is given below:

```
$ Open/Append File Rri_Disk:[Raj]Kiwi.Dat
$ Begin:
$ Inquire Record -
$ "Enter A New Record (Press Return To Exit) "
$ If Record .Eqs. ""Then Goto End_Loop
$ Write File Record
$ Goto Begin
$ End_Loop:
$ Close File
$ Exit
```

4.5.12   Handling file I/O errors

All input/output errors, file organization errors, and other types of errors are, by default, processed by the Record Management Services of OpenVMS. This default way of handling errors results in the display of errors and abortion of the command procedure. Hence, the user needs to include error handling action routines in the command procedure if he/she wants to continue the command execution, even if there are file errors.

Use the /ERROR qualifier with OPEN, READ, WRITE, and CLOSE to direct control to a labeled action routine if and when the I/O error occurs. This will suppress the display of RMS error messages, and the command procedure will obey the user action to continue or halt the procedure. Also, the choice for the user's error action overrides other error actions in the command procedure requested, using the ON ERROR THEN type of command string (discussed in the next section). An example template for error processing the file input/output is provided below:

```
$ Open/Read/Error=Eop File Hirohito.Txt
  :
$ Eop:
$ Write Sys$Output "File Error"
```

The global symbol $STATUS maintained by the operating system retains the error code. You can use the F$MESSAGE lexical to display the error message corresponding to the error code in this global symbol. Here is a template to illustrate this:

```
$Open/Read/Error=Check File 'p1'
  :
  :
```

```
$ Check:
$ Er_Mesg = F$Message($Status)
$ Tell "Error In File Opening: ",P1
$ Tell Er_Mesg
```

If end of file occurred, and no control action for end of file was specified, then the user-provided action indicated with the ON ERROR command is performed. If neither of these is provided by the user then OpenVMS RMS takes control and displays the corresponding error message. You can pass error condition values with the EXIT command as follows:

```
$@b
$   :
    :
File b.com starts here:

$on warning then goto error
    :
    :
$ error:
$ exit 1
```

Using the STOP command. You can stop execution of a command procedure. This is different from exiting from the command procedure. When you STOP a process you cannot resume it using the CONTINUE command. A typical usage of a STOP command would be:

```
$ on severe_error then stop
```

4.6   ERROR HANDLING

General error handling in DCL command procedures can be performed using the commands ON, SET ON, and SET NoOn.

There are three types of errors that can occur in a command procedure execution. These errors are called conditions in OpenVMS jargon. They are SEVERE_ERROR, ERROR, and WARNING. You can specify your own action for these types of errors using commands like the following:

4.6.1   ON commands

You can override the interpreter's default error handling using the ON command. The general syntax for the ON command is:

```
$ ON condition_type THEN command
```

where "condition_type" can be SEVERE_ERROR, ERROR, WARN-ING, or SUCCESS, and "command" can be a DCL command like EXIT or a GOTO statement.

Using ON WARNING will pass control to the command even if an ERROR and WARNING type of condition is resulting, i.e., conditions of higher levels are processed. If you use ON SEVERE_ERROR, then ERROR and WARNING types of conditions are ignored, i.e., conditions of lower levels are ignored. Therefore, for exiting on warning, error, and severe error, execute: ON WARNING THEN EXIT.

Remember that only one statement can be in effect at any one time. If more ON conditions are requested only the last one is marked for the condition handling.

4.7 $STATUS GLOBAL SYMBOL

All errors are captured in the global symbol called $STATUS. Only the latest error conditions are maintained in $STATUS. Therefore, if the user wants to take action based on the contents of this error variable, the user should assign its value to a local variable before continuing with the command procedure as its value may change depending upon the execution of the next step.

The $STATUS global symbol is a 32-bit-long word. The bit contents for $STATUS are as follows:

Bits 0–2 contain the severity level.

Bits 3–15 contain the message number.

Bits 16–27 contain the number associated with the facility generating the message.

Bits 28–31 contain internal control flags.

Success is indicated by bits 0–2 with values 1 or 3. 1 means success and 3 means information. Errors are indicated by bits 0–2 containing a 0, 2, or 4. 0 means warning, 2 means error, and value 4 indicates a fatal error.

$SEVERITY is another global symbol mapped to bits 0–2 of the $STATUS global symbol. It holds the logical value TRUE if its value is odd, which means success or information. You can use it as follows:

```
$ if $severity then goto display_success
```

Or you can use the $STATUS symbol itself as follows:

```
$ if $status then goto display_success
```

The interpreter maintains and displays the current hexadecimal value of $STATUS. Its ASCII translation can be displayed using F$MESSAGE as follows:

```
$ show symbol $status
$ write sys$output f$message()
```

If they complete successfully, the following commands do not affect $STATUS contents: CONTINUE, DECK, DEPOSIT, EOD, EXAMINE, GOTO, IF, SET SYMBOL/SCOPE, SHOW STATUS, SHOW SYMBOL, STOP, and WAIT.

If these commands result in error off-course, the code will be placed in $STATUS, and the severity level is placed in $SEVERITY.

After exiting because of error or severe error, the interpreter returns control to the previous level. If the condition is warning, success, or information, the procedure continues to execute. For GOTO commands, if the associated label does not exist in the procedure, then the condition is treated as warning. Hence, the user must process such procedural commands using the ON WARNING command.

When the command procedure exits as part of an error-handling routine, the value of $STATUS is passed back to the previous level with the high-order bit of $STATUS set so that the message is not redisplayed.

ON command action is executed only once, i.e., the default error action is reset after performing the ON action. For example:

```
$ on error then goto err_process.
```

After an error, err_process is executed, $STATUS and $SEVERITY are set to success, and the default error action is reset. If a second error occurs and if no ON or SET NoOn command is available, the procedure exits to the previous command level. ON action is only local to the procedure; it does not apply to the procedures executing in other levels.

SET NoOn prevents error handling specified in the ON command, and SET ON restores error handling. These commands have no meaning when executing commands interactively, i.e., not in command procedures.

4.8 HANDLING CTRL/Y INTERRUPTS

You can interrupt the execution of any command, command procedure, program, or system utility in OpenVMS using the CTRL/Y command. A CTRL/Y command level is maintained by OpenVMS Supervisor. By default, OpenVMS suspends the task in question upon the CTRL/Y command and returns control to the CTRL/Y command level. Now, you can execute certain DCL commands and CONTINUE the task execution or STOP the task.

For command procedures and other images, the supervisor stores the status of all previously established command levels, making possible the resumption with correct status. After interrupting, you can issue commands like SET VERIFY, SHOW TIME, etc.

You can override CTRL/Y action by using the ON CONTROL_Y action command. For example:

```
$ on control_y then exit
```

will override the default action of command input at the Control/Y command level. In the above example, the procedure exits upon CTRL/Y and the control is passed to the previous command level.

When CONTROL/Y is pressed, a procedure that uses ON CONTROL_Y completes the command and then the CONTROL_Y action is taken. If it is an image it is forced to exit and the CONTROL_Y action is taken. If the image declared an exit handler, it is executed before the CONTROL_Y action is taken. The image cannot continue after CONTROL_Y action. A CONTROL_Y action is in effect until (a) the procedure terminates (because of CONTROL_Y, EXIT, or STOP or a default error condition); (b) another ON CONTROL_Y is executed; or (c) the procedure executes the SET NOCONTROL_Y command. The ON CONTROL_Y action is local to the procedure.

Disabling and enabling CONTROL_Y action is done using the command SET NOCONTROL=Y or SET CONTROL=Y. You can use these SET commands at any command level; they affect all command levels. Digital does not recommend these uses of Control_Y except for special applications.

4.9 ITERATIONS AND RECURSIONS

Iterations in DCL are executed using the GOTO statement. A label indicates the start of the iteration loop and GOTO keeps passing control to the start of the iteration loop until certain conditions are met. An example follows:

```
$ count = 0
$ loop:
$       count = count + 1
$       if count .eq. 9 then exit
$       if p'count' .eqs. ""then exit
$           :
$           :
$ goto loop
```

Recursions are procedures which call themselves repeatedly until a condition within the same procedure terminates the procedure. A classic example is computing the factorial of a given integer:

$$n! = n * (n - 1) * \ldots\ldots\ldots 4 * 3 * 2 * 1$$

which can be computed as: Fact (n) = n * Fact (n - 1).

Here is a procedure which does a similar task. This example computes the factorial of an integer. Execute it as @factorial n—if you include this code in a file, factorial.com, where n is an integer.

```
$! File FACTORIAL.COM
$! A Recursion example on DCL: Computing Factorial of an input
$! integer
$! Execute the procedure as @file n -- where n is an integer
$! whose factorial
$! is to be returned
$     Fs == 1
$     N = P1
$     Call Fib 'p1
$     Write Sys$Output "The "n'th Factorial Is: "fs"'
$     Exit
$ Fib: Subroutine
$ Fs == 'p1 * Fs
$ P1 = P1 -1
$ If 'p1 .Gt. 1 Then Call Fib 'p1 ! **** Recursive Call
$ Exit
$ Endsubroutine
```

4.10 SUMMARY

The symbol substitution, lexicals, block-structured programming, and simplicity of the DCL interface encourage one to write many useful procedures in DCL itself instead of resorting to a programming language. For actual usage and syntax of all DCL commands, refer to the *DCL Dictionary* of Digital Equipment Corporation.

5

Logical Names
and Lexical Functions

This chapter gives a general introduction to logical names, their types, and usage, and lexical name types and their usage. There are new lexical functions introduced in OpenVMS which are of interest only to system management and networking personnel.

5.1 LOGICAL NAMES

Logical names are OpenVMS standardization for identifying input and output devices, files, areas on memory, and other system resources. Logical names provide a means of flexibility in addressing the system resources. For example, if a device, say a disk, is associated with a logical name called USER_DISK, the users and the system can now refer to the device by this logical name. If the contents of the disk are transformed to a different disk unit at some later time, then one need only to redefine the logical name USER_DISK. No references in the user or system procedures will be changed. Thus logical names help in maintaining resource independence for procedures, commands, and programs.

The logical names are classified into four types called *logical name tables:* process level, job level, group level, and the system level.

5.1.1 Process logical name table

Logical names in the process level logical name table are private to the process and they contain logical names that are defined for the process. There are four standard logical names already defined for every process. These are:

- SYS$OUTPUT

- SYS$INPUT

- SYS$COMMAND

- SYS$ERROR

These logical names are normally assigned to the login terminal. The process logical name table exists for the life of a process.

5.1.2   Job logical name table

In OpenVMS a job is typically a family of processes. The job level logical name table contains logical names which are private to the job. This includes the parent and all subprocesses existing in the job. The job logical name table exists until the job is completed.

5.1.3   Group logical name table

In OpenVMS a group is identified by the User Identification Code (UIC). The UIC contains two integer codes; the first one identifies the group and the second identifies the member of the group. The group logical name table defines logical names which are private to the group. They are permanent to the extent that the last process is active in the system.

5.1.4   System logical name table

The system level logical name table defines logical names which are available to all processes in the system. These logical names are permanent until the reboot of the system. To search for the requested logical name, OpenVMS observes a search order with the process logical name table first in order, followed by the job logical name table, group logical name table, and finally the system logical name table.

5.1.5   Using the logical name tables

In addition to the standard logical name tables, there can be many application-specific logical name tables and names also. Some of these are created by OpenVMS by default. Shareable tables are cataloged in the system directory table. Private tables are cataloged in the process directory table (one for each process).

Figure 5.1 lists the default logical name tables. Note that the JIB address in the name of the JOB table is a system-defined address of an area in memory called the *Job Information Block* (JIB). The system creates one JIB for each job, i.e., for each detached process and its subprocesses. The system uses the information in a JIB to manage the processes in a job.

Table	Name	Time of Creation	Logical Name
SYSTEM	LNM$SYSTEM_TABLE	At system initialization	LNM$SYSTEM
GROUP	LNM$GROUP_group_uic	At initialization of first process in group	LNM$GROUP
JOB	LNM$JOB_JIB-address	At initialization of first process in job	LNM$JOB
PROCESS	LNM$PROCESS_TABLE	At process initialization	LNM$PROCESS

Figure 5.1 Standard logical name tables in OpenVMS.

DCL can show the structure of logical name tables. For example, the following command can be used:

```
$ SHOW LOGICAL/STRUCTURE
(LNM$PROCESS_DIRECTORY)
   (LNM$PROCESS_TABLE)
   (LNM$SYSTEM_DIRECTORY)
   (LNM$GROUP_000006)
   (LNM$JOB_80703D44)
   (LNM$SYSTEM_TABLE)
```

You can create your own logical name table. The CREATE/NAME_ TABLE command can be used to create a logical name table. An example is shown here to create a logical name called VMS_EXAMPLE:

```
$ CREATE/NAME_TABLE VMS_EXAMPLE
```

Now, if you execute the SHOW LOGICAL/STRUCTURE command, you will see a new entry in the list output by DCL:

```
$ SHOW LOGICAL/STRUCTURE
(LNM$PROCESS_DIRECTORY)
   (LNM$PROCESS_TABLE)
   (VMS_EXAMPLE)
(LNM$SYSTEM_DIRECTORY)
   (LNM$GROUP_000006)
   (LNM$JOB_80703D44)
   (LNM$SYSTEM_TABLE)
```

After defining your own logical name table, you can include your application-specific logical names into the logical name table. To do this, you can use the ASSIGN command, which takes the name of the logical name table, the new logical name, and the equivalent definition of the logical name as inputs. An example is shown here:

```
$ ASSIGN/TABLE=VMS_EXAMPLE TEST.TXT TEST_FILE
  "TEST_FILE"="TEST.TXT"
```

But, initially the new table is unknown to the logical name parser of OpenVMS. It must be made known in the search list for OpenVMS to recognize the new logical name table and hence the new logical names defined therein. For example, if you invoke a DCL command to type TEST_FILE as defined, the system comes up with an error indicating no such logical name was found in the path for logical name tables. The search path is defined by a supervisor-level logical called LNM$FILE_DEV. Note that LNM$SYSTEM_DIRECTORY is not defined at the supervisor level and hence not modifiable by the users. If you notice the definition for LNM$FILE_DEV, you will see four tables defined in the search list: LNM$PROCESS, LNM$JOB, LNM$GROUP, and LNM$SYSTEM, which correspond to the four types of logical name tables discussed earlier. To include the new logical name table VMS_EXAMPLE into the search list, you can use the ASSIGN command, which takes a list of the logical name tables to newly define the search order:

```
$ ASSIGN/TABLE=LNM$PROCESS_DIRECTORY VMS_EXAMPLE,_
$_LNM$PROCESS,LNM$JOB, LNM$GROUP, LNM$SYSTEM LNM$FILE_DEV
```

Now if you execute the DCL command TYPE to type TEST_FILE, it will work. You can deassign a table using the DEASSIGN/TABLE command.

Usually, in OpenVMS whenever information about a file is requested as in the case of the DCL command DIRECTORY, the system outputs not just the filename, but also its location in terms of the device name and the name of the directory. For logical names defined by the system, the name of the device and in some cases the name of the directory are normally concealed. Instead, the logical name equivalent is output along with the filename. You can also conceal the device name for logical names defined by you. For this, you have to use the CONCEALED attribute with the TRANSLATION_ATTRIBUTES qualifier for the DEFINE command. Here is an example:

```
$ DEFINE/TRANSLATION_ATTRIBUTES=CONCEALED PRIVATE_DISK DUA2:
$ SHOW LOGICAL/FULL PRIVATE_DISK
  "PRIVATE_DISK [super] = "DUA2" [concealed] (LNM$PROCESS_TABLE)
$ COPY/LOG TEST.TXT [.SUB_DIR]*.*
%COPY-S-COPIED, PRIVATE_DISK:[YOU]TEST.TXT;4 copied to
PRIVATE_DISK:[YOU.SUB_DIR]TEST.TXT;4
```

The second command above, SHOW LOGICAL/FULL PRIVATE_DISK, indicates that the equivalent disk is DUA2, whereas the COPY command, after copying the file, displays that it has copied the file to PRIVATE_DISK. The name DUA2 is not displayed by the COPY command output. The physical device name remains transparent to the user, unless you explicitly request to display the device name by translating its logical name.

The CONCEALED option is useful when developing programs and command procedures or when performing other command operations. You need not be concerned about which physical device is being accessed for the file access operations. In addition, the option allows you to specify more descriptive names for the device.

You can establish a chain of logical names, i.e., one logical name defining another logical name. In such cases, OpenVMS gives you a feature to stop translating after getting the first logical name. This is known as noniterative translation. The translation becomes "terminal" or completed after the first translation. To do this, you can use the TERMINAL command as in the following example:

```
$ DEFINE/TRANSLATION_ATTRIBUTES=TERMINAL PRIVATE_3 DUA3:
```

When the logical name PRIVATE_3 is used, the physical device DUA3 is referred. Although another logical name defined as DUA3 may be existing. To avoid possible confusion with the usage of the TERMINAL attribute, it is wise to avoid using the physical device names in a chain of logical names.

Just like LNM$FILE_DEV maintains a search list, you can also define your own search lists using the DEFINE command. A search list is basically a logical name that has more than one equivalence string. For example:

```
$ DEFINE SAMPLE_LIST
PRIVATE_DISK:[YOU.VENUS],PRIVATE_DISK:[YOU.ORION]
$ SHOW LOGICAL LIST
   "SAMPLE_LIST" = "PRIVATE_DISK:[YOU.VENUS]"
(LNM$PROCESS_TABLE)
           = "PRIVATE_DISK:[YOU.ORION]"
```

In the above example, the logical name PRIVATE_LIST is a search list with two equivalence strings. Whenever you can use logical names, you can also establish a search list containing the logical names.

When you use search lists, the logical name is translated a number of times by the system. Every time the system translates the logical names, the system scans the search list one by one. If the first logical name translation getting the equivalence device name is not the right one, the next string is translated, and so on, until the translated string giving the device name is successful. With SAMPLE_LIST assumed to be defined as above, the following example illustrates the way the system scans the list and translates the logical names in the list:

```
$ DIRECTORY SAMPLE_LIST:TEST.TXT
Directory PRIVATE_DISK:[YOU.VENUS]
TEST.TXT;1
Total of 1 file.
Directory PRIVATE_DISK:[YOU.ORION]
TEST.TXT;1
Total of 1 file.
Grand total of 2 directories, 2 files.
```

The above DIRECTORY command uses both equivalence strings for the search list SAMPLE_LIST when searching for TEST.TXT. The output shows that there is a file named TEST.TXT in both the directories. You can notice from the above output that the DIRECTORY command uses the equivalence strings for SAMPLE_LIST in the order the strings were listed when SAMPLE_LIST was defined.

You can define more complex search lists like nested lists and multiple lists. The following example shows a file specification which has two search lists defined, the first in the filename and the second in the device name:

```
$ DEFINE FILE TEST1.TXT, TEST2.TXT
$ DEFINE PRIVATE_DISK DBDISK1:[KARL], DBDISK2:[KARL]
$ SET DEFAULT DISK
$ DIRECTORY FILE
Directory DBDISK1:[KARL]
TEST1.TXT;6              TEST2.TXT;1
Total of 2 files.
Directory DBDISK2:[KARL]
TEST1.TXT;2              TEST2.TXT;5
Total of 2 files.
Grand total of 2 directories, 4 files.
```

The above example shows that the directory listing for each filename is given first for DBDISK1:[KARL] and second for DBDISK2:[KARL].

You can also have iterative or nested search lists when one string in a search list translates to another search list. If this occurs, then the system will use each string in a sublist before continuing on to the next upper-level string. For example:

```
$ DEFINE NESTING TEST1.DAT, LIST1, TEST2.DAT
$ DEFINE LIST1 TEST3.DAT, TEST4.DAT
```

The search order for the search list NESTING would be: TEST1.DAT, TEST3.DAT, TEST4.DAT, and TEST2.DAT.

Figure 5.2 summarizes some frequently used DCL commands to work with logical names.

Command	Function
DEFINE	Creates a logical name and places it in the process, job, group, or system logical name table. The /PROCESS, /JOB, /GROUP, and /SYSTEM qualifiers specify the table in which the name is to be placed.
DEFINE/USER_MODE	Creates a logical name for the execution of the next image only. The name is automatically deleted following the completion of the next command or program.
ASSIGN	Similar to the DEFINE command. But, the order of the command parameters is reversed.
DEASSIGN	Deletes a logical name from the process, job, or system logical name table.
SHOW TRANSLATION	Displays the result of translating a logical name and displays the name of the table in which the logical name was found.
SHOW LOGICAL	Displays the logical name tables. If used with a logical name as a parameter, it has the same functionality as the SHOW TRANSLATION command.

Figure 5.2 Frequently used DCL commands for logical names.

5.2 LEXICAL FUNCTIONS

The lexical functions of OpenVMS are available at the command level. The lexical functions are so called because they are processed by the command interpreter during its lexcal processing of the command string. They can be used in command lines or command procedures to extract various information. The lexical functions can be broadly classified into four types corresponding to:

1. Manipulating and formatting character strings

2. Getting information about a process

3. Getting information about the system

4. Getting information about files and directories.

Every lexical function takes an argument and begins with F$. For example, F$TIME is a lexical function. If you use a symbol as one of the items in the argument, you do not have to force symbol substitution; DCL performs the substitution automatically. If a keyword is required in the argument, you must enclose it in quotation marks to distinguish it from a symbol.

There are many uses of lexical functions. You can embed the lexical functions in command procedures to develop useful and interesting command programs. The lexical functions are generally used to perform housekeeping operations, application installations, and query procedures, and to display various information about the system, process, etc. These functions include:

- Saving, manipulating, and restoring characteristics of a process within a command procedure
- Obtaining and displaying information about the system
- Extracting parts of character strings, time strings, or file specifications.

5.2.1 Getting file and directory information

Figure 5.3 lists the lexical functions used to obtain information about files and directories. Two of the lexical functions listed in Fig. 5.3 are useful for checking whether or not a user has entered a valid file specification. You can use the F$PARSE lexical function to extract specific fields from the file specification. Use the F$SEARCH function to check if the specified file exists. If the file exists, F$SEARCH returns the complete file specification. If the file does not exist, a null string is returned. An example use of lexical functions is shown below:

```
$ A = F$DIRECTORY()          ! Return the current default
                             ! directory in symbol A.
$ SHOW SYMBOL A              ! Display the directory string
A = "USER$DISK:[SAMPLE]"
```

5.2.2 Getting information about a process

Figure 5.4 lists the lexical functions used to obtain information about a process. An example of using one of these lexical functions is shown here:

```
$! Save the current protection
$ PROT_NOW = F$ENVIRONMENT("PROTECTION")
```

Lexical Function	Function Description
F$DIRECTORY	Returns the current default directory as a character string. Does not return the associated device.
F$FILE_ATTRIBUTES (file-spec, -item)	Returns attribute information for a specific file.
F$PARSE(file-spec, [default-spec] -[related-spec], [field], [parse-type])	Invokes the $PARSE Record Management Service (RMS) to parse a file specification and return either the expanded file specification or the particular field you request.
F$SEARCH(file-spec, [stream-id])	Invokes the $SEARCH RMS to search a directory file and return the full file specification of a named file.

Figure 5.3 Lexical functions for files and directories.

Lexical Function	Function Description
F$ENVIRONMENT	Returns information about the DCL command environment.
F$GETJPI (process-id, item)	Invokes the $GETJPI System Service to return process information on the specific process.
F$MODE	Returns a character string indicating the mode in which a process is running (INTERACTIVE, NETWORK, or OTHER).
F$PID (context-symbol)	Returns the Process Identification (PID) number of a process on the system.
F$PRIVILEGES (privilege-list)	Returns the value of TRUE or FALSE depending on whether your process has a privilege in the specified list.
F$PROCESS ()	Returns the current process name.
F$SETPRV (private-list)	Invokes the $SETPRV System Service to set the specified privileges for the process, and returns the status of the privileges before the privileges were set.
F$USER ()	Returns the current User Identification Code (UIC) in name format.
F$VERIFY ([procedure-value], -[image-value])	Returns an integer value indicating whether procedure verification is enabled or disabled. When arguments are specified, F$VERIFY turns procedure and image verification on or off.

Figure 5.4 Lexical functions to obtain information on processes.

You can use these functions in a command procedure. For example, the variable PROT_NOW can be used in a command procedure to restore the original default protection after creating certain files. And the new files being created can have protections that are set temporarily in the command procedure.

5.2.3 Getting the system information using lexical functions

Figure 5.5 shows the set of lexical functions used for obtaining the system-related information. Note that the function F$TIME takes a null parameter. It returns current date and time. An example of using some of the lexical functions is shown below:

```
$! Get today's date and time. Assign it to symbol TIME
$ TIME = F$TIME ()
$! Get the day number of the week from TIME.
$ WEEK = F$CVTIME(TIME, "WEEKDAY")
$! Get month from TIME.
```

Lexical Function	Function Description
F$CVTIME ([input-time], [format], -[field])	Returns information about absolute, combination, or delta time strings.
F$GETDVI (device-name, item)	Invokes the $GETDVI System Service to return information about a device.
F$GETSYI (item, [node])	Invokes the $GETSYI System Service to return status and identification information about your system, or a node in your cluster.
F$LOGICAL (logical-name)	Returns the equivalence string associated with the logical name. Does not perform iterative translation automatically.
F$MESSAGE (status-code)	Returns the message text associated with a specific system status code.
F$TIME()	Returns the current date and time string.
F$TRNLNM (logical-name, [table], -[index], [mode], [case], [item])	Returns the equivalence string or requested attributes associated with the logical name. Does not automatically perform iterative translation.

Figure 5.5 Lexical functions to obtain system information.

```
$ MONTH = F$CVTIME(TIME, "ABSOLUTE", "MONTH")
$! Get the day of the week from TIME.
$ DAY = F$CVTIME(TIME, "DAY")
$! Get hour from TIME
$ HOUR = F$CVTIME(TIME, "HOUR")
$! Get minute from TIME.
$ MINUTE = F$CVTIME(TIME,,"MINUTE")
```

This example illustrates how different attributes for the lexical function F$CVTIME can be specified.

The lexical functions can also be used as in-line code in a DCL command line or procedure. Here is an example:

```
$!
$! Print the process name.
$!
$ WRITE SYS$OUTPUT " "
$ WRITE SYS$OUTPUT F$PROCESS()
```

5.2.4 Lexical functions for manipulating strings

Figure 5.6 lists a summary of the lexical functions for manipulating and formatting character strings. There are many functions that use lexical functions to manipulate and format character strings. For

Lexical Function	Function Description
F$CVSI (bit-position, width,- string)	Extracts bit fields from character string data and converts the result, as a signed value, to an integer.
F$CVUI (bit-position, width,- string)	Extracts bit fields from character string data and converts the results, as an unsigned value, to an integer.
F$EDIT (string, edit-list)	Edits a string expression.
F$ELEMENT (element-number,- delimiter, string)	Extracts an element from a string. The elements must be separated by a delimiter. The first element is number zero.
F$EXTRACT (offset, number,- string)	Extracts a substring from a character string expression.
F$FAO (control-string,- [arguments])	Invokes the $FAO System Service to convert the control string to a formatted ASCII output string.
F$IDENTIFICATION (identifier,- conversion-type)	Converts an identifier from a character string to an integer, or vice versa.
F$INTEGER (string)	Returns an integer equivalent of the specified string.
F$LENGTH (string)	Returns the length of a string.
F$LOCATE (substring, string)	Locates the substring and returns the offset position.
F$STRING (expression)	The expression is equated to string after evaluating.
F$TYPE (symbol)	Returns the data type of the symbol.

Figure 5.6 Lexical functions for string manipulation.

example, if your command required the user to enter a filename without a file type, you should use the F$LOCATE lexical function to be sure the user did not enter the file type by mistake. The example given below shows a sequence of commands that perform this task.

```
$ INQUIRE FILE "Filename"
$ PERIOD_LOC = F$LOCATE(".",FILE)
$ IF PERIOD_LOC .EQ. F$LENGTH(FILE) THEN GOTO FILE_IS_OK
```

In the example above, the F$LOCATE lexical function returns the position of the period in the character string that is stored in the symbol FILE. If the period is not found, then the length of the string is returned.

5.3 SUMMARY

The lexical functions and logical names can be effectively used to write modular procedures. Logical names provide a flexible means of addressing resources. Lexical functions provide an easy way of obtaining various information related to the system, processes, files, devices, and other resources.

6

Application Development Using OpenVMS

6.1 INTRODUCTION

The first step in any application development after the software design cycle is to write the code in the chosen language link: MACRO, FORTRAN, C, etc. In OpenVMS one normally uses the editors EVE or EDT to create the program text files. The next steps are to compile the program files using the compiler, and to link it with user routines, user libraries, and system libraries; the program is then executed. For large or complex programs, the code is usually debugged using the debugger.

This chapter will describe the features of compilers, the linker, and the RUN command to execute your programs on OpenVMS. The next chapter will describe the debugger. Note that other optional tools for software engineering like code management and software module level management are available from DEC. Frequently used tools for this are CMS (Code Management System) and MMS (Memory Management System). These are typically used in medium- to large-scale software projects because they help tracking the software development cycle and provide encouraging features for software recyclability.

Compiling a program translates the source code into an object code; linking a program organizes storage and resolves external references, for example, calling the timer function from one of the system services. Running the program executes the linked image. Some important sequences we discuss here include the COMPILER command and its generally available qualifiers, the LINK command and its qualifiers, the RUN command and its qualifiers, run-time errors, and program interruption.

The source module is typically a program code written in a particular programming language like FORTRAN, C, COBOL, PL/I, etc. The object modules are the compiled versions of programs. You can perform mixed language programming, i.e., the components written in different programming languages can be linked together. Other components of a software module can be text modules and shareable images that are already supplied with the compiler software. For example, there are many libraries and option files shipped with VAX C software.

6.2 COMPILATION

Typically, a compiler goes through a preliminary phase that involves some preprocessing of the input source file. This stage prepares the input for actual compilation. The compilation procedure then begins involving two or even three passes before building an object version of the program. These different phases perform the following functions.

Modify and interpret any INCLUDE statements in the program file. INCLUDE statements may demand the compiler to consider one or more sets of code from other files for compilation. In this case, the compiler will prepare a composite file in its work area to resolve all such INCLUDEs. Also, it will define parameters as directed by definition statements in the code. For example, in VAX C you can use the '#define' statement to declare a generic code or a parameter. This phase is not exactly a compilation phase. It can be called the preprocessor phase for the compiler since it prepares an input for the actual compiler.

The actual compilation phase then begins with checking the validity of the source program and generating warning, information, or error messages for invalid statements. The next phase of compilation translates the source code into machine-language instructions. Then, the compiler groups data and machine-language instructions into program sections. Finally, the compiler writes the object version of the source code that will be input to the linker.

When an object module is created, various information related to the program and data regions of the program are generated for use by the linker. Important information used by the linker is the standard name for the module, which is usually the same as the filename (you can override this with the /OBJECT qualifier). For example, if you are compiling a file called TEST.PAS, an object version called TEST.OBJ is created with the object module named TEST.

A set of entry points is generated indicating the entry addresses for various external and internal functions referenced in the source program. The details of the data structures for functions and variables, along with their relative addresses, are also generated. The linker needs this information for linking two or more modules to form an executable image.

A list of compiler-generated program sections, their parameters and characteristics, the machine instruction equivalent of the original source code, and the relative addresses of different sections of the program are generated when it is compiled.

To help debugging the code and to make available any active blocks of the program at the time of execution for tracing back, the compiler optionally generates the *traceback information* for the source program. This is usually used by the OpenVMS default condition handler when a run-time error occurs.

Optionally, the compiler also generates a symbol table (with the /DEBUG qualifier). It is used by the OpenVMS Symbolic Debugger, and it provides a list of module names of both internal and external functions referenced in the program, along with their definition and locations in the code.

For a list of generally available qualifiers with a typical OpenVMS compiler, see Fig. 6.1.

With the SHOW option several optional parameters can be specified. These specifications can provide source listing, statistics, cross-reference listings, etc. A summary of these optional parameters is shown in Fig. 6.2.

Command Qualifiers	Default
/[NO]CROSS-REFERENCE	/NOCROSS_REFERENCE
/[NO]DEBUG=[OPTION]	/DEBUG=TRACEBACK
/DIAGNOSTICS	/NODIAGNOSTICS
/G_FLOAT	/NOG_FLOAT
/LIBRARY	
/[NO]LIST	/NOLIST (interactive mode)
	/LIST (batch mode)
/[NO]MACHINE_CODE[=option]	/NOMACHINE_CODE
/[NO]OBJECT	/OBJECT
/[NO]OPTIMIZE[=NODISJOINT]	/OPTIMIZE
/SHOW[=(option, . . .)]	/SHOW=(NOBRIEF)
	NODICTIONARY
	NOEXPANSION
	NOINCLUDE
	NOINTERMEDIATE
	NOSTATISTICS
	NOSYMBOLS
	NOTRANSLATION
	SOURCE
	TERMINAL
/[NO]WARNINGS	/WARNINGS

Figure 6.1 OpenVMS compiler options.

Option	Usage
ALL	Includes symbol table records and traceback records. This is equivalent to /DEBUG with no option.
NONE	Does not include any debugging information. This is equivalent to /NODEBUG.
NOTRACEBACK	Does not include traceback records. This option is used to exclude all extraneous information from thoroughly debugged program modules. This option is equivalent to /NODEBUG.
NOSYMBOLS	Includes only traceback records. This is the default if the /DEBUG qualifier is not present on the command line.
SYMBOLS	Includes symbol table records, but not the traceback records.
TRACEBACK	Includes only traceback records. This is the default if the /DEBUG qualifier is not present on the command line.

Figure 6.2 Options in the SHOW qualifier for OpenVMS compilers.

The compiler identifies any invalid syntax in the code as well as any invalid program constructs not adhering to the programming rules set out in the programming language that is used. If it locates any errors, the messages corresponding to these are written to either SYS$OUTPUT or SYS$ERROR (unless these logical names are redirected by you to some other device or filename; see the chapter on logical names for such redirection commands). Usually, in an interactive session the messages appear on the screen; for a batch job, the messages appear in the batch log file. If a listing file is generated by the compiler, the error messages, warning messages, or informational messages appear in the list file in addition to the screen output (in an interactive session) or the log file (for a batch job).

The message from the compiler has the following form:

```
%<compiler_name>-s-ident, message-text
          Listing line number nnnnnn
          At line pppppp in name_of_the_module
```

The mnemonic 's' appearing in the first line of the message indicates the severity of the error. In OpenVMS it has four categories:

F   **Fatal error**   The compiler stops execution when a fatal error occurs and does not produce an object module. You have to make corrections in the source code and invoke the compiler again.

E   **Error**   The compiler continues the compilation process. No object file is created. You have to make corrections in the source file and compile again.

W   **Warning**   An object module is created in this case. The compiler has tried to correct some code that is either inconsistent syntactically or something that cannot be classified strictly as an error. But this may generate execution errors. Normally, you need to check the warning lines of the code and compile the code again.

I   **Information**   This is for your information only about the actions taken by the compiler.

If the compilers come up with only informational messages or no messages, it means that the compiler's different phases were successfully passed and the resultant object code is ready to be linked.

The message also gives a small descriptive text indicating the type of error or information, in addition to giving two or three lines of text. The listing line number refers to the line number in the list file. The list file can be generated using the /LIST qualifier. You can find the list of messages and the corrective actions from the manuals related to the particular programming language that you are using.

If you use the /NOWARNINGS qualifier when compiling, no warning messages appear either on the display screen or in the compiler-generated list file. Also, the DCL command SET MESSAGE allows you to shorten the message reporting by the compiler. For example, if you use the following command:

```
$ SET MESSAGE/NOFACILITY
```

then the compiler name as described in the above format for messages is cancelled from appearing in the compiler-generated list file and on the terminal until you either issue the SET MESSAGE command once again or end the interactive session.

6.3 LINKING

The OpenVMS linker is invoked using the LINK command, which takes the name(s) of the object file(s) and library file(s) as the primary input and optional number of qualifiers. The linker prepares an executable image from the input object files and libraries. The basic function of the linker involves the allocation of virtual memory for the image, resolving references to external variables and assigning values to global symbols. The linker allocates storage for user-defined values, variables, and functions in program sections, whose locations, names, and characteristics depend on the data structure of the variable.

The space for executable code is also allocated by the linker. Any external references like function definitions and external data definitions are available for reference by the other modules specified in the linker command as one of the primary parameters. This feature is useful when you are doing mixed-language programming involving references to an external variable from a code in, say, PASCAL as well as a code in C.

The LINK command has the following format:

```
LINK[/qualifier ....] file-specification[/qualifier ...], ...
```

Here, the file specification is one or more files containing object modules to be linked and, optionally, libraries containing user-created object code. You can separate the file specifications with commas or plus signs. Unlike the COMPILER command, in either case all the specified files are used to create a single executable image. If the file specification does not contain a file extension and is not qualified by /LIBRARY, /INCLUDE, or /OPTIONS, the linker assumes a default .OBJ file extension.

The /qualifier specification indicates that you can specify one or more of the several linker options on the command line. The /LIBRARY, /INCLUDE, and /OPTIONS qualifiers can only be specified following the specification of an input file. All other qualifiers listed can be specified following either the LINK command or any input file specification.

Figure 6.3 provides information on different qualifiers available in the OpenVMS linker.

Function	Qualifiers	Defaults
Request output files and define a file specification	/EXECUTABLE[=file-spec]	/EXECUTABLE=xxxxx.exe where xxxxx is the name of the first input file
	/SHAREABLE=[file-spec]	/NOSHAREABLE
	/SYMBOL_TABLE=[file-spec]	/NOSYMBOL_TABLE
Request and specify the contents of a memory allocation listing	/BRIEF	
	/[NO]CROSS_REFERENCE	/NOCROSS_REFERENCE
	/FULL	
	/[NO]MAP	/NOMAP (interactive) /MAP=yyyyy.MAP (batch) where yyyyy is the name of the first input file
Specify the amount of debugging information	/[NO]DEBUG	/NODEBUG
	/[NO]TRACEBACK	/TRACEBACK
Indicate that input files are libraries and specifically include certain modules	/INCLUDE=(module_name)	
	/LIBRARY	
	/SELECTIVE_SEARCH	

Figure 6.3 OpenVMS linker options.

The object modules specification on the linker command file can be done in any of the following ways.

Individual object modules with the .OBJ file extension produced by the compiler can be specified by filename alone. The linker assumes the file extension to be .OBJ if the file is not associated with any qualifying file extension other than .OBJ.

You can specify one or more object module libraries to be searched in order to resolve references to external functions and variables. These libraries are searched for all references that are not resolved among the modules specifically included in the compilation. You must qualify the file specification of the library with the /LIBRARY qualifier.

Specify explicit modules from an object module library to be included in the image. You have to qualify the file specification of the library with the /INCLUDE qualifier and specify the names of the object modules to be included.

You can create an options file containing the linker commands, qualifiers, and the program and library file specification. The linker recognizes the default file extension .OPT for option files. When you specify the option files with the LINK command, you must qualify its file specification with the /OPTIONS qualifier.

The following file extensions are used as defaults by the linker:

Object module	.OBJ
Object library	.OLB
Options file	.OPT
Shareable images	.EXE

For example, you can specify the object modules and libraries like this one:

```
$ LINK EXAMPLE1, -
_$ EXAMPLE_LIBRARY/INCLUDE=(TEST1, TEST2), -
_$ [YOU.SUBDIR]GRAPH_LIB/LIBRARY
```

In this LINK command the object module EXAMPLE1 is linked with the modules TEST1 and TEST2 from the library EXAMPLE_LIBRARY. OLB. The external procedures and variables not available in these modules are fetched from the GRAPH_LIB.OLB library from the area [YOU.SUBDIR]. Then the system libraries are scanned to call system functions which are referenced by the functions in the programming language like input/output functions (print, read, etc).

Note that the sequence in which you specify the input files, whether object files or library files, is important because that is the order in which the linker scans the files. You can specify any number of object files and libraries. The same module can be defined in more than one

library module. The library files are searched only if there is any unresolved module that is referenced by modules specified earlier. If more
than one library module is specified, the linker searches these library
files in the order they are specified. In this example,

```
$ LINK TEST1, TEST_LIB/LIBRARY, TEST2
```

the library TEST_LIB is searched only to look for modules specified by
TEST1 and not TEST2. Whereas, if you change the order of specification:

```
$ LINK TEST1, TEST2, TEST_LIB/LIBRARY
```

the library TEST_LIB is searched to locate all unresolved references
made in both the TEST1 and TEST2 modules.

When you specify logical names which are defined to be library files,
the linker follows a hierarchy for searching the library files. The process, then the job, then the group, and then the system logical name
tables are searched for the logical name LNK$LIBRARY. Once the
modules are resolved, the search is stopped. If the search fails even
after going through these four logical name tables, then the linker
looks for the unresolved reference module(s) in the process, then the
job, then the group, and then the system logical name tables for the logical names LNK$SYSTEM_1 through LNK$SYSTEM_999. The search
stops once the module is located. The search, however, is repeated for
each reference that remains unresolved.

The linker map file, also known as the storage map or memory allocation map, describes the arrangement of object modules, global data,
etc., in the image file. Information about the entry points that give the
virtual memory addresses for various functions in the image is also
provided in the map file. When you specify the /MAP qualifier, you can
control the type of map file, i.e., whether a brief map or a full map, by
specifying the /BRIEF and /FULL qualifiers. Note that the map file is
generated by default for a batch job. There can be four different kinds
of map files:

- A brief map obtained using the /MAP/BRIEF qualifiers
- A default map obtained using just the /MAP qualifier
- A full map obtained using the /MAP/FULL qualifiers
- A cross-reference map obtained using the /MAP/CROSS_REFER-
  ENCE qualifiers.

The type of information contained in the map is shown in Fig. 6.4.

Two qualifiers that you can specify in the LINK command line,
/DEBUG and /TRACEBACK, incorporate necessary details into the
image file to make it available for debugging. The information content

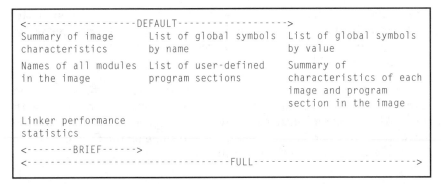

Figure 6.4 The linker map information.

obtained using these two qualifiers is used by the OpenVMS Symbolic
Debugger and the run-time, error-reporting mechanism. The traceback information is included by default. The run-time system uses
the information obtained by using this qualifier to list all procedure
invocations active at the time of a fatal error. You can cancel this functionality by using the /NOTRACEBACK qualifier. The traceback information is included if you use the /DEBUG qualifier even though you
had not specified it when you compiled the file(s). However, in this case
you cannot examine variables, as the symbol table is not available
because /DEBUG was not mentioned during compile time. If you want
to examine, change, and perform other debug functions on the variables, you must have used the /DEBUG qualifier when you compiled
the source file(s). For more details see the chapter on debugging.

If the linker detects an error while linking object modules together,
it shows the error by displaying a message indicating cause and error
severity. No image file is produced if any fatal condition or error has
occurred. Some of the common linker errors are caused by one of the
following reasons:

- *The compilation for the object module had generated a warning.*
  Usually such modules can be linked in spite of warning, but the
  resulting image may not behave as expected. You need to check this,
  preferably using the debugger.

- *The modules define more than one transfer address.* The linker warns
  you if more than one function in the program is named identically.
  The image, however, can be run in this case. But, the function specified first will carry the actual transfer address, i.e., that function is
  actually referenced when you run the program.

- *Unresolved references to symbolic names.* If you omit the required
  module or library in the LINK command line, it will cause the linker

to declare the module as an unresolved reference. Although the image is built in this case, it is not guaranteed to run correctly. Usually you correct such errors by reentering the command with correct modules or libraries.

The image file produced by the linker has an .EXE extension. If you specify the /MAP qualifier with the LINK command, a map file with the .MAP extension is also generated. If you specify more than one file for linking, then the image filename is the same as the filename of the first file specification in the command line. For example,

```
$ LINK X, Y, Z
```

produces an image file called X.EXE.

In a batch job the map file is generated by default in addition to the executable image file.

The /MAP and /EXECUTABLE qualifiers also optionally take a file specification as input. You can use them to override the default-naming convention of the linker for the map and the executable image files. For example,

```
$ LINK/MAP=[YOU.MAP]SAND TEST
```

will produce a SAND.MAP map file in the subdirectory [YOU.MAP] instead of TEST.MAP in your current directory. However, the file TEST.EXE is generated in your current directory. You can also use this technique to directly print out the map file on a printer instead of generating a file on the disk. For this, you can specify a printer name like LP: or the queue name of the printer at your installation, instead of specifying the filename and directory (i.e., something like LINK file_name/MAP=SYS$PRINT). In this case, the map file is generated, spooled to the printer, and then deleted.

6.4   RUN COMMAND

The image generated by the linker can be executed using the RUN command. For example,

```
$ RUN TEST
```

executes the image TEST.EXE. The OpenVMS Image Activator locates the file TEST.EXE and passes the control to the main function of the program. You can enhance the execution capabilities of the image if you incorporate commands from the Command Definition Utility (CDU), which is discussed in the next chapter. The image can also be run in an alternate way by defining a foreign command using DCL. For example, you can execute by invoking just a foreign command, say, 'RT', using the DCL assignment:

```
$ RT == $ DUA1:[YOU]:TEST.EXE
```

In this definition, note the usage of "==" and "$"; the definition must include the device and directory specification.

The image is terminated once it executes a programming language equivalent or system function equivalent of an exit, or if an error is encountered which is not handled in the program, or when the control encounters the end of the outer block in the main function. Upon exit from the image, the system performs various housekeeping operations like closing opened files and freeing the allocated system resources like the tape drive.

The system may force image exit for several reasons. One of them is the user typing <control/y> when the image is being executed, and then executing another image. If you do not start execution of another image, the current image is still executing although you may see '$' prompt (if you are expecting an output from the program and if you have accidentally typed <control/y>, you can resume the output by issuing the CONTINUE command). The image can also exit when you issue a STOP command. STOP does not result in the housekeeping operations that the system performs for normal exits. Also, a system service function SYS$EXIT called in the program can result in image exit and housekeeping operations. Another way the image exits is by invoking a process-level system service called SYS$FORCEX in the system causing the exit of the process itself.

For more details on the actions OpenVMS takes upon image exit and for details on SYS$EXIT and SYS$FORCEX system service refer to the OpenVMS System Services Reference Manual.

Generally, register 0 is used to pass the status of the exit to the command language interpreter for issuing a proper message on the terminal.

When an error is encountered during the image execution, the system terminates the program execution and the OpenVMS condition handler displays one or more messages on the SYS$ERROR device. You can redirect this logical to a file if you so desire. The message is appended with traceback information. For each module in the image that has this information, the condition handler lists the modules that were active and the sequence in which the modules were called. For example, if an integer-divide-by-zero has occurred, a run-time message like the following is displayed:

```
%SYSTEM-F-INTDIV, arithmetic trap, integer divide by zero
   at PC=0000125F,    PSL=0420004D
```

This message is followed by traceback information which may look something like this:

```
%TRACE-F-TRACEBACK, symbolic stack dump follows

module name    routine name   line   rel PC      abs PC
TEST_1         TEST_A         16     00005432    000031FD
TEST           main           1034   00007F02    0000208F
```

Information in the traceback indicates the sequence in which the routines were called. First TEST, the main program, was executed, and TEST, at line number 1034, called the TEST_1 module which resulted in an error at its line number 16. The module name and the routine name columns will help you to locate the filename and the function name that called the other function which resulted in the error. The 'rel PC' information gives the location relative to the virtual memory. Using this information and the information from the map file, you should be able to figure out if declaration of a particular variable is causing the error, and if so what variable it is, and so on. If you can find the erroring variable, changing the data type or length for the variable may fix the problem. The column named 'abc PC' provides the absolute PC locations. This may be useful in analyzing more critical reports like Crash Dump Analysis reports, etc. Normally, the traceback information is provided by default for many compilers as well as the linker in OpenVMS. If you want to exclude traceback, you can specify the /NOTRACEBACK qualifier when you link the file(s). It is generally recommended to have the traceback enabled until your program is thoroughly tested.

The program execution can be interrupted by typing <control/y>. The program space and its status are still maintained by the system even after typing <control/y>, which means that you can restart the program execution. To restart, you can issue the CONTINUE command. Commands from a subset of the DCL command set can be executed after interrupting and before issuing the CONTINUE command. These commands are =, ALLOCATE, ASSIGN, ATTACH, CLOSE, DEALLOCATE, DEASSIGN, DEBUG, DECK, DEFINE, DELETE/SYMBOL, DEPOSIT, EOD, EXAMINE, GOTO, IF, INQUIRE, ON, OPEN, READ, SET CONTROL_Y, SET DEFAULT, SET ON, SET PROTECTION/DEFAULT, SET VERIFY, SET UIC, SHOW DAYTIME, SHOW DEFAULT, SHOW PROTECTION, SHOW QUOTA, SHOW STATUS, SHOW SYMBOL, SHOW TIME, SHOW TRANSLATION, SPAWN, WAIT, and WRITE.

6.5 SYSTEM SERVICES AND RUN-TIME LIBRARIES

OpenVMS provides many system services for use at run-time for users' programs. This is called the Run-Time Library (RTL) located in the object libraries SYS$SHARE:IMAGELIB.OLB and SYS$SHARE:STAR-LET.OLB. The OpenVMS linker automatically links the user programs with these libraries; you do not have to specify any special qualifier to link RTL functions. Functions like SYS$GETTIM are located in one of these two library files. All programming language compilers supported under OpenVMS can use the RTL functions. While using these functions, the data structure requirements for them need to be handled in user programs. You can find out the call format for the RTL functions using the on-line help facility:

```
$ HELP RTL
```

In order to maintain a uniform standard to call almost all OpenVMS products and system-level functions like RTL functions, OpenVMS adheres to a calling standard that is similar to the VAX calling standard. This enables the programs written in any programming language to access the RTL functions or any permitted system module. Normally, the programming language constructs for statements like CALL incorporate the necessary requirements of the calling standard; the user need not be concerned about this standard. But, this becomes an important issue with mixed-language programming.

The machine code generated by the compiler conforms to the OpenVMS calling standard. Some of the conditions of the calling standard met by these compilers are:

The parameters need to be passed as an argument list that can be found either on stack or memory.

OpenVMS-specified data types for its function parameter should be used in the calling programs.

The return code from system functions is available in register R0.

The parameters are to be passed in one of three ways depending on the data type:

- By value
- By reference
- By descriptor

By value is trivial; the value passed is typically an integer. By reference means that the address of the memory location containing the parameter is passed. By descriptor means the address of the descriptor of the parameter is passed to the function.

Commonly, for passing character strings, descriptors are used. They are also used for passing many other data types like arrays of integers, data and time information, etc. The descriptor occupies 8 bytes of memory containing the length of the string passed. The attributes of a descriptor are:

Length	An unsigned word containing the length of the string passed
Size	2 bytes
Data type	An unsigned byte containing the code for data type
Size	1 byte
Class	An unsigned byte containing the class of data
Size	1 byte
Address	An unsigned longword containing the address of the parameter
Size	4 bytes

6.6 SUMMARY

The OpenVMS compilers, linkers, and the editor (EVE or EDT) together form the necessary tool to write application programs. Various information that the compilers and the linker can provide may be used in conjunction with the debugger to develop error-free programs in a shorter time.

Command Definition Utility

7.1 INTRODUCTION

The input parameters for an executable image in OpenVMS can be provided either interactively, via terminal, or through a file. Command Definition Utility (CDU) provides a tool to expand the DCL command functionality. This command-level programming can be used to pass parameters to a program in terms of qualifiers (as you would do with a typical DCL command like LINK/MAP=filename). This chapter illustrates some techniques of programming using CDU.

The DCL tables contain the standard command set definition and pointers to locations of the corresponding system programs on the disk or memory. For example, when you issue the COPY command, the system searches the DCL table to see if such a command exists. Once it finds the entry in the table, it will fetch the address of the COPY.EXE (see Fig. 7.1) system program on the disk. Then the process scheduler invokes the COPY.EXE program from the disk. DCL command tables are copied into the P1 address space when you begin an interactive session. However, some commands are interpreted from within the image for the DCL table. For example, the command SHOW STATUS does not have any image associated with it. It is executed in the command language interpreter.

Command Definition Utility allows you to create and add new commands to the DCL command table. It also allows you to delete the added commands in the DCL table. The master DCL command table resides in SYS$LIBRARY in a file named DCLTABLES.EXE.

To add a command you must:

- Define the command in a format that DCL understands
- Provide an image to execute the new command

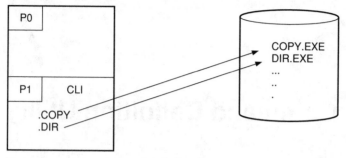

Figure 7.1 Image access using DCL tables.

7.2 DEFINE VERB COMMAND

Programming in CDU chiefly uses the DEFINE VERB command, which defines a command. DEFINE VERB has additional parameters to specify the qualifiers. The command specification file in CDU has a default file extension .CLD.

Following is an example of programming in CDU:

```
1    !
2    DEFINE VERB color
3    IMAGE DUA1:[YOU]:color
4    PARAMETER P1, PROMPT='Template color',
5    LABEL=template
6    VALUE(REQUIRED)
7    PARAMETER P2, PROMPT='Background',
8    LABEL=background
9    VALUE(DEFAULT='GREEN')
10   QUALIFIER state, VALUE(REQUIRED)
```

Assume that the above code is contained in a file called COLOR.CLD. There is a Pascal program named COLOR.PAS that takes parameters along with a qualifier from the command line when run and simply prints the parameters and the qualifier values on the screen. Note that the filenames for the source program and the Command Language Description file must be identical.

To run the program using the new command COLOR, you must let the Command Language Interpreter know about the new command. To do so, you can use the SET COMMAND command:

```
$ SET COMMAND GRAPH_DIR:COLOR.CLD
```

where GRAPH_DIR is the logical name defined as DUA1:[YOU] using the following command:

```
$ ASSIGN DUA1:[YOU] GRAPH_DIR
```

After compiling and linking your Pascal program, you can run it using the new command called COLOR. This is possible because the CLD file has defined the image to be your Pascal program executable image. The CLD command procedure features the *parameter passing* to your program. Because you have already indicated the image address in the Command Language Description file, you do not have to issue a DCL assignment command as above after you have enabled the new command using the SET command.

The program can be run in many different ways using the parameters and qualifiers shown here:

```
$ COLOR/STATE=BLUE GREEN YELLOW
```

For this command, the program may print:

```
GREEN
BLUE
YELLOW
```

The variables named template, state, and background take the input from the command line; the program is assumed to type these values in that order on the terminal. In the above command, two things are to be noticed: first, the command invoked is your own command called COLOR to run the program and not the RUN command. Second, the usage of the qualifier called STATE is described in the command description file COLOR.CLD.

```
$ COLOR/STATE=MAGENTA
_Template color: RED
_Background: GREEN
      RED
      MAGENTA
      GREEN
```

In this example, note that the prompt as declared in the command description is displayed if the required values for the parameters are not provided in the command line.

```
$ COLOR
_Template color: ORANGE
```

```
_Background:
   ORANGE
   GREEN
$
```

In this example, note that two parameters and the qualifier are not specified. But the parameters are required as declared in the command description procedure. So the corresponding prompts are displayed. Because no specification was made for background, the program takes the default value of GREEN as specified in the command procedure above.

The command language definition file with the default file extension .CLD defines the syntax of a command by describing the command line syntax and specifying what image to invoke. The image specification using the DEFINE VERB statement in the command procedure can also have parameters and qualifiers.

If you want to add many commands to the DCL command table, you can issue a command like the following:

```
$ SET COMMAND/TABLE:SYS$LIBRARY:DCLTABLES.EXE
/OUTPUT=YOURAPP_DCL.EXE *.cld
```

and then you can make this new composite command table which contains both the DCL table and the command definitions from all of your .CLD files with the following command:

```
$ SET COMMAND/TABLE=USER_DISK:[YOU]USERAPP_DCL.EXE
```

The command interpreter looks for this new table instead of the DCL table whenever you execute a command.

You can replace a command definition using the SET COMMAND/REPLACE command.

An example to indicate the syntax of the DEFINE command is:

```
DEFINE VERB ERASE
   IMAGE "USER_DISK:[YOU]ERASE"
   QUALIFIER SCREEN
   QUALIFIER LINE, SYNTAX=LINE
```

7.3   DEFINE SYNTAX CLAUSE

The DEFINE VERB defines the verb ERASE. This verb accepts two qualifiers, /SCREEN and /LINE. The qualifier /LINE uses an alternate syntax specified with the SYNTAX=LINE clause. If you issue the command ERASE/LINE, the definition in the DEFINE SYNTAX LINE statement overrides the definitions in the DEFINE VERB ERASE statement. However, if you issue the command ERASE/SCREEN, or if you do not specify any qualifiers, the definitions in the DEFINE VERB ERASE statement apply.

An example of a DEFINE SYNTAX statement is shown below:

```
DEFINE SYNTAX LINE
    IMAGE "USER_DISK:[YOU]ERASE"
    QUALIFIER NUMBER, VALUE(REQUIRED)
```

The DEFINE SYNTAX statement defines an alternate syntax called LINE. If you issue the command ERASE with the /LINE qualifier, the image LINE.EXE is invoked from the directory [YOU] on the logical device USER_DISK. The new syntax allows the qualifier /NUMBER, which requires a value.

There are several built-in types available for value clauses (see Fig. 7.2). A description of them is given here:

$ACL   The value must be an access control list.

$DATETIME   The value must be an absolute or a combination time. DCL converts truncated time values, combination time values, and keywords for time values such as TODAY to absolute time format. If

Built-in Type	Description
$ACL	The value must be an access control list.
$DATETIME	The value must be an absolute or a combination time. DCL converts truncated time values, combination time values (such as TODAY) to absolute time format. If the value is missing any date fields, DCL fills in the current date. If the value is missing any time fields, DCL fills these fields with zeros.
$DELTATIME	The value must be a delta time. If the value is missing any time fields, DCL fills these fields with zeros.
$FILE	The entity value must be a valid file specification.
$NUMBER	The entity value must be an integer. The command string can contain decimal, octal, or hexadecimal numbers. However, DCL converts all numbers to decimal.
$QUOTED_STRING	DCL uses the default method of processing the entity, with one exception: DCL does not remove quotation marks when processing the string.
$REST_OF_LINE	Everything until the end of the line is equated to the entity value.

Figure 7.2 Built-in types in CDU for value clauses.

the value is missing any date fields, DCL fills in the current date. If the value is missing any time fields, DCL fills these fields with zeros.

$DELTATIME   The value must be a delta time. If the value is missing any time fields, DCL fills these fields with zeros.

$FILE   The entity value must be a valid file specification.

$NUMBER   The entity value must be an integer. The command string can contain decimal, octal, or hexadecimal numbers. However, DCL converts all numbers to decimal.

$QUOTED_STRING   DCL uses the default method of processing the entry, with one exception: DCL does not remove quotation marks when processing the string.

$REST_OF_LINE   Everything until the end of the line is equated to the entity value.

The example given below shows a parameter that must be specified as a file specification:

```
DEFINE VERB PLAY
    IMAGE "DISK_A:[DIR_A]PLAY"
    PARAMETER P1, VALUE(TYPE=$FILE)
```

7.4   DISALLOW CLAUSE

When you specify qualifiers, you can disallow certain combinations of them using a clause called DISALLOW. For example, a command definition may contain a DEFINE VERB statement that defines the verb BREAKFAST with three qualifiers: /BREAD, /BUTTER, and /JAM. However, you may want to make the qualifiers mutually exclusive. The following example shows how to use the DISALLOW verb clause to put this restriction into the command definition file:

```
DEFINE VERB BREAKFAST
    IMAGE "DISK_F:[FOOD]BREAKFAST"
    QUALIFIER BREAD
    QUALIFIER BUTTER
    QUALIFIER JAM
    DISALLOW ANY2(BREAD, BUTTER, JAM)
```

The DISALLOW verb clause indicates that a command string is invalid if it contains more than one of the qualifiers /BREAD, /BUTTER, or /JAM.

The disallow feature of the DEFINE VERB clause can be used in programs for menu-driven applications.

7.5 SUMMARY

The Command Definition Utility gives a programmable mechanism for interfacing the user programs with the Command Language Interpreter.

8

OpenVMS Symbolic Debugger

OpenVMS Symbolic Debugger is a run-time tool which helps test executable images. It supports several programming languages and has advanced features to help the programmer debug the code quickly and conveniently. Debugging usually results in resolving logic errors and errors related to data structures of program variables and functions.

The symbolic debugger has about 100 commands which will assist you in:

- Controlling execution of the image
- Manipulating the program variables
- Displaying source code and error messages, along with line numbers
- Controlling the screen format

The debugger has two modes: line mode and screen mode. You can invoke the debugger in one of the following two ways:

1. Compile and link your program with the /DEBUG qualifier. See Fig. 8.1 for debug specifications that go with the /DEBUG qualifier of OpenVMS compilers.

2. Run your program with the /DEBUG qualifier.

8.1 MODES OF THE DEBUGGER

OpenVMS debugger supports the application keypad of the VT100 and VT200 series terminals. The keypad entries are used on the screen to

Option	Usage
ALL	Includes symbol table records and traceback records. This is equivalent to /DEBUG with no option.
NONE	Does not include any debugging information. This is equivalent to /NODEBUG.
NOTRACEBACK	Does not include traceback records. This option is used to exclude all extraneous information from thoroughly debugged program modules. This option is equivalent to /NODEBUG.
NOSYMBOLS	Includes only traceback records. This is the default if the /DEBUG qualifier is not present on the command line.
SYMBOLS	Includes symbol table records, but not the traceback records.
TRACEBACK	Includes only traceback records. This is the default if the /DEBUG qualifier is not present on the command line.

Figure 8.1 Debug options during compilation.

execute a debug command by using only a few keys. The key assignment diagram can be displayed at any time using the help feature. Figure 8.2 shows the key assignment for debug commands. The keypad mode can be enabled using:

```
DBG> SET MODE KEYPAD
```

PF1	PF2	PF3	PF4
GOLD	HELP NOCOLOR	SET MODE SCREN	BLUE
GOLD	HELP GOLD	SET MODE NOSCR	BLUE
GOLD	HELP BLUE	DISP/GENERATE	BLUE
KP7	KP8	KP9	MINUS
DISP SCR/INST	SCROLL/UP	DISPLAY next	DISP nxt AT FS
DISP INST/REG	SCROLL/TOP		DISP, SRC OUT
KP4	KP5	KP6	COMMA
SCROLL/LEFT	EX/SOU .0\%PC	SCROLL/RIGHT	GO
SCROLL/LEFT: 132	SHOW CALLS		
SCROLL/LEFT x	SHOW CALLS 3	SCROLL/RIGHT x	SEL INST next
KP1	KP2	KP3	ENTER
EXAMINE	SCROLL/DOWN	SEL SCROLL nxt	
EXAM (prev)	SCROLL/BOTTOM	SEL/OUTPUT nxt	
	SCROLL/DOWN x	SEL/SOURCE nxt	
KP0		PERIOD	ENTER
	STEP	RESET	
	STEP/INTO	RESET	
	STEP/OVER	RESET	

Figure 8.2 Debugger keypad functions.

It can always be cleared by:

```
DBG> SET MODE NOKEYPAD
```

The commands

```
DBG> SET MODE SCREEN
```

and

```
DBG> SET MODE NOSCREEN
```

enable and disable the screen mode, respectively. For a summary of commands to access the keypad operations see Fig. 8.3.

The debugger effectively uses the windowing feature on VT series terminals. A window is a region on the terminal screen through which you may view a display. It is defined by a starting line number and by the number of text lines that you want to view through that window.

8.2 STEPPING THROUGH THE CODE

The STEP command, which can take many qualifiers (see Fig. 8.4), is one of the main debug functions used for controlling the flow of program execution. STEP is used for:

- Executing code
- Finding out program behavior
- Stepping into each function called

You can issue the STEP command either by typing STEP (see Fig. 8.5) at the DBG prompt or by typing '0' on the numeric keypad when the keypad mode is enabled:

Command	Description
SET MODE KEYPAD	The keypad mode is activated.
SET MODE NOKEYPAD	The keypad mode is ended.
DEFINE/KEY	A specified debug command is associated with a key from the keypad.
DELETE/KEY	The specified key definition is deleted.
SHOW KEY	The definition of a specified key is displayed.

Figure 8.3 Debugger commands to access the keypad mode.

Command	Description
STEP/OVER	The function is not entered for debugging. The current stream of debugging is resumed after executing the function. This is the default stepping mode.
STEP/INTO	The called function is entered for debugging.
STEP/SYSTEM	Debugger enters the OpenVMS system service that is referenced. But, no breakpoints or examining the data within the service is possible.
SET STEP	Sets a default mode for stepping (INTO, OVER, or SYSTEM).
SHOW CALLS	Displays a traceback of the calling sequence. This is particularly useful when returning to the debugger after a CTRL/Y interrupt. The debugger displays a traceback list that shows you the sequence of calls leading to the current module. If you specify a value, that value determines the number of calls to be displayed.
CALL	A function can be called by specifying its arguments.

Figure 8.4 The STEP command qualifiers in the debugger.

Command	Description
STEP	One or more instructions of a program are executed at a time. The following step modes are available:
	/INTO, /OVER, /SYSTEM—For stepping through or passing over user-defined functions, or whether you step through system routines.
	/SOURCE, /NOSOURCE—For displaying source statements in addition to the debugger outputs.
	/NOSILENT, /SILENT—For enabling or disabling the display of debugger message as commands are executed.
SET STEP	Changes the default mode for STEP commands. Simply, this command specifies the number of lines of code to step.
SHOW STEP	Shows the step modes that are in effect.

Figure 8.5 Accessing the debugger STEP command.

```
DBG> step 3
stepped to GAUSS\main\%LINE 18
    12: random = 7568
DBG>
```

8.3 BREAKPOINTS AND WATCHPOINTS

You can set breakpoints in the debug mode, which results in stopping at those breakpoints. This is used to execute a part of the code and then test variables to know whether they have the expected values.

Some examples of the SET BREAK command are:

```
DBG> set break OPEN
DBG> set break/after:10 %line 106
DBG> set break %line 1098 do (examine perim, limit, volume; go)
```

You can verify where the breakpoints are set by using the SHOW command:

```
DBG> SHOW BREAK
```

and you can cancel breakpoints using

```
DBG> CANCEL BREAK
```

Watchpoints set for a program entity notify you whenever the entity is modified. For example,

```
DBG> SET WATCH COUNT
```

This command notifies the user, whenever the value of COUNT is changed, with the appropriate message, which may look like this:

```
1436 move 187 to COUNT.
1436 COUNT = 2
old value: 186
new value: 187
DBG>
```

Also,

```
DBG> SHOW WATCH
```

will show the watchpoints set by you. And

```
DBG> CANCEL WATCH
```

cancels all watchpoints.

You can check for unexpected control transfers using the TRACE command (see Fig. 8.6 for a list of TRACE commands):

```
DBG> SET TRACE %LINE 1042
```

The SHOW TRACE command shows all the tracepoints set by you. You can cancel the tracepoints with the CANCEL TRACE command. The tracepoints do not stop execution of the code.

Command	Description
SET TRACE	The address, label, line number, or name of the function can be specified for suspending the execution momentarily. You can also use a /LINE, /INSTRUCTION, or /CALL qualifier to set a tracepoint at every line, instruction, or call.
SHOW TRACE	Displays the locations in the program where tracepoints are currently set.
CANCEL TRACE	Remove one or more tracepoints currently set in the program.

Figure 8.6 The debugger TRACE commands.

8.4   ACCESSING PROGRAM VARIABLES

You can examine the contents of program variables using the EXAMINE command:

```
DBG> EXAMINE J
```

will type contents of the variable *J* in the program that is being debugged. You can also examine string variables, arrays, and any special data structures supported in the programming language that you are using, like unions and structures in C language. For example, you can examine an array with the following command:

```
DBG> EXAMINE DIME2(*,1)
```

This command gives only column values. There are many options you can use with the EXAMINE command. The general syntax for this command is:

```
EXAMINE[/qualifiers]address-expression[:address-expression]
```

Using the symbolic debugger, you can change the value of a program variable. You can use the DEPOSIT command to do this. The general format for the DEPOSIT command is

```
DEPOSIT[/qualifiers]address-expression=expression
```

Figure 8.7 summarizes the EXAMINE, DEPOSIT, and SHOW SYMBOL commands.

You can evaluate source expressions or simply use the debugger for calculator-like arithmetic functionality using the EVALUATE command. You can also perform comparisons between program variables. For example,

```
DBG> EVALUATE I>J
```

Command	Description
EXAMINE	The contents of a specified variable are displayed. More than one variable can be specified. The data type qualifiers ASCII, BYTE, DECIMAL, and so forth, can be used to display the data. Decimal is the default radix.
DEPOSIT	Modifies the contents of a variable. Only one variable can be modified at a time. The variable name and the new value must be separated by an equal sign. The data type qualifiers can be used to specify the type of new data.
SHOW SYMBOL	With /TYPE qualifier displays the data type of a variable.

Figure 8.7 The debugger EXAMINE command.

This command results in displaying 1 if the condition is true and 0 if it is false. Other examples of using the EVALUATE command are:

```
DBG> EVALUATE K+M
DBG> EVALUATE 18*1024
```

To evaluate a source language expression, use the EVALUATE command. The command format for EVALUATE is:

```
EVALUATE[/qualifiers]language-expression[,expression,...]
```

You can declare additional symbols, other than those defined in the main program, to make them available before the routine is called, using the SET MODULE command:

```
DBG> SET MODULE FUNCTION_DRAW.
```

This example adds symbols in FUNCTION_DRAW to the image's symbol table. Note that in keeping with the OpenVMS environment, the linker converts the names of the object modules into uppercase letters. When using the debugger to access object modules, express the module name in uppercase letters.

8.5 OPTIMIZER

To execute a program with the debugger, you must compile and link the program with the /DEBUG qualifier. Unless you compile your program with the /DEBUG qualifier, you cannot access all of the program's variables. You should use the /NOOPTIMIZE qualifier to turn off compiler optimization that may interfere with debugging. If you desire a minimal amount of optimization that would not interfere with your debugging session, use the /OPTIMIZE=NODISJOINT qualifier.

Sometimes, especially in the case of large programs (even after the program is thoroughly tested with the debugger with the /NOOPTI-MIZE option), you may encounter bugs when the program is run without the debugger and with the optimizer enabled. In such cases, the problem is generally due to data section misalignment that results from an improper optimization. To resolve such problems, you can build the program without the debugger and without the optimizer enabled and run the program again. This way, you will avoid the side effect that the optimizer might have introduced in your program.

An example of building a program image with the debugger option is given below:

```
$ FORTRAN/DEBUG/LIST=(SYMBOLS, INCLUDE, EXPANSION)-
-$ /OPTIMIZE=NODISJOINT EXAMPLE.FOR
$ LINK/DEBUG EXAMPLE
```

When debugging your program with more than one module, use the SET MODULE command to make additional symbols available for debugging.

8.6 INITIALIZING

The logical name DBG$INIT can be used to specify a command file that is to be executed whenever you start a debugging session. This is similar to the concept of using LOGIN.COM that is executed at the time of login.

The following commands are commonly used in initialization files:

```
SET OUTPUT    LOG,  VERIFY
SET LOG    filename
SET MODE    SCREEN
SET STEP    SILENT
SET MODULE/ALL
SET MODULE[/qualifiers]module_name[,module_name...]
```

You can maintain a history of your DEBUG session by directing the debugger to output to a log file. The following example for a command called SET OUTPUT illustrates this:

```
DBG> SET OUTPUT LOG
```

This command stores the debug session in a log file called DEBUG.LOG. It will not record a 'DBG>' prompt. The debugger responses begin with an '!'. You can also use this log file as the debugger command procedure or as a journal file in case the debugging image abruptly exited due to a system failure. You can execute the logged information from the log file as a command procedure using the command:

```
DBG> @DEBUG.LOG
```

Or if you had created a command procedure containing the debugger commands in a file called, say, DBGTEST.COM, then you can execute it by issuing "@DBGTEST" at the "DBG>" prompt.

A debugger logical called DBG$INIT can be used to automatically execute certain debug commands from a command procedure file by assigning the file to the logical name. Here is an example:

```
$ ASSIGN USER$DISK:[KARL]DBGTEST.COM DBG$INIT
```

8.7 SHOW AND SET COMMANDS

The SHOW CALLS command can be used to see the path of calls leading to the current location that is about to be executed. You can also use this command to display information about the sequence of currently active procedure calls or the number of call frames in the stack. The command format is:

```
SHOW CALLS [n]
```

You can find out the location of a symbol, i.e., the module name containing the symbol. The SHOW SYMBOL command, which takes the symbol name as its parameter, can be used for this function:

```
DBG> SHOW SYMBOL FRACTION
Module1 Fraction
    :
    :
Modulen Fraction
```

You can find various information about the symbol, like where it is defined in the modules, using several qualifiers that you can apply to the SHOW SYMBOL command. The general syntax for this command is:

```
SHOW SYMBOL[/qualifiers]name_specification
```

You can specify a path for searching a variable for examining, depositing, etc. The syntax to do this is:

```
DBG> EXAMINE MODULE2\FRACTION
```

You can default to a particular module if you have to execute a series of 'examine' and 'deposits' commands. The command you would use is SET SCOPE. For example,

```
DBG> SET SCOPE MODULE2
```

You can specify more than one module in the above commands. Then, the program variable is searched in modules according to the order in which they are specified in the SET SCOPE command line. See Fig. 8.8 for a summary of SCOPE commands. The command format for this is:

```
SET SCOPE[/qualifiers]location[,location ...]
```

The compiler-generated list file is accessed by the debugger whenever the image is executed with the debug option. This enables the debugger to provide the source file information. You can see lines of code from the original program when executing the program in the debug mode. The TYPE command takes the line number, path, and range of line numbers as parameter(s), and displays the code corresponding to that line number in the list file. For example,

DBG> TYPE 109	types line number 109 of the program file
DBG> TYPE 15:23	types lines 15 through 23
DBG> TYPE DICTION\16:19	types lines 16 through 19 of the module called DICTION

If you want to know where the program counter is currently pointing to, you can use the debugger-defined variable called PC in the EXAMINE command. For example,

```
DBG> EXAMINE/SOURCE .PC
```

displays the location that the PC is currently pointing to. You can also use the variable PC to see the next line to be executed upon return from the current routine. For example,

Command	Description
SET SCOPE	Defines a new scope or path. This command can also be used to define a scope list, which specifies the order in which the debugger should search symbols to display the data. Decimal is the default radix.
SHOW SCOPE	Shows you the current scope.
CANCEL SCOPE	Resets the scope to the PC scope.

Figure 8.8 SET SCOPE command of the debugger.

```
DBG> EXAMINE/SOURCE .1\PC        displays the contents of the memory
                                 location one level above the stack
DBG> EXAMINE/SOURCE .2\PC        two levels above the stack
     :
     :
     :
```

If you want to see the first line of code in a routine you are about to call, you can use the /SOURCE qualifier with the EXAMINE command. The following example displays the first line from the module GAUSSIAN:

```
DBG> EXAMINE/SOURCE GAUSSIAN
```

You can examine memory locations using the EXAMINE command. Generally, you would check the contents of a memory addresses listed by the traceback handler. Normally, the hexadecimal address is provided to the EXAMINE command for such purposes. For example,

```
DBG> EXAMINE/SOURCE %HEX 1245DF
```

You can use the SEARCH command to locate a string in your program modules. An example is:

```
DBG> SEARCH MODULE_1 "CYCLOTRON"
```

If the source has been moved since the file was compiled using the /DEBUG qualifier, then you can specify a search order to be used by the SEARCH string. An example to specify the search order using the SET command is given here:

```
DBG> SET SOURCE/MODULE=MODULE_A [],USER$DISK:[KARL]
```

8.8 DISPLAY CONTROL

You can use the screen mode to see more information, to maneuver through the program text, and to debug more conveniently. The screen mode divides the screen into two windows: one containing the program text along with the line numbers, the other containing debug messages indicating the program line being executed, any error messages, and the status and output of the debug commands. In addition, the bottom is reserved for the debug command line with a DBG> prompt. You can invoke the screen mode with the SET MODE SCREEN command.

The window that displays the source code listing is called SRC. The other categories of windows are OUT (for debugger output), REG (for register values), and INST (for displaying the assembly instructions).

If you are using the MACRO-32 assembler in the debug mode, then REG provides information on register values. In this case, another default display, INST, is also used for showing assembly instructions.

Note that the REG display is not displayed initially. However, if the language you are using is MACRO-32, then the REG display is shown by default instead of the SRC display. Otherwise, it is not visible unless you request that display.

You can see a display on the screen using the DISPLAY command. For example,

```
DBG> DISPLAY REG
```

shows registers on screen. See Fig. 8.9 for a brief summary of screen mode commands.

To remove a display you would use the /REMOVE qualifier with the DISPLAY command:

```
DBG> DISPLAY/REMOVE REG
```

You can scroll through a window using the SCROLL command. An example for its use is:

```
DBG> SCROLL/BOTTOM
```

This command scrolls to the bottom of the currently selected scrolling display. You can select which window to scroll using the SELECT command. An example is:

```
DBG> SELECT/SCROLL OUT
```

You can use the flexible features of the symbolic debugger to define your own display for continuously monitoring one or a range of variables. You can use the SET DISPLAY command to define your own dis-

Command	Description
SET MODE SCREEN	The debugger screen mode is activated.
SET MODE NOSCREEN	Ends the screen mode and returns to line mode.
SHOW MODE	Displays the mode in effect.
DISPLAY REG	Paces register window REG on the display.
SCROLL display	Scrolls a specified screen display in the screen. By default, the SRC display is scrolled. Qualifiers /UP[:n], /DOWN[:n], /RIGHT[:n], or /LEFT[:n] can be used to specify the direction and the number of lines or columns to be scrolled.

Figure 8.9 A summary of the debugger screen mode commands.

play where you can specify the window size and also a DO action to execute a debug command in that window. For example,

```
DBG> SET DISPLAY EX_DISPLAY AT (14,3) DO (EXAMINE COUNT, INCR)
```

You can use the SHOW display and CANCEL DISPLAY commands to show and delete the display definition, respectively.

8.9 KEYPAD INPUT

You can use numeric keypad keys to enter debugger commands, provided you are in the keypad mode. Each keypad key is associated with up to three debugger commands or functions. Figure 8.2 shows the debugger commands and functions associated with each key on the keypad.

You can define your own key using a DEFINE/KEY combination. For example, the following command defines the keypad key '0' as a debug command—to examine variables COUNT and INCR and then STEP by one instruction to execute the next line of code. Whenever you press the numeric keypad key '0', this debug action takes place:

```
DBG> DEFINE/KEY/NOECHO/TERMINATE KP0 "EXAMINE X,Y,Z;STEP"
```

8.10 SPAWNING DCL COMMANDS

You can use the SPAWN command to interrupt the debugger and go back to the DCL environment. You can resume the debugger by logging out from the spawned process:

```
DBG> spawn mail
$ MAIL
MAIL>
   :
   :
MAIL>EXIT
$ LOGOUT
%DEBUG-1-RETURNED, control returned to process process_name
DBG>
```

8.11 CONTROL STRUCTURES

The symbolic debugger allows the control structure for command procedures. You can use constructs like the IF-ELSE condition, FOR loops, and WHILE-DO loops. Some examples are shown below:

IF-ELSE condition:

```
DBG> IF J.EQ.0 THEN (EXAMINE I) ELSE (EXAMINE I, J)
```

FOR loop:

```
DBG> FOR COUNT = 1 TO 5 DO (EXAMINE I, J;STEP)
```

WHILE-DO loop:

```
DBG> WHILE I.GE.J DO(STEP/SILENT;EXAMINE I,J)
```

When you are finished with the debugging session, you must not restart a program from the beginning unless you first exit from the debugger. Otherwise, unpredictable results can occur.

The following is an example of the GO command:

```
$ RUN GAUSS
        (DEBUGGER version messages)
%DEBUG-I-INITIAL, language is Pascal, module set to 'GAUSS'
DBG>go
%DEBUG-I-EXITSTATUS, is '%SYSTEM-S-NORMAL, normal successful
                completion'
DBG>
```

8.12   RUN-TIME SYMBOL TABLE

The debugger can access the symbols from the Run-Time Symbol Table to which you can refer during a debugging session. You can refer to the following items:

- The debugger's permanent symbols
- Global symbols and function names
- Program variables
- Program locations, including defined symbolic references to program locations

You may not be able to access function parameters and local variables unless you use either the /NOOPTIMIZE or the /OPTIMIZE=NODIS-JOINT qualifier on the compilation command line.

Symbols can be variable references or values. The debugger interprets them according to the following rules:

1. If a symbol begins with an alphabetic character, the debugger assumes that the symbol is a program variable or a symbolic reference to an address.

2. If a symbol begins with a numeric character (0 through 9), the debugger assumes that it is a character-string constant.

General register 0 through R11, argument points (AP), frame pointer (FP), stack pointer (SP), program counter (PC), and processor status longword (PSL) are all treated as permanent symbols by the debugger. Hence, these symbols are available at any time during the debugging session.

You can refer to program locations in the following ways:

- By function name
- By label name
- By listing line number, preceded by the %LINE keyword

The debugger does not recognize all line numbers. In particular, it does not recognize those line numbers associated with nonexecutable statements, such as declarations. If you specify such a line number, the debugger responds with a message indicating that no such line exists:

By line number within a function, using the %LINE keyword with the function name.

By virtual address, which can be the virtual address returned by the EVALUATE/ADDRESS command, or a symbolic name assigned to the virtual address with the DEFINE command.

8.13 EXAMINING ARRAYS

```
DBG> examine oned
ARRAY\main\oned
    [0]:    -3
    [1]:    -2
    [2]:    -1
    [3]:     0
    [4]:     1
    [5]:     2
    [6]:     3
    [7]:     4
    [8]:     5
    [9]:     6
```

Simply specify the variable identifier as above, or individual members, using the bracket operator to specify the offset of the member of the array as below:

```
DBG> examine oned[4]
ARRAY\main\oned[4]: 1
DBG>
```

Examining strings

```
DBG> examine/az str
STRING\main\str: "alpha"
DBG>

depositing into strings

DBG> deposit/az str = "beta"
```

8.14 RESOLVING REFERENCES

When the debugger encounters a reference to a variable, it resolves the reference by going through the following steps:

1. If the specified symbolic name is unique within the Run-Time Symbol Table, then the debugger uses that name.

2. If the specified symbol is ambiguous—that is, not unique within the symbol table, but one of its occurrences is with the PC scope—then the debugger recognizes the symbol as it appears in the PC scope.

3. If the specified symbol is not defined in the symbol table, then the debugger issues an error message indicating that the symbol was not found. If the specified symbol is ambiguous and does not occur within the PC scope, then the debugger issues an error message indicating that the name is ambiguous.

Remembering these steps, you can specify the scope in one of three ways:

- By using the debugger's PC scope
- By explicitly specifying the scope of the variable, that is, by prefixing the variable's name with its pathname. The form of pathname is:

```
MODULE-NAME\function-name\variable-name
```

If you want to make frequent references to a location with a long pathname, you can define a symbolic name for it with the DEFINE command.

- By defining a new default scope or scope list

8.15 SUMMARY

The OpenVMS debugger provides powerful features to trace a running program and to remove logical errors in the program. The basic debugger commands, like STEP, EXAMINE, and DEPOSIT, can be easily used to study a program's behavior and to achieve a reliable, error-free code.

9

OpenVMS Record Management Services

9.1 INTRODUCTION

The file handling system in OpenVMS is Record Management Services (RMS). You can use subroutine calls in your program to set up the data file structures and access the same. The file handling in a typical program running on OpenVMS can be classified into two parts: one that uses the programming language-specific Run-Time Library functions and the other that uses the RMS functions that provide extra and advanced file handling techniques.

OpenVMS RMS supports three kinds of file structures: *sequential, relative,* and *indexed.* Once you create a file with a particular file structure you cannot change it. The structure determines the way the file is stored on the device and the file operations you can perform. However, other RMS utilities enable you to define the characteristics of a new file, and then transfer the contents of a file that has a different format to the new file. The File Definition Language (FDL) Editor and the CONVERT or CONVERT/RECLAIM utilities are used in such circumstances.

The records of a sequential file are arranged in a consecutive order. There are no empty records separating the records that contain data. Although this is a simple organization, it has certain operational limitations; you cannot position the file at a particular record randomly, you have to scan through the intervening records to reach the required record. Operations like reading data from any record at random or writing data at the end of a file are also limited for sequential files.

Files on a nondisk device like magnetic tape can be organized only sequentially.

In a relatively ordered file structure the records need not have the same length although records occupy numbered, fixed-length cells. These cells can be empty or can have data. In a relative file, unlike the sequential files, you can perform some random file operations like positioning the file at a particular record, reading a record from any cell, deleting, and writing records from any cell. Only disk-based files can have relative file structure.

Indexed file organization allows usage of keys in its file structure. The records can also contain the data and carriage-control information. There can be more than one key defined for the records, which can be fields of character strings, packed decimal numbers, and 16-bit, 32-bit, or 64-bit signed or unsigned integers. Every record has at least one key, the primary key, the value of which cannot be changed in each record. But, the values of any secondary or other keys can be changed. When a file is created, you can indicate whether the records can have duplicate keys to allow the particular key to have the same value in different records. Key definitions indicating the length and the position within a record hold good for the complete file.

RMS maintains the keys defined as indexes in a fixed-file organization. The key value-updating mechanism enables RMS to order the key values in an ascending order whenever a key value is inserted into the record. Indexed-file organization enables several random file operations, like positioning the file at a particular record, by direct access, reading any record, including sequential reads controlled by a key's index, deleting any record, updating an alternate key's value if the key's definition permits its value to change, and writing records selectively, depending on the value of a key and, when allowed in the key's definition, based on duplicate keys. For writing records selectively, if duplicate values are permitted, you can write records containing key values that are already present in the key's index. Otherwise, such write operations are rejected.

Only disk-based files can use the indexed-file structure of RMS.

RMS supports three types of record access: sequential access, direct access by key, and direct access by record file address. The direct access is possible only for disk-based files. The way you access records from a file is independent of the file structure. You can access one record using one type of access and another record using another access type, provided it is permitted. For example, typically, in an indexed file you would locate a record randomly and from that record onward you may read sequentially all the indexed records in ascending order of their key values. This method of accessing records in an indexed file is known as the indexed-sequential access method (ISAM).

The following formats for records in files are supported by RMS:

Fixed-length format   The record length for all records of the file is defined when the file is created. You can use this format for any file type.

Variable-length format   The maximum length that any record in the file can have is defined at the time the file is created. Any file type can have this format.

Variable-length format with a fixed-length control (VFC) area   Every record in the file is prefixed by a fixed-length field. Only sequential and relative files can use this format.

Stream format   Special terminators delimit each record in the file. Terminators are part of the record. There are three types of stream formats: Stream variation, where records can be delimited with any special character; Stream_cr, where the records are delimited with the carriage return character; and Stream_lf, where records are delimited with the line feed character. The third type of stream format, stream_lf, is the default format when you create files using the standard I/O functions.

In addition to RMS functions to define different file types supported by RMS, a set of higher-level system functions can be used in user-developed programs. Figure 9.1 provides a summary of these file processing functions.

9.2   RMS DATA STRUCTURES AND FUNCTIONS

There are many RMS functions which you can use to create and manipulate files. The RMS data structures that define file characteristics also imply the file operations that are allowed on the file by defining the file to be of a certain type and the type of access for its records. The RMS functions make use of the information on these data structures. However, these data structures need not be specified as parameters to RMS function calls. They are automatically declared when RMS first accesses the file by opening a file header.

Function	Description
sys$create	Creates and opens a new file of any organization.
sys$open	Opens an existing file and initiates file processing.
sys$close	Terminates file processing and closes the file.
sys$erase	Deletes a file.

Figure 9.1   RMS file processing functions.

Mainly, there are four RMS data structures:

File Access Block (FAB)   This defines the file's characteristics, such as file organization and record format.

Record Access Block (RAB)   Defines the way in which records are processed, such as the record access mode.

Extended Attribute Block (XAB)   Various kinds of extended attribute blocks contain additional file characteristics, such as the definition of keys in an indexed file. Extended attribute blocks can be specified optionally.

Name Block (NAM)   Defines all or part of a file specification to be used when an incomplete file specification is given in an OPEN or CREATE file operation. This data structure is optional information.

All RMS file operations and record access functions make use of the above data structures.

Figure 9.2 shows some of the common RMS functions used for run-time processing of files and records.

The first step in performing I/O using RMS is initializing the file access block. The following example in VAX C illustrates a way of initializing FAB.

```
#include rms
struct FAB fabex

main ( )
{
  fabex = cc$rms_fab
    :
    :
}
```

Function	Description
sys$connect	Associates a file access block with a record access block to establish a record access stream; a call to this function is required before any other record processing function can be used.
sys$get	Retrieves a record from a file.
sys$put	Writes a new record to a new file.
sys$update	Rewrites an existing record to a file.
sys$delete	Deletes a record from a file.
sys$rewind	Positions the record pointer to the first record in the file.
sys$disconnect	Disconnects a record access stream.

Figure 9.2 RMS run-time functions for processing files and records.

In this example, the 'include' statement declares all RMS data structures. The 'struct' statement defines a file access block. And 'cc$rms_fab' is a VAX C-specific RMS prototype data structure for the file access block (each programming language has its own construct like this to access RMS data structures). The assignment initializes FAB.

Similarly, you can initialize record access blocks (RABs). The record access block specifies how records are processed. For example, in VAX C you use a structure construct called RAB and declare a variable to have this structure (just like FAB in the previous example). Then you can use an RMS prototype called 'cc$rms_rab' to initialize the structure just as you used 'cc$rms_fab' in the above example.

There is an extended attribute block structure (XAB) which you can initialize in many different ways. XAB defines additional file attributes. For example, the key extended attribute block is used to define the keys of an indexed file. All XABs are appended to a file access block in the following manner:

In a FAB, you initialize the 'fab$l_fxab' field with XAB's address.

Initialize the field 'xab$l_nxt' with the next XAB's address in the chain. You chain each XAB in order by the key of reference (first the primary key, then the first alternate key, then the second alternate key, and so on).

To indicate the end of the chain of XAB, the field xab$l_nxt of the last XAB is equated to 0.

The usage of RMS prototypes in the language you are programming and the RMS data structures to initialize XAB is similar to the VAX C example shown above for FAB and RAB.

The name block defines filename specification details like device, directory, filename, etc. If you do not specify one of the parts of the file specification when you open the file, RMS uses the values contained in the name block to make up a complete file specification and places this information in an array. The initialization procedure for the name blocks is similar to the one shown for FAB.

RMS allocates disk blocks in a dynamic way as new records are added to files. This causes an additional overhead on the disk to look for free blocks that are available to write new records. This overhead can be minimized if some disk blocks are already allocated at the time of file creation. Also, when the disk space is allocated in a dynamic way the chances of the disk running out of space are higher, and this may cause the programs to forcibly exit. By preallocating the exact amount of disk space in terms of 512-byte blocks when the file was created, the disk overhead can be totally eliminated. If more disk blocks are required to be written when you open the file for the second time, the allocation of disk blocks is made dynamically.

RMS refers to the disk's free-block list when allocating disk space dynamically. The allocation is made in small increments when the file becomes full, before adding a new record. This allocation mechanism may repeat for a long time when updating a file with a large number of new records. By allocating a larger number of blocks initially, the over-head due to the repeated allocation of disk blocks in small increments can be reduced. A parameter called 'extend size' is defined by RMS to specify the increment size. This size can be replaced by a new value when the disk is mounted by using the /EXTENSION qualifier with the MOUNT command. For example, the following command overrides the system default value for the 'extend size' parameter by specifying a size of 10 blocks.

```
$ MOUNT/EXTENSION=10 device_name
```

You can see the value of the 'extend size' parameter using the command

```
$SHOW DEVICE device_name: /FULL
```

The 'extend size' parameter can also be specified at the time of file creation.

For example, you can consider a file of fixed-size records of record length 250 bytes and extend size of 10. When the file is created, RMS allocates 10 blocks, i.e., 5120 bytes. Because each record contains 250 bytes, the initial allocation for the file is enough to hold 20 records amounting to 5000 bytes. When the twenty-first record is added to the file, because there are only 120 bytes left free in the file to accommo-date the new record, RMS extends the file by allocating another 10 blocks, or 5120 bytes, to make the total available space 5120 + 120 (left over) = 5240 bytes.

If you specify large extend sizes you may waste a lot of disk space because, after writing the last record, there may be a large empty space left at the tail of the file. The default extend size is equal to that defined for the device when the device was initialized.

9.3 DISK CLUSTER

The root directory [000000] of every disk on your system has two system files called INDEXF.SYS and BITMAP.SYS. These contain information about the blocks used by the files on the disk. The information about the free number of blocks and the allocated number of blocks on the disk is available from BITMAP.SYS with one entry per block. With a large number of blocks on a disk, the size of the BITMAP.SYS file may be too large to maintain an entry for each block. To reduce the size of this file, RMS uses the concept of disk cluster, which specifies a minimum allocation quantity. A disk cluster is nothing but one or more contiguous blocks. For example, if the disk cluster size is 6, then you would effectively reduce the disk allocation table size by one-sixth, because each entry in the disk allocation table now contains an entry for six blocks instead of one block. When a file performs a write operation requiring more blocks, RMS determines the number of blocks required using the extend size parameter. The required clusters are allocated to fit the allocation implied by the extend size parameter. There is one drawback with the concept of disk cluster. Just as the possible empty space left at the tail of the file due to allocation of blocks is determined by the extend size parameter, allocation of the whole cluster may result in a larger empty tail at the end of the file. This is the price to be paid if one prefers a faster allocation of disk blocks during write operations.

9.4 BUCKET

RMS employs a data buffering technique called a *bucket*. For RMS a bucket is more like a cache memory for physical memory. If you want to access a record from a file, RMS may not pick the requested record alone, but it reads the neighborhood records in a sequential order. This set of records contains a contiguous number of records in addition to the requested record. These records are buffered into a portion of physical memory. This buffer space in the memory is called a bucket. The bucket concept is employed with the assumption that in a sequential access, the records are read one after the other as a set of read operations and not just one record at a time. This is practically true for many sequential access read or write operations. And a bucket-like buffering mechanism cuts down the disk access time because the data is available in the memory, which has a faster response than a disk.

But, the bucket is not a universal solution to cut down the disk access time. For example, in a random access, one might be interested in accessing just one record from a bucket and another record subsequently which may not be found in the bucket. In such cases the bucket has to be replaced with a new set of records. There are two overheads here. First, whenever the bucket size is more than the record size, more than one record was read when the first record was required to be accessed by the user. Second, when the user requested to access a second record, because the record was not in the bucket, a second set of records instead of one record was read from the disk to replace the bucket. Therefore, in the case of random access, larger bucket sizes are more likely to slow down RMS functions.

Bucket size is measured in 512-byte units or blocks. A certain number of buckets are allocated for each area in a file. The key bucket carries data corresponding to the key values. Whenever records are inserted, keys are inserted in these key buckets. When a bucket is full, the bucket is split to accommodate any new key information. This bisection of the bucket follows a binary-tree structure each time, increasing the depth of the tree. This causes an overhead on the CPU, because the memory–CPU interaction increases with increasing depth of the bucket tree. On the other hand, having a large bucket size causes a different type of overhead—bringing a larger chunk of data into memory although only a small portion of it is used. This reduces the performance again. Typically, you can increase the bucket size by a small amount whenever the bucket size splits. This has to be done by monitoring the disk input/output and paging faults whenever the I/O-intensive large programs involving the indexed files are executed.

The records cannot span across buckets. A maximum bucket size of 32 blocks is allowed in RMS. Note that a bucket size of 0 means that the bucket holds just one record.

9.5 SPANNING AND NONSPANNING RECORDS

There are two ways that records can be written in terms of blocks: records which span the blocks and those which do not span the blocks, i.e., nonspanning records. Recall that a block contains 512 bytes of storage unit. In the first case of spanning, a record of size, say 400 bytes, is accommodated in the first block as well as the partial data from the second record stored on the same block (in fact, 512 − 400 = 112 bytes of the second record). The rest of the data from the second record (288 bytes) is written in the second block. Then the second record is said to be spanning the two blocks. Normally, this is the default way of storing records in blocks.

In the second case of nonspanning records, an integer multiple of blocks is allocated per record. If a record is 1000 bytes long, two blocks (1024 bytes) are allocated to the record although 24 bytes of storage are wasted.

Having spanned records has the advantage of conserving space at the cost of expensive access time. On the other hand, nonspanning records have the advantage of faster access at the cost of fragmented and, hence, initialized storage space on the disk. Note that for variable-length records, the effective size of a block will be 510, because 2 bytes of the record header are maintained for every record. Also, for indexed files, to provide information about key indices, the file-structuring mechanism of RMS may reserve more than 2 bytes for each record.

RMS uses the concept of protection flags and locking to support the security for the files. The user can set protection to files to declare:

- no read and no write accesses
- read access
- read and write access

for other users.

To resolve a deadlock situation resulting from the possibility of two or more users attempting to simultaneously access the same record, RMS has employed the concept of record locking. There are two ways of locking records against such deadlock situations:

- *Automatic record locking*
- *Manual record locking*

In case of automatic record locking, RMS is responsible for automatically locking and unlocking the records. By default, if a file is declared as read-only access, then any record from that file can be read by other users also. And, if a file is opened for write or update, other users are prohibited from having read access to the records from that file.

In manual record locking, the user locks and unlocks records. In this case you have the advantage of locking and unlocking each record or a group of records from the same file. You can also have control to provide no-read or read-only access to records by other users when the file is kept open by you.

9.6 INDEXED FILES

In order to store multiple records with the same primary key value in an indexed file, a DUPLICATE key has to be associated with the key value. You can specify this during the file creation. DUPLICATE keys can be associated with any primary key. Using duplicate keys, first you have to access the first record with the same key value. The rest of the records having the same key value can be fetched in a sequential order.

All update operations which change the value of the primary key have to be done with two operations: First, deleting the record and then inserting a new record having the new primary key value. When the alternate keys are used, the prevailing records can be updated for these alternate keys. RMS takes care of handling such updates by updating the alternate indexes suitably. For this one has to use the CHANGEABLE KEY option for the alternate keys.

Normally, the data and indexes in an indexed file are kept together as records in terms of blocks, but it is preferable to have the keys arranged in a logically sequential order so that searching for keys can become faster. RMS makes use of designated areas within the file to accommodate the keys as a separate set for easy accessibility. An area is basically a logical partition within the file. It is possible to group each class of keys in this way. Areas can be assigned at the time of file creation using the File Description Language utility (invoked as EDIT/FDL).

The indexed files are normally used as sequential files when opened the first time for write operations. Subsequent opening of the file may involve randomly picking the records for reading or writing the records randomly. Therefore, the key buckets initially are contiguous with sequentially ordered key values. Whenever a random access of a record is requested, the key buckets are split, reducing the performance. A *fill factor* of 100% defines the buckets which are not split. This is the initial condition. By specifying a lower fill factor, say 40 percent, at the time of file creation, it is likely that the bucket splits are reduced and a uniform I/O performance is maintained. Whenever a record is added randomly, the corresponding key value is inserted into already available space in the bucket. The only price that is paid for a lower fill factor option is that a large chunk of mostly empty space is allocated for the buckets with the assumption that the space will be used by subsequent write operations. The fill factor has to be tuned after monitoring the typical write operations on the concerned file for program execution. If this becomes critical, a new file with a slightly larger fill factor has to be created with a similar file structure, and the contents of the old file have to be transferred to this new file.

9.7   RMS UTILITIES

There are three important file utilities of RMS which are used in maintaining RMS-created files:

FDL	File Definition Language, used for creating files
CONVERT	Program to convert format of specified file to another specified format
DUMP	Program to display the file contents

9.7.1   FDL

In RMS the file definition is made using a simple language known as FDL that specifies the structure of the file and various attributes related to the file. For normal operation, the open statement in most of the programming languages interfaces with RMS to automatically create the file for the user, with attributes specified as parameters in the open statement. In special circumstances, when you are designing a large file or modifying one, or when you are concerned about the file input/output performance, you would resort to FDL for specifying customized file structures rather than default file structures provided by RMS.

When you open a file in your program you need not specify all attributes of a file. Most of the attributes are associated with certain default values, which are normally sufficient for many regular file operations. Also, you cannot specify all possible RMS parameters when using the open statement of the programming language. To specify any of the allowed RMS parameters you have to use FDL. You can then open the file in your program and resume the update operations.

You can also modify the structure of an existing file or specify new RMS attributes using FDL. For example, if you want to extend the record size to place an extra field, you can use FDL (using the ANA-LYZE/RMS/FDL command). You can make the necessary changes using the EDIT/FDL command and finally the file created with modified structure using the CREATE/FDL command. The new file needs to be updated with the contents of the old file. This can be done using the CONVERT utility.

You can create or modify a file by invoking FDL as follows:

```
$ EDIT/FDL file_name
```

The default file extension .FDL is assumed.

FDL is a query-answer program. It asks many questions to receive the RMS parameter specifications and then it constructs the file definition file.

Using an editor like EDT or EVE, the file created by FDL can be edited to make suitable changes using the MODIFY option.

After defining the file, i.e., once you have your .fdl file, the actual file can be created using the CREATE utility. The syntax for invoking CREATE is:

```
$ CREATE/FDL=file_specification
```

The file that was created will have the file specification mentioned in the FDL file. But you can mention any other name to the file by specifying it in the CREATE command line:

```
$ CREATE/FDL=fdl_file_specification create_file_specification
```

Using the DIR/FULL command, you can verify if the file is created properly.

To collect information regarding the file structure of an existing file, you can use the ANALYZE utility of RMS. This utility takes the existing file as an input parameter. It scans the file header and collects the file structure information and all RMS parameter specifications. Then, it creates a .FDL file containing all the collected information. Now you can go through the sequence of editing the file using EDIT/FDL and CREATE/FDL to edit the file definition suitably and create the file. To invoke ANALYZE, use the following syntax:

```
$ ANALYZE/RMS/FDL file_specification
```

Note that here the file_specification is for the actual file referred to in your programs. The output is a .fdl file with the same name.

The DUMP utility can dump the contents of a file, as well as header information, in a variety of ways.

9.7.2 CONVERT utility

The CONVERT command is used to convert data from an old structure to a new structure. This stage is usually a continuation of the sequence ANALYZE, EDIT, and CREATE. After creating the new file with new organization, the data from the old file need to be transferred to the new file, which differs in its file structure. CONVERT is a support that RMS provides to make differing file structures compatible with each other. The format for using the CONVERT utility is:

```
$ CONVERT/qualifiers input_file output_file
```

9.8 SUMMARY

RMS functions can be directly accessed in programs to achieve an efficient file input and output. Several I/O functions of RMS define various attributes. These attributes can be declared when specifying the function to achieve an efficient organization of the files. Also, RMS generally helps in giving an improved throughput compared to that achieved using the I/O functions provided in programming languages.

10

Utilities

The standard distribution of OpenVMS includes several utilities. Typically, these utilities are routinely used for file management, text comparison, and interactive communication via software utilities that simulate phone, mail, and some conferencing systems. Some important and popular OpenVMS utilities are discussed here. They are:

- MAIL
- PHONE
- SORT and MERGE
- DIFFERENCES
- DUMP
- SEARCH
- NOTES

10.1 MAIL UTILITY

MAIL is one of the most frequently used utilities. It is used for sending messages to not only other users on the same node or cluster but also to the Wide Area Network to send messages to users across the world. MAIL is the command you would issue at the '$' prompt to invoke the MAIL utility:

```
$ MAIL
MAIL>
```

The SEND command of MAIL requires a username. Then the text to be sent to the other user has to be entered. The message is terminated by typing <control/z>. The message is sent to the mail file of the receiving user. If the user is logged on the system when the mail message is sent, his or her terminal will display a line of message indicating the arrival of the mail. An example:

```
New mail on node ORION from GAUTAM::RAJ
```

If the receiver is not logged onto the system, the user, when logged into the system, will receive a message issued by the MAIL utility which looks something like:

```
Username: JOHN
Password:
                :
        {  OpenVMS Welcome Messages }
                :
You have 5 new Mail messages.
```

To read mail from another user, invoke the MAIL utility and enter just <return> or type READ. Continue issuing <return> until you see all pages of all messages. Here is an example:

```
MAIL> send
To: CIACCIO
Subj: Printer queue.
[EOB]
*i
    I want to know the parameter for the printer queue
    LASER$101 to get landscape outputs. Please call me or mail.

    Dave (Ext: 365)

[EOB]
*exit

MAIL> exit
```

Note that MAIL uses the EDT editor by default. If you wish to use another editor, say EVE, then use

```
MAIL> SET EDITOR TPU
```

The setting will be in effect until it is changed again.

Mail can also be sent using just one DCL command line, as in

```
$ MAIL /SUBJECT="Please confirm tomorrow's meeting"
MEETING6.TXT HAWTHORNE
```

where MEETING6.TXT is the file containing the mail message and HAWTHORNE is the username of the receiver.

You can extract a message to a file for printing or some other purpose by reading the message and then entering something like:

```
MAIL> EXTRACT MAIL.DOC
```

where MAIL.DOC is the file where the message will be stored.

The SEARCH command can be used to search for a string in all the mail messages in the current folder:

```
MAIL> SEARCH "TOKEN"
```

This command searches for messages in the currently active folder containing the string "token".

10.1.1 Sending mail

To send mail to a user on another node, precede the username by the node name:

```
MAIL> send
To: YUSAKA::POLYI
          Your message
```

To execute the SEND command, type <control/z>.

10.1.2 Responding to messages

The REPLY command is to be used while reading the message or just after reading the message. It sets up the receiver's name and subject (taking this information from the message header of the message that is being read). Then you can enter the response message similar to the example shown for send, using either EDT or EVE that is set as a default editor. Some frequently used MAIL commands are summarized in Fig. 10.1.

10.1.3 Mail characteristics

You can associate personal information like a telephone number, room number, etc. For example, a brief message can be displayed at the receiver's terminal by setting the PERSONAL_NAME parameter:

```
MAIL> SET PERSONAL_NAME "East is lux, West is lex"
```

Command	Description
HELP	Enters MAIL's on-line system.
READ	Reads next MAIL message.
SELECT NEWMAIL	Accesses folder of unread messages.
SEND	Sends mail to specified user.
SEND filespec	Sends the specified file contents to the specified user.
DELETE	Deletes the messages just read.
DIR	Lists directory of current MAIL messages.
ANSWER or REPLY	Replies to MAIL message currently being read.
CTRL/Z	Completes the message that is being typed.
EXTRACT filespec	Sends MAIL message currently being read to the specified file.
FORWARD	Forwards current message to specified user.

Figure 10.1 Frequently used MAIL commands.

Then when the mail is sent to another user, the receiving user will see a message like this one:

```
New mail on node SQUIRREL from SQUIRREL::WILSON "East is lux.
West is lex"
```

The WASTEBASKET folder contains deleted messages and it is purged when you exit from MAIL. You may want to keep all your old messages. The next command will do this:

```
MAIL> set noauto_purge
```

Later if the WASTEBASKET folder needs to be cleaned, the command is:

```
MAIL> purge ! Purge WASTEBASKET (This is different from
           ! DCL's PURGE command)
```

You can keep a copy of every message you mail by using a command similar to

```
MAIL> set copy_self send
```

For multiple users you can use MAIL to send messages to more than one user. You need to specify the names separated by commas:

```
MAIL> send
To: MADHAV,XIONG,SULLIVAN
```

A file containing the distribution list of usernames can also be used. The file is then specified with the @ command:

```
MAIL> send
To: @dist.mai

$ TYPE LIST.MAI

MADHAV
XIONG
SULLIVAN
```

10.1.4 Folders

Each user has a file MAIL.MAI in their login directory. Mail is stored in this file. The file consists of folders, and folders contain mail messages. Folders can be thought of as subdirectories within MAIL.MAI. To see a list of folders, the command is:

```
MAIL> DIR/FOLDERS
```

You can create your own folders. The MAIL utility uses three folders:

MAIL	Contains messages which have been read.
NEWMAIL	New messages are stored here.
WASTEBASKET	Messages which have been deleted are stored here.

When a message arrives, it is stored in the NEWMAIL folder. Once you read the message it is stored in the MAIL folder. When a message is being read, the DELETE command can be issued to send it to the WASTEBASKET folder. The WASTEBASKET folder is purged when you exit from the MAIL utility.

To see messages in the current folder, use the following command:

```
MAIL> directory
#  From            Date         Subject
1  ORION::WILSON   23-NOV-1993  Comments about SN1993s
              :
              :
              :
MAIL>
```

To select another folder, enter

```
MAIL> SELECT WASTEBASKET
```

To read a particular message just enter the message number

```
MAIL> 35 ! read message number 35
```

To delete a particular message, use the message number

```
MAIL> DELETE 18 ! delete message number 10
```

If a message is being read, it can be deleted using

```
MAIL> DELETE ! delete current message
```

10.2 PHONE UTILITY

This utility is used to communicate with another user interactively. Users on any node in a network can be addressed using the PHONE utility. The message text is transferred across the two users' terminal displays just like voice is transferred across a phone. One user types text on his/her screen which is instantly displayed by PHONE on the receiver's display. To respond, the user at the receiving terminal need not wait for the sender to issue a carriage return; the message can be typed while the text is being output on the receiver's terminal. The receiver's response and the sender's input are displayed in separate windows.

You can call another user by ringing. The PHONE ring is initiated using the receiver's username as follows:

```
$ PHONE PRADIP
```

The other user must be logged into the system for the phone to ring at his/her terminal. If the user is logged in, the phone ring is simulated at the receiver's terminal by issuing a message at a regular interval. The ring message looks something like this:

```
MARS::STEVE is phoning you on MARS:: (10:56:03)
```

The message is repeated every 10 seconds on PRADIP's terminal until the receiving user invokes the PHONE utility to answer the call as below:

```
$ PHONE ANSWER
```

The display on both the terminals will be divided into two regions, one allocated to send messages and the other to receive messages. After the conversation, you can end the phone session with the 'bye' command followed by <control/z> twice. To call a user on another node, use a command similar to the following:

```
$ PHONE NAUKA::FEYNGOLD
```

Command	Description
HELP	Enters PHONE's on-line system.
DIR or DIR nodename::	Obtains directory of users currently logged in the system you are using or the node you have specified.
DIAL username	Places a call to the user with specified username.
ANSWER	Answers when some other user calls you.
REJECT	Tells a caller that you do not want to answer.
HANGUP or CTRL/Z	Disconnects the call.

Figure 10.2   PHONE utility commands.

Figure 10.2 shows a summary of frequently used PHONE commands.

10.3   SORT AND MERGE UTILITIES

The SORT utility can be used to sort files of any type: sequential, relative, or indexed. Consider an input file TEST.INP which is to be sorted for names occurring in the fifth column and having a length of 5 characters. For this example, the SORT command can be used as follows:

```
$ SORT/KEY=(POSITION=5, SIZE=5) test.inp sample.srt
```

To sort the file on two keys, the primary keys being the first number and the second number in each record, use:

```
$ SORT/KEY=(POSITION=5, SIZE=3) /KEY=(POSITION=10,SIZE=5)-
_$                              test.inp sample.srt
```

You can specify up to 255 sort keys. The input file can have any file structure, including sequential, relative, or indexed. The output file will also have the same file structure. If large files are to be sorted, SORT will create temporary work files on the disk SYS$SCRATCH.

To merge files, the command is similar to SORT except that multiple input files are specified. A maximum of 10 files is allowed:

```
$ MERGE/KEY=(POSITION=5, SIZE=5) /KEY=(POSITION=11, SIZE=4) -
_$ SAMPLE.SRT1, SAMPLE.SRT2 SAMPLE.MRG
```

Note that the input files specified in the above command were ASCII characters. Keys can be of any data type including packed decimal. The key type can be specified as in

```
$ SORT/KEY=(POSITION=7, SIZE=3, PACKED_DECIMAL) TEST.INP
SAMPLE.SRT5
```

The key data types are

- CHARACTER (default)
- BINARY (signed)
- BINARY, UNSIGNED
- F_FLOATING
- DECIMAL
- DECIMAL, LEADING SIGN

10.4 DIFFERENCE UTILITY

The DIFFERENCE utility is used to compare the contents of two text files. Each set of differences is displayed between two lines with 10 asterisks. The lines which are different in the two files are displayed, separated by 6 asterisks. One extra line is displayed so that the context in the file can be easily determined.

Blank lines can be ignored by using /BLANK=BLANK_LINES.

This utility is used to compare two versions of the same file. This feature is particularly useful when you want to know code changes between two versions of the same file.

10.5 DUMP UTILITY

The DUMP utility is used to print out the contents of binary data files. It is used to dump such files from either disks or tapes. The dump output from this utility will display the file header, end of block, and the binary contents of the file along with a translation to ASCII-equivalent text. In case of dumps from tape files, the tape header, tape marks, and contents of every block are displayed. Files may be displayed in terms of 512-byte blocks or by logical records in the file. Starting and ending records can also be specified to dump selected portions of the file.

The DUMP utility supports many formats of tape files. Some of the qualifiers used in DUMP are:

```
/ASCII
/DECIMAL        !Specifies the data representation for display
/HEX            !This is default
/OCTAL
/BYTE
/LONGWORD
/WORD
/RECORD         !Specifies logical record display
```

/BLOCK   !Specifies display of blocks of the file
                        !Optionally the starting
                        !record or block number and the ending or count of
                        ! the number of records or blocks can be specified.

Two examples of using DUMP to dump a range of blocks from a file are
shown below:

```
$ DUMP/RECORD=(START:12, END:17) FERMAT.TXT
$ DUMP/RECORD=(START:7 END:10) FERMAT.TXT
```

10.6 SEARCH UTILITY

The SEARCH command searches for lines in specified files which contain the specified string(s). For example, if you wanted to find the filenames and the lines of text containing a string "spring", then you can
use SEARCH as follows:

```
$ SEARCH *.TXT spring
```

Search strings should be specified in quotes if they contain blanks
and tabs:

```
$ SEARCH *.TXT "spring and autumn"
```

Multiple searches can be specified by separating the search strings
by commas. The example given below uses a SEARCH qualifier
/MATCH with a logical operator AND to search for lines of text containing both the strings "spring" and "autumn" (on the same line):

```
$ SEARCH *.TXT/MATCH = AND spring, autumn
```

The wild card (*) usage above is one way of specifying a search from
multiple files. Another way you can specify multiple files for search is
by explicitly specifying files separated by commas:

```
$ SEARCH abc.txt, xyz.txt
```

Other frequently used SEARCH qualifiers are:

/EXACT
/FORMAT
/STATISTICS
/WINDOWS

The /MATCH qualifier allows other logical operators like OR, NOR, and NAND in searching strings.

By default, the lowercase and uppercase characters are not distinguished in SEARCH. However, you can override this condition by specifying /EXACT to make SEARCH case-sensitive. The following example makes SEARCH case-sensitive:

```
$! Get the lines of text containing the string "Quorum" only,
$! not "quorum"
$ SEARCH/EXACT *.TXT Quorum
```

The qualifier /FORMAT with an attribute called DUMP, i.e. /FORMAT=DUMP, interprets nonprintable characters to output a printable mnemonic form. The /STATISTICS qualifier provides summary information on the search performed by the SEARCH utility. /WINDOWS displays a number of lines above and below the line which has a matching string. This is useful to find out the context of the search string:

```
$ SEARCH *.TXT remnants/window=4
```

10.7 NOTES UTILITY

The OpenVMS NOTES is a frequently used utility that provides many features similar to the bulletin board system (BBS) that is widely used on PC platforms. The command to invoke this program is NOTES at the '$' prompt. NOTES uses a file called NOTES$NOTEBOOK.NOTE in your login directory just like MAIL.MAI is used for the MAIL utility.

Once you invoke NOTES, you will see the primary display of NOTES, which has four classes of information:

- Command line
- Message line
- Heading
- Viewing area

The prompt Notes> appears in the command line. The message line is reserved for displaying error messages, copyright message, and any other system messages, link mail notifications, etc. The heading lists the type of information displayed in the columns below. The viewing area is used for various purposes, like displaying a notification about the conferences in your notebook.

There is extensive on-line help available in NOTES. Many NOTES functions can be invoked using one or two keys in the keypad mode.

Each user of NOTES can have notes for many conferences in his or her NOTEBOOK. Each conference in turn can have many topics. The concept of conference in NOTES is slightly different from the real-life conferences. In NOTES, the conference on a selected topic is created by a user who associates several NOTES attributes to the conference. The attributes determine the reading privileges, writing privileges, etc., for different classes of users of the conference, like supervisor and group members. Typically, the first note of a topic in the conference lays out the scope of the topic and any rules to be observed in using the conference.

The DIRECTORY/CONFERENCES command lists all the conferences you have in your notebook. The OPEN command opens the specified conference for you to review or reply. Any response to the topic discussed in the conference is called a reply; replies are arranged in the order they are received. An opened conference can be closed using the CLOSE command or by exiting from NOTES using the EXIT command.

To read notes from other conferences, first you have to make your notebook aware of the conference address. You can do this by using the ADD ENTRY command, which takes the conference name to be included as its argument. Then you can use the UPDATE command to keep the conference topics current. To read the topics from the conference, you need to use the READ command.

You can save the contents of the notes replies being read; use the EXTRACT command where you can specify a filename in which the reply contents will be placed. This command is similar to the EXTRACT command in MAIL.

The WRITE command is used to post a new topic. To delete a note that you have posted, use the DELETE NOTE command. The REPLY command is used to reply to a note or to comment on a note that you are reading.

10.8 SUMMARY

The utilities discussed here are some of the popular ones being used on OpenVMS. In particular, utilities MAIL and NOTES can be powerfully used to speed up the software development. Together, they help in corresponding quickly, setting up discussion meetings, etc. For various other utilities, the reader may consult the OpenVMS manuals and guides.

OpenVMS Architecture

A Process in OpenVMS

11.1 INTRODUCTION

A process is the basic working environment in OpenVMS. It is defined for the user to facilitate standard operations like using several resources including the CPU, memory, and I/O devices. This is in addition to default processes provided by the job controller like the Digital Command Language (DCL) and others. The process creation involves the following steps:

1. Checking the user's privileges and quota parameters by referring to the *user authorization file* (UAF). The UAF is a system database containing all information about user accounts.

2. Performing the process initialization procedures with reference to the UAF. This results in the creation of the *process control block* (PCB), the *job information block* (JIB), and the *process quota block* (PQB).

3. Updating the scheduler database with the data structures describing the new process.

The sequence in which a new process context is created is depicted in Fig. 11.1. Execution of the new process is suppressed until the swapper process moves the new process into the authorized portion of the physical memory. This quota of physical memory is called the *balance set*. The initial scheduling state of the new process is called *computable out-swapped* (COMO). The following steps are performed in the context of the swapper process:

1. Moving a template for the new process context into the balance set from an executive image.

1. Terminal Driver communicates with the context of the requesting process. This occurs in the System Context.
2. In the requesting Process Context, $CREPRC System Service prepares the PCB, JIB and PQB. The input to $CREPRC is from the Batch Processing DCL command $SUBMIT, Job Controller, Application Image, $SPAWN or $RUN/DETACH DCL commands.
3. In the context of the Swapper Process, the PHD and address spaces are allocated and initialized.

Figure 11.1   Process creation in OpenVMS.

2. Building the process header (PHD) according to the values of SYS-GEN parameters for the current configuration.

3. Requesting that the new process be scheduled for execution.

The final step of process initialization takes place in the context of the new process in a system routine that results in updating the process's P1 space and the process header, and loading the image.

The environment of a process consists of virtual address space, hardware, and software contexts represented by the process control block (see Fig. 1.2). Within the context of a single OpenVMS system, each process is identified with a process identifier (PID). A process can delete itself or any other process in the system that it has the privilege to affect. For a process to be deleted, a number of cleanup actions are necessary:

- All resources allocated to the process must be returned to the system.
- Accounting information must be sent to the job controller.
- Any subprocesses of the process being deleted must be deleted.
- If the process being deleted is a subprocess, all quotas and limits taken from its parent (owner) process must be returned.
- If the owner requested notification of the process's deletion through a termination mailbox, the deletion message must be sent.

Process deletion occurs in three stages: first, in the context of the process requesting the deletion; second, in the context of the process being deleted; and finally, in the system context.

When a process owns subprocesses, the deletion of the owner process is delayed until all its subprocesses are deleted. The prior deletion of subprocesses ensures that any quotas taken from the owner process are returned. In early versions of OpenVMS, prior to the existence of the JIB and its jobwide pooled quotas, several quotas were charged against a process when it created a subprocess. At deletion of the subprocess, the subprocess returns those quotas. All the quotas treated in this way are now pooled except for the CPU time limit, which is the only quota returned at subprocess deletion.

11.2 PROCESS COMMUNICATIONS

In applications involving more than one process, the processes commonly share data or transfer information from one process to another. The executive provides various mechanisms that accomplish this information exchange. These mechanisms vary in the amount of information that can be transmitted, transparency of the transmission, and amount of synchronization provided by the operating system. Event flags, lock management system services, mailboxes, logical names, global sections, file sharing, and DECnet task-to-task communication are some of the means of establishing interprocess communication.

Commonly used system services for process control are shown in Fig. 11.2.

Function	Service Name	Scope of Processes Affected	Special Privileges Required (if any)
Hibernate Process	$HIBER	Issuing Process	None
Wake Process from Hibernation	$WAKE	Same VMScluster	GROUP or WORLD
Schedule Wakeup	$SCHDWK	Same VMScluster	GROUP or WORLD
Cancel Wakeup	$CANWAK	Same VMScluster	GROUP or WORLD
Suspend Process	$SUSPND	Same VMScluster	GROUP or WORLD
Resume Process	$RESUME	Same VMScluster	GROUP or WORLD
Exit	$EXIT	Issuing Process	None
Force Exit	$FORCEX	Same VMScluster	GROUP or WORLD
Create Process	$CREPRC	Same node	DETACH for different UICs
Delete Process	$DELPRC	Same VMScluster	GROUP or WORLD
Set AST Enable	$SETAST	Issuing Process	Access mode check
Set Power Recovery AST	$SETPRA	Issuing Process	Access mode check
Set Priority	$SETPRI	Same VMScluster	ALTPRI, GROUP or ALTPRI, WORLD
Set Process Name	$SETPRN	Issuing Process	None
Set Resource Wait Mode	$SETRWM	Issuing Process	None
Set System Service Fail Mode	$SETSFM	Issuing Process	Access mode check
Set Process Swap Mode	$SETSWM	Issuing Process	PSWAPM
Reschedule Process	$RESCHED	Issuing Process	None
Get Job/Process Information	$GETJPI	Same VMScluster	GROUP or WORLD
Process Scan	$PROCESS_SCAN	Same VMScluster	GROUP or WORLD

Figure 11.2 System services for controlling processes.

11.2.1   Lock management system services

The lock manager or the lock management system services enable a process to name a resource (for example, a printer that is being shared by many users in the cluster) and share it VMScluster-wide. A process can request locks on the named device in a variety of ways known as lock modes. By locking a device, the process can control the manner in which the process shares the device with other processes. In each lock request, the process can declare a blocking procedure that is invoked by the lock manager whenever the lock blocks another request for the device. The process can also specify the lock manager's behavior when access to a resource cannot be granted immediately, either that it wait until the resource is available, or return immediately with notification of the failure.

11.2.2   Mailboxes

Mailboxes are software-implemented I/O devices that can be read and written through Record Management Services (RMS) requests or the Queue I/O Request ($QIO) system service. Although process-specific or systemwide parameters may control the amount of data that can be written to a mailbox in one operation, there is no limit to the total amount of information that can be passed through a mailbox with a series of reads and writes.

Typically, one process reads messages written to a mailbox by one or more other processes. In the simple method of synchronizing mailbox I/O, the receiving process initiates its read of the mailbox and waits until the read completes. The read completes when another process writes to the mailbox. Since the receiving process cannot do anything else while waiting for data, this technique is restrictive.

In most applications, the receiving process performs other tasks in addition to servicing the mailbox. Putting such a process into a wait state for the mailbox prevents it from servicing any of its other tasks. In such an application, the receiving process could read the mailbox asynchronously with a notification, using the *asynchronous system trap* (AST) mechanism and OpenVMS (see Sec. 12.3). Alternatively, the receiving process could queue a read attention AST request to the mailbox driver. These techniques allow a process to continue its mainline processing and to handle mailbox requests from other processes only when there is data in the mailbox.

11.2.3   Logical names

The executive makes extensive use of logical names to provide device independence in the I/O subsystem. Logical names can be used for many other purposes also. For example, one process can pass information to another process by creating a logical name that is shared.

Chapter 5 provides more details on the usage of logical names.

11.2.4   Global sections

Global sections provide the fastest method for one process to pass relatively large amounts of information to another process on the same system. Because the processes map the data area into their address space, no movement of data takes place; the data is shared. The sharing, however, is not transparent. Each process must map to the global section, and the participating processes must agree upon a synchronization technique to coordinate the reading and writing of the global section and provide notification of new data. It can be implemented with event flags, lock management system services, or some similar mechanism.

A global section implemented on a multiprocessor system can be simultaneously accessed by multiple processes. Synchronization in such an environment requires use of MACRO-32 interlocked instructions, their high-level language equivalents, or a protocol based on event flags or locks. Note that a global section cannot be shared between processes on different VMScluster members.

11.2.5   Event flags

Common events flags can be treated as a way for several processes to share single bits of information. A common event flag is typically used, however, as a synchronization tool for other, more complicated, communication techniques. Common event flags can be shared by processes in the same user identification code (UIC) group executing on processors accessing common memory, that is, processors participating in a symmetric multiprocessing system (SMP). They cannot be shared by processes on different VMScluster nodes.

Many OpenVMS I/O operations and interprocess communications use event flags for synchronization. Event flags are status bits maintained by the OpenVMS operating system for general programming use. Each event flag can be either set or clear, and its status can be tested.

System services read, set, and clear event flags. A process can specify that an event flag be set at the completion of an operation such as an I/O request. When the process can proceed no further until the request is complete, the process can request a system service to wait for the event flag to be set.

An event flag can be used within a single process for synchronization with the completion of certain system services, such as I/O, lock, information, and timer requests (Fig. 11.3). Each of these services includes an argument identifying the event flag associated with the request.

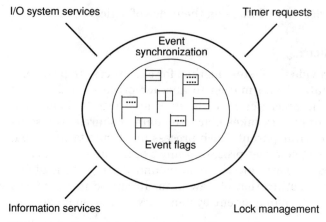

Figure 11.3 Synchronization using event flags.

When a process requests such a system service, that event flag is cleared. It is subsequently set when the request has been completed as a signal to the process that the operation is complete. Event flags can also be used as application-specific synchronization tools.

Event flags can be local to one process or shared among processes in the same UIC group. Shared event flags are called *common event flags.* Processes sharing common event flags must be running on a single OpenVMS cluster member, that is, common event flags are not visible clusterwide.

Each process has available to it 64 local (process-specific) event flags, in two clusters of 32 flags each, and can access 64 common event flags at once, in two clusters of 32 flags each. Before a process can refer to the flags in a particular common event flag cluster, it must explicitly associate with the cluster, specifying which numbers it will use to refer to the flags. For example, when a process requests the $QIO system service, specifying event flag 10 as one of the arguments, the process can subsequently wait for completion of that I/O request by waiting for event flag 10 to be set. After the process's wait is satisfied, the meaning of event flag 10 is undefined. Use of the Run-Time Library procedures LIB$GET_EF and LIB$FREE_EF can help prevent inadvertent concurrent use of the same flags.

The services for which an event flag argument can be specified include

$BRKTHRU[W]	Breakthrough [and Wait]
$ENQ[W]	Enqueue Lock Request [and Wait]
$GETDVI[W]	Get Device/Volume Information [and Wait]
$GETJPI[W]	Get Job/Process Information [and Wait]

$GETLKI[W]   Get Lock Information [and Wait]

$GETQUI[W]   Get Queue Information [and Wait]

$GETSYI[W]   Get Systemwide Information [and Wait]

$QIO[W]   Queue I/O Request [and Wait]

$SNDJBC[W]   Send to Job Controller [and Wait]

$SETIMR   Set Timer

$SYNCH   Synchronize

$UPDSEC[W]   Update Section File on Disk [and Wait]

The 64 local event flags are contained in each process's PHD. Local event flags 0 to 31 make up cluster 0; event flag numbers 24 through 31 are reserved for system use, i.e., they can be set or cleared at any time by OpenVMS executive software and should not be used by application software.

Event flags 32 to 63 make up cluster 1. OpenVMS VAX local event flags are in the PCB. Their relocation in OpenVMS AXP to the PHD makes it possible for the wait-for services to test them in an outer mode. Event flag 0 is the default event flag. Whenever a process requests a system service with an event flag number argument, but does not specify a particular flag, event flag 0 is used. Consequently, it is more likely than others to be used incorrectly for multiple concurrent requests.

A process creates a common event flag cluster dynamically, using the Associate Common Event Flag Cluster ($ASCEFC) system service. Each common event flag cluster is described by a nonpaged pool data structure called a common event block (CEB). The process specifies whether it will access the flags in that cluster using event flag numbers 64 through 95 (cluster 2) or 96 through 127 (cluster 3).

When a process waits for more than one flag, all the flags so used for process synchronization must be in the same cluster. A process waits for event flags by requesting $WAITFR (wait for single event flag), $WFLOR (wait for logical OR of event flags), or $WFLAND (wait for logical AND of event flags). It may also wait by requesting Record Management Services as a synchronous operation which results in requesting $WAITFR.

A process sets an event flag directly by using the Set Event Flag ($SETEF) system service. A process can use this service at AST level to communicate with its mainline code. It can also use this service to set common event flags to communicate with other processes.

The executive sets event flags in response to I/O completion, time expiration, the granting of a lock request, and completion of many system services.

11.3 INPUT/OUTPUT

The portion of a processor's physical address through which it accesses hardware interface registers is known as its *I/O space.*

A *hardware interface register,* or *interface register* for short, is the place where software interfaces with a hardware block. Every hardware block on an Alpha system, including CPU and memory, has a set of interface registers. The term *control/status register* (CSR) is sometimes used instead of the generic terminology "interface register."

A device driver typically interacts with an I/O device controller in the following manner to accomplish I/O:

1. The driver requests and initiates a device function.
2. The controller carries out the requested function.
3. The controller informs the driver of request completion.
4. The driver determines the status of the completed operation.

During an I/O operation, a controller can access data, command, and response buffers in memory without the intervention or assistance of the processor. Such an access is called *direct memory access* (DMA).

The major components of the OpenVMS I/O subsystem are device drivers and their data structures, ancillary control processes, I/O support routines, and I/O system services.

User programs initiate most VMS I/O operations. The OpenVMS executive initiates I/O operations for swapping, paging, file system, and other miscellaneous functions. All I/O operation requests are eventually handled by a system software component called a *device driver,* or simply a *driver.* The driver is primarily responsible for communicating system and user I/O requests to the I/O hardware and ensuring that they are carried out correctly within a reasonable time. Each type of device has a separate driver. User programs and most VMS components request an I/O operation through the $QIO system service. User programs can indirectly request the $QIO system service using RMS or a higher-level language interface such as a FORTRAN WRITE statement or the C language printf ().

The $QIO system service provides a device-independent user interface to drivers. If the device-independent parameters of a user's I/O request are valid, the service allocates and builds an I/O request packet (IRP). The IRP describes the I/O request and its context until the request completes successfully. The $QIO system service passes the IRP to the driver's I/O preprocessing routine for device- and function-specific validation. This I/O preprocessing routine may, for example, check the accessibility of the $QIO requestor's buffer in preparation for a DMA transfer. Steps to be followed for performing input/output, using system services, is shown in Fig. 11.4.

Step 1:	Allocate the device using $ALLOC system service, if appropriate.
Step 2:	Assign a channel to the device using $ASSIGN system service.
Step 3:	Use $QIO or $QIOW to specify the I/O function to perform.
Step 4:	Use $SYNCH or $WAITFR if a synchronous service is desired.
Step 5:	If more I/O is desired, go to step 3.
Step 6:	Deassign the channel using $DASSGN system service.
Step 7:	Relinquish the device using $DALLOC, if appropriate.

Figure 11.4 Input/output using system services.

The driver's I/O preprocessing routine, also known as a function decision table (FDT) routine, delivers the IRP to the driver's start I/O routine if all the following conditions are met:

- The I/O request is valid.
- No ancillary control process (ACP) assistance is required.
- The requested function cannot be completed by the I/O preprocessing routine.
- No further I/O preprocessing is required.

The start I/O routine interacts with the controller to perform the requested I/O operation. If the I/O preprocessing routine requires ACP assistance, it delivers the IRP to the ACP. An ACP assists a device driver with its complex functions. For example, the network ACP (NETACP) assists the network device driver (NETDRIVER) with creating links to other systems, performing routing, switching functions, and so on. The ACP can issue $QIO requests of its own to process a user's I/O request, or it can deliver the IRP to the driver's start I/O routine.

The I/O database describes individual I/O hardware components, such as devices, controllers, adapters, and widgets, as well as device drivers. The database also describes the configuration and interrelations among I/O hardware components, and it maintains the context of I/O operations.

VMS maintains the context of a user I/O request in the channel control block (CCB) and the IRP. Before an image can perform I/O operations to a device, it must assign an I/O channel to the device. It does this by requesting the $ASSIGN system service, which allocates a CCB to describe the channel. Unlike other I/O data structures, CCBs are located in the P1 space of each process. An I/O channel, described by the CCB, is the software mechanism that links a process to the target device of an I/O operation.

A device driver is a collection of routines and tables that assist OpenVMS in performing I/O operations on a device. An ACP is a separate thread of execution running in process context that implements complex driver functions. A complex function request, such as opening a disk file or establishing a network logical link, for example, is typically handled by an ACP.

An ACP image usually hibernates, waiting to be awakened by service I/O requests. An I/O request is passed to the ACP by queuing the IRP to the ACP queue block (AQB) and waking up the ACP if necessary. Some of the ACPs provided by OpenVMS are magnetic tape ACP (MTAACP), DECnet-VAX ACP (NETACP), and remote terminal ACP (REMACP). The term *volume* refers to a set of one or more devices that is treated as a single entry by an ACP; an ACP is responsible for maintaining the structure of data on a volume.

A volume control block (VCB) describes a volume. A device's unit control block (UCB) points to the VCB for the volume to which the device belongs. A VCB may be known by a different name within the ACP. For example, the DECnet ACP's VCB is known as a routing control block (RCB). Typically, a VCB contains information about the organizational structure of a device.

11.3.1   I/O system services

An image performs I/O operations on a device by requesting I/O system services. System components such as Record Management Services, ancillary control processes, and the Files-11 Extended QIO processor (XQP) also request I/O system services on behalf of a process. The basic I/O system services are:

Allocate Device ($ALLOC):	Reserves a particular device for exclusive use.
Deallocate Device ($DALLOC):	Relinquishes a device.
Assign I/O Channel ($ASSIGN):	Creates a logical link to a device.
Deassign I/O Channel ($DASSGN):	Deletes the logical link.
Queue I/O Request [and Wait] ($QIO[W]):	Requests an I/O operation on a particular device.
Cancel I/O on Channel ($CANCEL):	Cancels outstanding I/O requests on a particular logical link to a device.

An I/O device can be declared shareable or nonshareable by its driver. A disk, for example, is typically declared shareable so as to allow concurrent access to multiple users, whereas a line printer is always declared nonshareable because access to it must be serialized. A device is typically declared nonshareable if its I/O is inherently sequential; such a device is designed to service I/O requests from one user at a time. OpenVMS allows multiple processes to access a shareable device concurrently.

Before a process can issue an I/O request to a nonshareable device, it must allocate the device for its exclusive use. A process can also allocate a device that is declared shareable, thus temporarily acquiring exclusive access to it. Only the subprocesses, and any other process with SHARE privileges, can use such an allocated device by a process.

The software mechanism that links a process to a device is called a *channel*. To perform I/O on a device, an image first creates a channel to it by requesting the $ASSIGN system service. The image then identifies the device to the $QIO system service through its channel number. When the image is done with the device, it requests the $DASSGN system service to break the link between the process and the device.

The $QIO system service performs device-independent preprocessing and, via FDT routines, the device-dependent preprocessing. It then queues an I/O request to the driver for the device associated with a channel. Any additional work to be done is performed by the device driver's start I/O routine.

The $QIOW system service is the synchronous form of the $QIO system service. It takes the same arguments as the $QIO system service.

The I/O postprocessing routine is an interrupt service routine. It implements the device-independent steps necessary to complete an I/O request. Some I/O postprocessing operations, for example, unlocking buffer pages and deallocating buffers, are performed by the postprocessing interrupt service routine. Other operations, such as writing the I/O status block (IOSB), are performed by a special kernel-mode AST routine.

11.3.2 I/O processing

Once a user's I/O request is preprocessed and validated by the $QIO system service and a device driver's FDT action routine, the VMS executive invokes the driver's start I/O routine to perform the requested function.

The core of a driver is its start I/O routine. The start I/O routine services I/O requests by interfacing with the device controller. Allocating controller and device-specific resources, initializing device activity, waiting for device activity completion, deallocating controller and device-specific resources, and initializing I/O request completion processing are some of the main steps that a start I/O routine performs.

For every I/O that OpenVMS initiates, it creates a fork process (not to be confused with OpenVMS processes) thread of execution in which driver code executes. A fork process's context is maintained in the fork block, which is usually part of a larger data structure such as the UCB or the IRP. A driver fork process that requires more context can execute as a kernel process. A kernel process has a private stack on which it can maintain context across stalls and restarts.

A VAX MACRO driver being ported from OpenVMS VAX to OpenVMS AXP can be converted to use the kernel process mechanism through macros provided by OpenVMS AXP.

11.4 MAILBOXES

An OpenVMS mailbox is a virtual I/O device for interprocess communication. One process writes a message to a mailbox for another process to read. A process reads or writes mailbox messages using standard I/O mechanisms. The Alpha AXP hardware mailbox should not be confused with the type of mailbox mentioned here.

OpenVMS mailboxes are virtual I/O devices implemented in software. Mailbox data structures are created dynamically in response to a process's Create Mailbox and Assign Channel system service request. Mailbox messages are read and written through the standard I/O mechanisms. The mailbox driver, MBDRIVER, services $QIO system service requests to mailbox devices. The driver stores messages written to a mailbox device in pool space of the physical memory until they are read.

Two or more processes running on the same system can share a mailbox. The executive allows the I/O driver processes to write to mailboxes, although it does not allow them to read from mailboxes. Processes sharing a mailbox generally identify it by a predetermined logical name, which translates to the mailbox device name. Processes running on different VMScluster system members cannot share a mailbox.

Typically, a mailbox is used as a one-way communication path between two or more processes; one process reads messages written to the mailbox by one or more other processes. By default the mailbox driver associates each write request with a single read request. Mailbox messages are read in the order in which they are written. A message written to a mailbox cannot be broadcast to other processes; it is read by only one process. There are no restrictions on the order in which read and write requests can be issued, although the order influences the order of request completion.

A mailbox is created with a specified maximum byte count to buffer messages written to it that have not been read. Thus, a process can write a message to a mailbox whether or not there is a pending read request. If there is a pending read request, the message is read immediately; otherwise, the message is buffered. By default a write request does not complete until another process reads the entire message, although a process can specify that its write request complete immediately.

When a process issues a read request to a mailbox, a buffered message may or may not be present. By default, a read request does not complete until another process writes a message to the mailbox, although a process can specify that its read request be completed immediately.

The executive provides two forms of mailbox I/O: the traditional record I/O and a new form called *stream I/O*. With record I/O, the mailbox driver matches a read request with at most one write request, even if the size of the read data buffer and the amount of data provided by the buffered write message are not the same. With stream I/O, a process can specify exactly how much data is to be read. The driver matches as many writes as necessary.

The mailbox driver can handle any sequence of stream and record I/O operations to a mailbox predictably; an application performing the I/O operations must ensure that the sequence is meaningful.

There are two kinds of mailboxes, temporary and permanent. A temporary mailbox is deleted automatically when no more processes have channels assigned to it. A permanent mailbox must be explicitly marked for deletion using the Delete Mailbox ($DELMBX) system service. Once marked for deletion, a permanent mailbox is deleted when no more processes have channels assigned to it.

11.5   TIMER SUPPORT

To support time-related activities, the Alpha architecture requires that each Alpha system provide a battery-backed watch, an interval timer interrupt that repeats at a system-specific interval, and a process cycle counter. Console software and the privileged architecture library code (PALcode) cooperate to provide a system cycle counter based on the process cycle counter.

Using these hardware features, the Alpha VMS operating system keeps time and services time-dependent requests from processes and system threads of execution. OpenVMS uses the battery-backed watch to initialize and maintain the system time across system bootstraps, power failures, and shutdowns. It uses interval timer interrupts to maintain the current date and time (the system time) as well as the time elapsed since the system was bootstrapped (the system uptime). VMS uses the system cycle counter for timing very short intervals, typically with a granularity of a few tens of nanoseconds or less.

In addition to maintaining the system time, the interval timer interrupt service routine is also responsible for checking whether the current process has reached quantum end and whether time-dependent requests must be serviced.

The system manager can adjust the system date and time using the SET TIME DCL command or the Set Time ($SETIME) system service. The Get Time ($GETTIM) system service enables users to read the current date and time. Several other services convert the date and time between ASCII and binary formats. Application software can also call a number of Run-Time Library procedures, described in DEC manuals or the OpenVMS Run-Time Library Routines Volume, to convert or format the date and time.

OpenVMS provides two system services, Schedule Wakeup ($SCHD-WK) and Set Timer ($SETIMR), to support users' time-dependent requests.

11.5.1   Timer support in OpenVMS AXP

Interval timer. All OpenVMS AXP systems provide an interval timer that generates an IPL 22 interrupt at the minimum rate of 1000 times per second, with a minimum accuracy of 0.0005%. An interval timer interrupt is sometimes called a *tick*. The interrupt rate is implementation-dependent and passed to VMS by console software through the hardware restart parameter block (HWRPB).

All currently available Alpha systems generate interval timer interrupts at the rate of 1024 per second.

Battery-backed watch. A battery-backed watch maintains the date and time across system reboots and power failures. At system initialization the operating system reads the battery-backed watch to determine the date and time.

11.5.2   Timekeeping in OpenVMS

During system initialization VMS determines the date and time from the battery-backed watch, from a value previously recorded on the system disk, or from a value entered by the operator. OpenVMS maintains the system time in a global location in increments of 100 nanoseconds from a known base time. The interval timer interrupt service routine updates this and other global locations that represent time.

OpenVMS maintains the system uptime in two different formats. One contains the number of seconds elapsed since system bootstrap, and the other contains the number of soft ticks elapsed during the same period. The term *soft tick* refers to a 10-millisecond event that simulates a VAX-style interval timer interrupt.

To facilitate the porting of VAX/VMS, the OpenVMS AXP interval timer interrupt service routine simulates a VAX-style 10-millisecond clock. As a result, a number of time-related VAX/VMS modules and interfaces are largely unchanged despite significant changes in the underlying hardware mechanisms. For example, parts of the interval timer interrupt service routine and time-related scheduling functions, such as quantum-end processing, work much the same in OpenVMS AXP as they do in OpenVMS VAX.

The 10-millisecond event is called a soft tick to differentiate it from the interval timer interrupt. Depending on the interval timer interrupt frequency, soft ticks may not occur precisely at 10-millisecond intervals. Therefore, the interval service timer interrupt service routine uses an algorithm that ensures that over a large number of interrupts, the average interval between soft ticks is 10 milliseconds. This imprecision does not affect the accuracy of any other clocks, such as system time, that depend on hardware mechanisms.

Any VAX/VMS software being ported to OpenVMS AXP that relies on an exact 10-millisecond duration for the 10-millisecond clock must be changed.

Application software can use two system services, $SCHDWK and $SETIMR, to request time-dependent services. Two complementary services, Cancel Wakeup ($CANWAK) and Cancel Timer Request ($CANTIM), cancel time-dependent requests.

Prior to OpenVMS VAX Version 5.5, the IPL 7 software timer interrupt service routine serviced the timer queue. In later versions of OpenVMS VAX and in OpenVMS AXP Version 1.0, the timer queue is serviced by an IPL 8 process running the software timer routine.

11.6 SUMMARY

A detailed understanding of the process creation and I/O system services like QIO is essential to perform system programming for such time- and space-critical applications like real-time systems and data acquisition systems. An understanding of the data structures for a process will help in efficiently designing system-level applications.

12

Executive

The term *executive* refers to those parts of the operating system that are loaded into the system space and execute from there. The executive includes the system base image, SYS$BASE_IMAGE.EXE (formerly known as SYS.EXE). In addition to the system base image, other components of the OpenVMS system include executive images, device drivers, command language interpreters, and utility programs.

12.1 SYSTEM SERVICES

Many of the operations that the VMS operating system performs on behalf of a user are implemented as procedures called *system services.* A user application requests system services directly, and components such as the file system request system services on behalf of the user.

Most system service procedures are contained in executive images and reside in system space; others are contained in privileged shareable images. System services typically execute in kernel or executive access mode so that they read and write data structures protected from access by outer modes.

A system service is a procedure in the VMS executive that performs a function for a process, usually at the process's request. An image running in the process requests a particular service by calling the associated procedure.

A major distinction between system service procedures and other procedures is that system services are generally provided by the executive. In early versions of VAX/VMS, system services were provided by system service procedures in SYS$BASE_IMAGE.EXE, the system image; Record Management Services (RMS) were provided by procedures in RMS.EXE. Since then, the system service mechanism has been extended to user-written services in privileged shareable images, and the system image has been reorganized into executive images, eliminating most distinctions between the system services and RMS services. Most system service procedures execute in kernel or executive mode.

12.2 PROCESS CONTROL

The executive provides a number of services that allow one process to control the execution of another. It also provides a variety of mechanisms by which processes can obtain information about each other and communicate with one another. Process control system services enable a process to affect its own scheduling state or that of another process, either on the local system or on a remote VMScluster node. These services also enable a process to alter some of its own characteristics such as name of the process, its priority, etc. The process information system services allow a process to obtain detailed information about other processes, both on the local system and on other VMScluster nodes.

The Set Process Name ($SETPRN) system service allows a process to change or eliminate its own process name. The new name cannot contain more than 15 characters. Note that this service allows more flexibility in establishing a process name than is available from the usual channels, such as the DCL command SET PROCESS/NAME.

When a process requests an inner-mode system service, it executes a system service transfer routine that serves as a bridge between the requestor's mode and the inner mode in which the service procedure executes. The external name of a system service transfer routine generally has the form SYS$service. A transfer routine executes in the mode of the caller. That procedure is typically part of an executive image and executes in an inner access mode. The name of a procedure that performs the actual work of the system service is usually of the form EXE$service or RMS$service.

Every OpenVMS procedure is described by a data structure called a *procedure descriptor* that contains the address of the procedure's entry point and information about its type and characteristics. A compiler generates a procedure descriptor for each procedure in a module and places them together in a program section called a *linkage section*. When an image that requests a system service is linked, the linker must resolve the system service transfer routine name. By default, it searches the file base image to resolve any unresolved symbols after it searches STARLET.OLB library.

The privileged architecture library codes (PALcodes) that are specially included in the Alpha architecture contain several advanced functions. OpenVMS uses two PALcodes, CALL_PAL CHME (change mode to executive) and CALL_PAL CHMK (change mode to kernel), instructions used exclusively to request system services. Their exception service routines are known as the change mode dispatchers.

CHMS (change mode to supervisor) and CHMU (change mode to user) exceptions are treated much like other exceptions that OpenVMS passes to a user-declared condition handler.

· Normally, system services perform their requested function and then return immediately to the process that requested the service. Others, called asynchronous system services, initiate some system activity on behalf of the requesting process and return before the activity is complete. To synchronize with completion of the initiated activity, the requestor can wait for an event flag associated with the system service request. A synchronous service initiates the activity, just as its asynchronous counterpart does, but waits for completion of the activity before returning to its requestor.

A trailing "W" in the name of the synchronous service distinguishes it from the corresponding asynchronous service: $QIO and $QIOW, for example. Many RMS services also have both synchronous and asynchronous forms. The two forms, however, are not distinct services with different names. Instead, an image requests either asynchronous or synchronous return from a particular RMS service through a bit in the file or record stream data structure associated with the request.

In OpenVMS AXP, a synchronous service is implemented as a mode of caller service that requests the asynchronous service, tests the return status to ensure that the service was initiated, and then waits for the activity initiated by the service to complete. An OpenVMS VAX synchronous system service in turn requests two or more other system services: the asynchronous form of originally requested service and, minimally, a wait service.

To guarantee completion of a synchronous system service request, the service requestor must specify both an event flag and a status block (I/O status block or lock status block). The asynchronous service-specific procedure clears the event flag and status block associated with the request. The synchronization routine tests the combination of event flag and status block for request completion, placing the process into event flag wait if the request is not complete.

12.3 ASYNCHRONOUS SYSTEM TRAPS (ASTs)

An asynchronous system trap (AST) is a mechanism that enables an asynchronous event to trigger a change in the control flow within a process. Specifically, as soon as possible after the asynchronous event occurs, a procedure or routine designated by either the process or the system executes in the context of the process.

A process can request an AST as notification that an asynchronous system service has completed. ASTs requested by the system result from operations such as I/O postprocessing, process suspension, and process deletion. These operations require that OpenVMS executive code executes in the context of a specific process. ASTs fulfill this need.

OpenVMS VAX support for enabling and disabling ASTs is implemented entirely in software. A process sets or clears AST by requesting the Set AST Enable ($SETAST) system service. Before dispatching to an AST procedure, the AST delivery interrupt service routine must check that delivery to that mode is currently enabled and, if it is not, dismiss the interrupt.

For OpenVMS VAX compatibility, OpenVMS AXP supports the $SETAST system service.

ASTs can be created in many ways. One such way is a process request for AST notification of the completion of an asynchronous system service, such as Queue I/O Request ($QIO) or Enqueue Lock Request ($ENQ). The arguments for these system services include an AST procedure value and an argument to be passed to the AST procedure. The system's ability to initiate the execution of code in a particular process context is crucial to OpenVMS operations. Only the AST mechanism provides this capability. The executive employs this mechanism primarily to access the process's virtual address space.

An AST procedure is called with the following arguments:

- AST parameter
- Contents of register R0 at the time of the interrupt
- Contents of register R1 at the time of the interrupt
- The PC of the interrupted thread of execution
- The PS of that thread

In OpenVMS AXP, the only argument directly intended for the AST procedure is the AST parameter, which was originally an argument to a system service such as $QIO, $ENQ, or $DCLAST (AST of the DCL). Although the other arguments are present for compatibility with OpenVMS VAX, they have no subsequent use after the AST procedure exits; modifying them in an OpenVMS AXP environment therefore has no effect on the thread of execution to be resumed at AST exit.

Special kernel mode ASTs differ from normal ASTs in several ways. They are dispatched at IPL 2 and execute at that level or higher. Special kernel mode ASTs result from the operations of kernel mode code. That is, a user cannot directly request special kernel mode AST notification of an asynchronous event.

Several executive features are implemented through normal ASTs. For example, the automatic working set limit adjustment to a process that takes place at the end of a CPU timeslice (called quantum) is implemented with a normal kernel mode AST. CPU time limit expiration is implemented with potentially multiple ASTs. Beginning in the user mode, the AST procedure requests the Exit ($EXIT) system service. If the process is not deleted, a supervisor mode time expiration AST is queued. This loop continues with higher access modes until the process is deleted. The executive also uses the AST mechanism for the $FORCEX, Suspend Process ($SUSPND), and Delete Process ($DELPRC) system services. Each system service procedure queues an AST to the target process. The $SUSPND system service queues either a supervisor or kernel mode AST to its target process, depending on the access mode of the suspension. A process suspended through a supervisor mode AST can execute kernel and executive mode ASTs.

Several OpenVMS device drivers queue an AST to notify a process that a particular attention condition has occurred on a device. The terminal driver, for example, queues an attention AST to notify an interested process that <control/c> or <control/y> has been typed on its terminal. The terminal driver can also queue an out-of-band AST as notification that a control character other than <control/c> and <control/y> has been typed. The mailbox driver can queue an attention AST as notification that an unsolicited message has been put in a mailbox or that an attempt to read an empty mailbox is in progress. To establish an attention AST for a particular device whose driver supports this feature, the user requests the $QIO system service with the I/O function. IO$_SETMODE or, for some devices, IO$_SETCHAR. The kind of attention AST requested is indicated by a function modifier. The out-of-band ASTs are similar to attention ASTs in that the terminal driver forks to queue an ACB to the process. The main difference between the attention AST mechanism and the out-of-band AST mechanism is that, once declared, out-of-band ASTs are delivered to the process for its lifetime or until the $CANCEL system service is requested to flush the AST list.

12.4 SYNCHRONIZATION TECHNIQUES

OpenVMS AXP uses a combination of the following Alpha mechanisms and software techniques to synchronize the actions of code threads that might otherwise interfere with each other:

- Atomic memory accesses to aligned longwords and quadwords
- Load-locked (LDx_L) and store-conditional (STx_C) instructions
- Interrupt priority level (IPL)
- Memory barriers to enforce order on reads and writes of data accessed by multiple processors (CPU and I/O processors)
- Queue support provided by privileged architecture library (PAL) routines (see Chaps. 16, 17, and 18)

- Spinlocks to synchronize access to executive data
- Mutual exclusion semaphores (mutexes)
- Lock management system services
- Event flags
- Parallel processing Run-Time Library routines

Atomicity and *mutual exclusion* are frequently described as different types of serialization, i.e., the coordination of events in such a way that only one event happens at a time. Atomicity refers to the indivisibility of a small number of actions, such as those occurring during the execution of a single instruction or a small number of instructions. Mutual exclusion refers to serializing the execution of groups of instructions so that one group completes before another starts.

12.5 MEMORY BARRIERS

Memory barriers can be inserted into code wherever necessary to impose an order on memory references. On a single processor system an instruction's read of a memory location always returns the data from the most recent write access to the same location, provided the memory is not overwritten by DMA I/O. However, reads and writes issued by a processor can complete out of order from the viewpoint of an I/O processor. Memory barriers are required for ordering reads from and writes to data shared with an I/O processor. If an Alpha system supports multiprocessing, memory barriers would also be required for ensuring the order in which other members of a symmetric multiprocessing system see writes to shared data and the order in which reads of shared data complete.

12.6 SPINLOCK

Essentially, spinlock is a flag that is set to indicate that a processor is accessing data. The flag is tested and set, or tested and cleared, atomically with respect to any other threads of execution on the same or other processors. A spinlock enables a set of processors to serialize their access to shared data. A processor that needs access to some shared data tests sets the spinlock associated with that data using an interlocked bit test and set instruction. If the bit is clear, the processor is allowed to access the data. This is known as *locking* or *acquiring the spinlock*. If the bit was already set, the processor must wait, because another processor is accessing the data. A waiting processor essentially spins in a right loop, executing repeated bit test instructions to test the state of the spinlock. This is known as a busy wait. It is from this spinning that the term spinlock derives. The busy wait ends when the processor accessing the data clears the flag with an interlocked operation to indicate that it is done. Clearing the flag is known as *unlocking* or *releasing the spinlock.*

12.7 MUTUAL EXCLUSION SEMAPHORES (MUTEXES)

The synchronization techniques described so far all execute at elevated IPL, thus blocking certain operations, such as a rescheduling request. However, in some situations requiring synchronization, elevated IPL is an unacceptable technique. One reason elevated IPL might be unacceptable is that the processor would have to remain at an elevated IPL for an indeterminately long time because of the structure of the data. For example, associating to a common event block cluster requires a search of the list of common event blocks (CEBs) for the specified CEB. This might be a lengthy operation on a system with many CEBs. Also, elevated IPL is unacceptable for synchronizing access to pageable data.

OpenVMS bugchecks if a page fault occurs at an IPL above 2. Thus, a pageable data structure cannot be protected by elevating IPL.

One synchronization mechanism that does not require elevated IPL is a *mutual exclusion semaphore,* or *mutex.* OpenVMS uses mutexes for synchronizing kernel mode accesses to certain shared data structures. Basically, a mutex is a counter that controls read or write access to a given data structure or database. OpenVMS allows either multiple readers or one writer of a data structure or database to synchronize through mutex acquisition. Typically, the threads of execution whose accesses are synchronized through a mutex are process context threads. A mutex is a data structure consisting of a single longword. The information contained in the mutex is the number of processes accessing the data, that is, the number of processes that have locked the mutex. It is called the *owner count value.*

12.8 MODULARITIES IN THE EXECUTIVE ORGANIZATION

The OpenVMS executive consists of two base images and a number of separately loadable executive images. Some of these images are loaded on all systems, while others support features unique to particular system configurations. The executive base images connect requests for system services and other system functions with the routines that provide them. These routines are located in separate loadable executive images.

```
Embedded System Routines
Library Procedures
Read-only Data for the Library Procedures
System Data
Procedure Descriptors for Executive Routines
SYSGEN Parameters
Symbol Vector
Linkage Section for the Library Procedures
```

Figure 12.1 Layers of OpenVMS executive.

The layout of the OpenVMS executive image consists of embedded system services, library procedures, read-only data for the library, etc. See Fig. 12.1 for a summary of the executive layout.

The concept underlying the OpenVMS VAX executive is similar to that of a VAX/VMS shareable image, which contains transfer vectors and routines. The VAX VMS system image has been split into a base image named SYS.EXE and a number of other images called executive images. Unlike transfer vectors for a standard shareable image, which are in the same image as the routines, all transfer vectors of executive images are collected in the base image.

Like the VAX/VMS executive, the OpenVMS AXP executive is modular and it is also based on the concept of shareable images. An OpenVMS AXP shareable image contains a global symbol table and a symbol vector. The global symbol lists the name of each universal symbol in the image along with the offset of its corresponding entry in the symbol vector. Although part of the image file, the global symbol table is not loaded into memory. The linker uses it to resolve symbolic references when another image links to the shareable image.

The modular organization of the executive makes it possible to have alternative versions of an executive image and to select the one to be loaded at system initialization. For example, there are three versions of the system synchronization image; during system initialization, the version appropriate to the configuration is selected and loaded.

Executive images are loaded much like user images. During system operation, a user image is mapped into its address space by the Image Activate ($IMGACT) system service, commonly known as the *image activator.*

Modular executive has a base image. It is the pathway to routines and data in other executive images. All images that refer to executive universal symbols link with the base image. For example, each executive image is linked with the base image to resolve references to routines and data in other executive images and in the base image. OpenVMS AXP and OpenVMS VAX differ in this regard; an OpenVMS VAX image links with a system symbol table to resolve base image references.

The offsets of entries in the base image's symbol vector are guaranteed to remain the same in subsequent versions of OpenVMS. It is thus possible that an image linked with SYS.EXE can continue to execute on a later version than the one with which it linked. Whenever algorithmic or data structure changes in an executive subsystem might prevent correct execution of an image that referenced the earlier version, the version category associated with that subsystem is updated. An image linked with an earlier version of that subsystem cannot then be activated on a system running the updated version.

The executive base image is nonpageable with two sections, one for read-only and the other a writable image section. The image sections contain several small system routines, library procedures, commonly accessed writable data and pointers to data structures in executive images, procedure descriptors for universally available routines in executive images, SYSGEN parameters, and a symbol vector with entries for the data, parameter, routine, and procedure names to be universally available through the base image.

The base image includes a number of procedures that implement low-level operations like division, character string operations, and field operations. Most calls to these procedures are compiler-generated. Although a typical image's reference to these procedures would be resolved through the Run-Time Library shareable image, an executive image cannot be linked this way. One alternative is for each executive image to link with an object library containing the procedures the image needs. A simpler and more efficient alternative is to build the executive with only a single copy of each procedure. Several areas in the base image are related to these procedures: one each for their code, read-only data, and linkage section.

The SYSGEN parameters area is defined in module SYSPARAM. This area contains all the SYSGEN parameters. For coordination with SYSBOOT, which copies the current parameters to this area during system boot, all SYSGEN parameters are virtually contiguous. SYSGEN parameters are part of the base image, rather than of a particular executive image, so that they can be referenced directly. No one executive image references them most often; they are widely referenced from many executive images and from other images linked with the base image.

The executive base image contains a symbol vector whose entries represent all the universally available names for system services provided by executive images. An image requests a particular system service by calling SYS$service_name, the universally available system service name. The linker resolves system service names using global definitions in the base image, which it searches by default. OpenVMS guarantees that the offsets of entries in the base image's symbol vector will remain the same in subsequent versions of OpenVMS. This ensures that an image can execute on a later version.

A system service transfer routine is a minimal procedure that executes in the mode of the caller and that serves as a bridge to the actual procedure implementing the service request. The actual procedures are within executive images and typically execute in an inner access mode. When an executive image is loaded, each system service in it that executes in an inner access mode is assigned a unique change mode number. Its system service transfer routine is overwritten to contain an instruction that loads this change mode number into R0 and executes a CALL_PAL CHMx instruction. When an image requesting a system service calls its transfer routine, the transfer routine executes these instructions, resulting in an exception. The change mode exception service routine uses the change mode number to index a table that contains the addresses of the actual system service procedure descriptor and its code entry point. It then calls the actual procedure. When an executive image is loaded that contains a mode of caller system service, the contents of the base symbol vector entry for that universal system service name are updated to point to the executive image. As part of executive image initialization, the procedure descriptor in base vectors is bound to the procedure in the executive image.

12.9 SUMMARY

The two base images contain relatively little executable code. Their executive image procedure descriptors generally cause dispatch to routines in loaded executive images. An executive image is implemented as a form of shareable image. Like any shareable image, it has a global symbol table, image section descriptors, and an image activator fixup section. Unlike other types of shareable image, an executive image does not contain a symbol vector. Instead, its universally available procedures and data cells are reached through entries in the loaded base image symbol vectors. The internal structure of an executive image is more constrained than that of a typical shareable image. An executive image can be mapped into system space either in contiguous virtual pages with the virtual layout created by the linker or with some of its sections in granularity hint regions and thus in discontiguous virtual addresses. By default most executive images are mapped with sections in granularity hint regions. This option provides better performance.

Chapter

13

Memory Management

13.1 INTRODUCTION

The *American Heritage Dictionary* defines *virtual* to mean something that exists in effect, though not in fact! Several trillion bytes of data addressability provided by the 64-bit architecture of Alpha is contrasted by the physical impossibility of installing such a large memory. Current memory technology can support a few hundred megabytes for the physical memory. As a result, for Alpha AXP–based systems the physical memory space is always smaller than the virtual memory.

Support for virtual memory enables a process to execute an image that only partly resides in physical memory at any given time. Only the portion of virtual address space actually in use occupies physical memory. This enables the execution of images larger than the available physical memory. It also makes it possible for parts of different processes' images and address spaces to be resident simultaneously. Address references in an image built for a virtual memory system are independent of the physical memory in which the image actually executes.

Virtual memory is implemented in such a way that each process has its own address space. The OpenVMS executive is mapped into the same address range in each process's address space and is shared among all processes. That address range is called *system space*. Only the process itself can access the nonshared part of its address space, which is called *process-private space,* or simply *process space.* Each process is thereby protected against references from other processes.

Physical memory consists of storage locations, each with its own address. Physical address space is the set of all physical addresses that identify unique memory storage locations and I/O space locations. A physical address space can be transmitted by the processor over the processor-memory interconnect, typically to a memory controller.

63	43 42	33 32	23 22	13 12	0
Sign extension bits	Level 1	Level 2	Level 3	Byte within page	

Figure 13.1 Alpha's virtual address components.

During normal operations, an instruction accesses memory using the virtual address of a byte. A virtual address (see Fig. 13.1) is an unsigned integer. The processor translates the virtual address to a physical address using information provided by the operating system. The set of all possible virtual addresses is called virtual memory, or virtual address space. In the Alpha architecture, a virtual address is represented as a 64-bit unsigned integer.

Virtual address space and physical memory are divided into units called pages. Each page is a group of contiguous bytes. The virtual page is the unit of address translation and the unit of memory protection. Each virtual page has protection bits specifying which access modes can read and write it.

For address translations from virtual address space to the physical address space, the memory management first uses a CPU component called the translation buffer and, if that fails, a set of software data structures is used. The data structures, known as page tables, provide a complete association of virtual to physical pages. A page table consists of page table entries (PTEs), each of which associates one page of virtual address space with its physical location, either in memory or on a mass storage medium. A translation buffer (TB) is a small cache of recently used PTEs. A TB can be accessed and searched faster than a page table.

The set of a process's valid virtual page is called its working set. OpenVMS limits the number of pages of physical memory a process can use at the same time by setting a maximum size for its working set. When this limit has been reached the process incurs a page fault.

The mass storage location from which a virtual page is read is called its backing store. If the virtual page is guaranteed not to change, if it contains code or read-only data, the page fault handler need not write the page to mass storage when it is faulted out to save I/O and can read it from the image file as often as required.

13.2 MEMORY MANAGEMENT IN ALPHA AXP AND OPENVMS AXP

OpenVMS AXP Version 1.0 has a page size of 8 KB (8192 bytes). In fact, the Alpha architecture is capable of supporting a page size of 8 KB, 16 KB, 32 KB, or 64 KB. In contrast, all VAX processors have the same page size, 512 bytes. This chapter describes virtual addresses and address translation in terms of a page size of 8 KB. To distinguish the two architectures' pages, the term pagelet identifies a VAX page, or a 512-byte unit of memory.

13.2.1 Alpha virtual addresses

The Alpha architecture supports a sparse virtual address space. Whether a particular virtual page is defined is independent of the state of its neighboring pages. Unlike the VAX architecture, the Alpha architecture has no page table length registers and does not require multiple physically contiguous page tables. Moreover, holes in the virtual address space need not be represented by page tables. The architecture requires only that the level 1 page table (L1PT) be resident; it permits L2PTs and L3PTs to be pageable. See Fig. 13.2 for Alpha AXP page table structures.

13.2.2 Translation buffer (TB)

A translation buffer is a CPU component that caches the result of recent successful virtual address translations of valid pages. Each TB entry caches one translation, a virtual page number, and, minimally, its corresponding page frame number (PFN), address space match, and protection bits.

Like a physical memory cache, a TB is a relatively small amount of relatively fast memory that the CPU can access more quickly than physical memory. Because there are considerably fewer TB entries

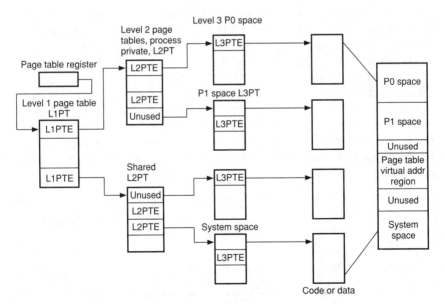

Figure 13.2 OpenVMS AXP page table structure.

than virtual pages, a one-to-one mapping between virtual pages and TB entries is impossible. The size and organization of a TB are CPU-specific. Some CPUs have both an instruction stream TB (ITB) and a data stream TB (DTB). The ITB caches translations performed as the result of instruction fetches. The DTB caches translations performed as the result of loading or storing memory operands. The information in each type of TB entry can be different.

13.2.3   Granularity hint regions

An Alpha TB optionally supports a feature called *granularity hint,* by means of which one TB entry can represent a group of physically and virtually contiguous pages with identical characteristics like protection, validity, and fault-on bits. Use of granularity hints improves the CPU performance by keeping anticipated portions of code and data in cache.

One region is always created for nonpaged dynamically allocated system data. The SYSGEN parameter ITB_ENTRIES and the flags in the SYSGEN parameter LOAD_SYS_IMAGES control whether other regions are created and what use is made of them.

The SYSGEN parameter ITB_ENTRIES specifies the maximum number of ITB entries to map granularity regions containing code. Its default value is 1, as a result of which a 512-byte page is created.

13.2.4   Virtual address space
in OpenVMS VAX

OpenVMS AXP virtual address space is largely based upon OpenVMS VAX virtual address space, which is defined by the VAX architecture. The VAX architecture defines a 32-bit virtual address space.

The virtual address in Alpha can use up to 64 bits. But, initial versions of AXP systems make use of a smaller number of bits for this purpose. Figure 13.3 shows the page size and virtual address for different systems.

The low half of the AXP virtual address space is called process-private space (see Fig. 1.3). This space is further divided into two equal pieces called P0 space and P1 space. The P0 space expands toward increasing addresses. The P1 space range expands toward decreasing addresses.

Page Size	Max. Bytes	Virtual Addr. Bits	Physical Addr. Bits
8 Kbytes	8 Trillion bytes	43	45
16 Kbytes	128 Trillion bytes	47	46
32 Kbytes	2,048 Trillion bytes	51	47
64 Kbytes	32,768 Trillion bytes	55	48

Figure 13.3 Page size and virtual addresses on Alpha.

The upper half of the VAX virtual address space is called system space. The lower half of system space is called S0 space. S0 space begins expanding toward increasing addresses. Although the original VAX architecture specified that the upper half of system space was undefined and reserved to digital, the architecture has since been modified to permit S0 space to expand. The expanded address range results in 2 GB of system space.

The VAX architecture associates a page table with each region of virtual address space. The processor translates system space addresses using the system page table. Each process has its own P0 and P1 page tables. A VAX page table does not map the full virtual address space possible; instead, it maps only the part of its region that has been created.

A key goal of OpenVMS AXP memory management is to maximize compatibility with OpenVMS VAX. For normal use, therefore, OpenVMS AXP Version 1.0 supports only the three VAX virtual address space ranges and the page table virtual address region.

The P0 and P1 virtual address space ranges are identical to their VAX counterparts. Thus, the Alpha 64-bit addresses are sign-extended versions of the VAX 32-bit ones. Alpha AXP instruction requires its address operands to be in registers.

OpenVMS allocates some pages of physical memory permanently—for example, the pages that contain the system page table or the system base images. Normally, OpenVMS allocates a physical page of memory for a particular need, such as a virtual page in a process's address space, and deallocates the page when it is no longer needed.

Virtual address space is created and recreated at different times during system operation. System space is formed once and mapped in each process's address space. Process-private address space is created for each process and mapped only when that process is current.

The VAX architecture limits P0 and P1 space to 1 GB each. In supporting VAX-like address regions, OpenVMS AXP enforces this limit. Their combined sizes may be further constrained by the SYSGEN parameter VIRTUALPAGECNT, the page file quota available to the process, and some additional factors.

13.3 MANAGEMENT OF PHYSICAL MEMORY

Historically, OpenVMS VAX has had two fundamental mechanisms to control its allocation of physical memory to processes: paging and swapping. Several auxiliary mechanisms, such as automatic working set limit adjustment and swapper trimming, supplement these basic mechanisms. Originally, the major goal of the early releases of OpenVMS VAX operating systems was to provide an environment for a variety of applications, including real-time, batch, and time-sharing, on a family of VAX processors with a wide range of performance and capacity. The memory management subsystem was designed to adjust to the changing demands of time-sharing loads and to meet the more predictable performance demanded by real-time processes. OpenVMS uses both paging and swapping to make efficient use of available physical memory. The page fault handler executes in the context of the process that incurs a page fault. It supports programs with virtual address spaces larger than physical memory. The paging mechanism can support more active processes than can fit into physical memory at one time. The swapper ensures that there are not too many processes which can cause too much paging. The swapper's responsibilities are more global and systemwide than those of the page fault handler.

OpenVMS provides the following system services for memory management:

$CRETVA   Create Virtual Address Space—A process can create demand zero pages in P0 space or P1 space.

$EXPREG   Expand Region—A process can create demand zero pages at the high end of P0 space or the low end of P1 space.

$CRMPSC   Create and Map Section—A process can create a process-private or global section that maps the blocks of a file to a portion of process address space.

$MGBLSC   Map Global Section—A process can map to an existing global section.

$DELTVA   Delete Virtual Address Space—A process can delete P0 or P1 pages.

$CNTREG   Contract Region—The upper end of P0 space or the lower end of P1 space is deleted.

$DGBLSC   Delete Global Section—A global section can be marked for deletion when no more processes are mapped to it.

$SETSWM   Set Process Swap Mode—A process can enable or disable swapping.

$SETPRT   Set Protection on Pages—The protection on a page of virtual address space can be changed.

Among the most basic memory management services are those that create process-private virtual address space: $CRETVA, $EXPREG, $CRMPSC, and $MGBLSC. The image activator requests these services during image activation.

13.3.1 Page fault wait state

The most obvious wait state is page fault wait, in which a process is placed when a read is required to resolve a page fault. An I/O postprocessing routine detects that a page read has completed and reports the scheduling event page fault completion for the process. As a result, the process is removed from the page fault wait state and made computable. No priority boost is associated with page fault read completion.

13.3.2 Free page wait state

If not enough physical memory is available to satisfy a page fault, the faulting process is placed in a free page wait state. A free page list is the list of pages available for processes waiting in the free page wait state. If the free page list was formerly empty, a memory management routine checks for processes in this state whenever a page is deallocated. It reports the scheduling event that a free page is available so that each process in the free page wait state is made computable. The routine makes no scheduling decision about which process will get the page. There is no first-in/first-out (FIFO) approach to the free page wait state; rather, all processes waiting for the page are made computable. The next process to execute will be the highest priority resident computable process.

13.3.3 Working set dynamics

The pages of physical memory in use by a process are called its working set. A data structure within the process header (PHD) called the working set list describes just those pages in a compact form. A valid page is one whose PTE valid bit is set. As a process executes an image, it faults code, data, and page table pages into its working set. Execution of AST procedures, condition handlers, and system services that touch pageable process space can cause additional faults into the working set. The working set continues to grow as the process faults pages until the process occupies as much physical memory as it requires or is allowed, whichever is smaller. Each subsequent page fault requires that a page be removed from the working set to make room for the new page.

The executive maintains a list of working set pages for each process, called the working set list. The list facilitates

- Selecting a page to remove from the working set when a process needs to fault in a page but already occupies all the physical memory it is currently allowed, or when the process's working set is being shrunk
- Determining which pages to write when a process is outswapped
- Determining which pages to read when a process is inswapped

The size of the working set list and the number of its entries constrain a process's use of physical memory. The working set list size varies over the process's lifetime. It can be affected by the authorization file entry for an interactive user, SYSGEN parameters, availability of physical memory, and the recent paging history of the process.

By requesting the following system services, a process can affect its own working set and working set list:

$ADJWSL   Adjust Working Set Limit

$LKWSET   Lock Pages in Working Set

$LCKPAG   Lock Pages in Memory

$ULWSET   Unlock Pages from Working Set

$ULKPAG   Unlock Pages from Memory

$PURGWS   Purge Working Set

13.3.4   The working set list

A process working set includes the process's P0 and P1 space pages and the system space pages that contain its header information (PHD). The working set also includes global pages in use by the process. Each of these pages is described by a working set list entry (WSLE). Pages that are part of a section mapped by the PFN are valid for the entire time the process maps such pages, and they do not appear in the working set list. The page containing a process's L1PT is dedicated to that use while the process is resident, but it has no virtual mapping and is not represented in the working set list.

When a process references an invalid virtual page, the page fault handler takes several steps to make the page valid. It uses the dynamic region of the working set list to determine which virtual page to discard. The executive uses a modified FIFO scheme for its working set list replacement algorithm.

When an empty WSLE is found, a memory management system service checks whether a page can be added to the working set. If there are fewer pages in the working set than in the user authorization parameter WSQUOTA, a new physical page may be added to the working set. It may also be possible to add physical pages to the working set above WSQUOTA, depending on the size of the free page list.

13.4   SUMMARY

To summarize, the OpenVMS memory management routines attempt to optimally use the available physical memory for the user and system processes. While doing so, many built-in data structures of the memory management module ensure the proper security and efficiency of handling the physical memory.

Chapter

14

Scheduling in OpenVMS

14.1 INTRODUCTION

Only one process can run on a VAX or AXP processor at any given time.
Scheduling is the mechanism that selects a process to run. The
OpenVMS scheduling mechanism is characterized by the process priority and scheduling state.

Running on a particular processor, the scheduler identifies and
selects for execution the highest priority process that can execute on
that processor and places it into execution. A process currently executing enters a wait state when it makes a direct or indirect request for a
system operation that cannot complete immediately. A waiting process
becomes computable as the result of system events, such as the setting
of an event flag or the queuing of an asynchronous system trap (AST),
and may preempt a current process.

The process control block (PCB) specifies the scheduling state and
process priority of a process and records many other process characteristics. When a process is created, a PCB is allocated for it from nonpaged pool space in physical memory. A process continues to use the
same PCB until the process is deleted and its PCB deallocated. All processes in the system are in the current (CUR) state, a wait state, a computable resident (COM) state, or a computable outswapped (COMO)
state. PCBs of processes in most scheduling states are linked with
those of other processes in the same states. There are queues for computable processes and for processes in different wait states.

A process waiting for one or more common event flags is queued to
a wait queue in the common event block (CEB), defining the common
event flag (CEF) cluster with which the process is associated. Having
a wait queue in each CEB makes it easier to determine which CEF
wait processes are computable when a common event flag is set. The

wait queue in the CEB contains both resident and outswapped processes.

Registers and other hardware data structures associated with a process constitute the process's hardware context. It includes the integer registers R0 through R29, the stack pointer (SP), and the floating-point registers F0–F30 (F31 is always read as zero), per-process stack pointers for kernel, executive, supervisor, and user mode stacks, program counter (PC) and processor status (PS), etc.

While a process is current, its hardware context is updated continuously. When a process is taken out of execution, its hardware context is copied from registers to memory, where it is saved until the process executes again. OpenVMS scheduling routines ensure that the integer registers, PC and PS, are saved on the process's kernel stack and, if necessary, the floating-point registers are saved in the PHD. The privileged architecture library code (PALcode) routine that implements the swap process context instruction (CALL_PAL SWPCTX) saves a subset of the hardware context in the hardware PCB (HWPCB).

14.2 PROCESS PRIORITY

Two different mechanisms whose names contain the term *priority* are associated with each process. The interrupt priority level (IPL) applies to process-based and system-based code alike (see Fig. 14.1 for a list of IPLs and the type of interrupts at those IPLs). IPL governs the precedence of interrupts. Process priority determines the precedence of a process for execution and memory residence. Throughout this book, the term *priority* used without qualification refers to *process priority*.

Process priorities have two different representations, an external one for presentation to the user and an internal one for use by most scheduling code. External priorities take on values from 0 to 63; 0 is the lowest priority, 63 the highest.

The range of 64 priorities is divided into two segments. The priorities from 16 to 63 are assigned to real-time processes; the priorities from 0

IPL	Type of Interrupt
20–23	Device-specific input/output interrupts
22	Interval timer interrupt
20	System-corrected error interrupt
20	Processor-corrected error interrupt
30	Powerfail interrupt
31	System machine check abort
31	Processor machine check abort

Figure 14.1 Interrupt priority levels (IPLs) and the type of interrupts at those IPLs.

to 15 are assigned to normal processes. The scheduling of a process is significantly affected by its type (normal or real-time) and its assigned priority level. Traditionally, OpenVMS priorities are in the range 0 to 31, which is divided into a real-time half and a normal half. The OpenVMS AXP priority range includes additional real-time priorities in preparation for future real-time Portable Operating System Interface (POSIX) support.

System utilities, such as the System Dump Analyzer (SDA), MONITOR, and the code that implements the Digital Command Language (DCL) command SHOW SYSTEM, convert internal priorities to external ones for display. The Get Job Process Information ($GETJPI) system service returns an external priority when a process priority is requested.

When a process is first created, its base priority is initialized from an argument to the Create Process ($CREPRC) system service. Subsequently, if the process executes the LOGINOUT.EXE image, it may reset the base priority using the value from the user's record in the system authorization file.

A process with the ALTPRI privilege can raise and lower its current and base priorities without constraint, using the Set priority ($SETPRI) system service or the DCL command SET PROCESS/PRIORITY. A process without the ALTPRI privilege may raise and lower its priorities only between 0 and that allowed in the user authorization file.

The current priority of a real-time process does not change over time unless there is a direct program or operator request to change it. No dynamic priority adjustment is applied by the executive.

A real-time process executes until it is preempted by a higher priority process or it enters a wait state. A real-time process is not susceptible to quantum end; that is, it is not removed from execution because some interval of execution time has expired. The real-time range of priorities provides a scheduling environment like traditional real-time systems: preemptive, priority-driven scheduling without a timeslice or quantum.

Most user processes are normal processes. All system processes except the swapper and the Files-11 Extended QIO processor (XQP) cache server process are normal processes. The current priority of a normal process varies over time, while its base priority remains constant unless there is a direct program or operator request to change it. This behavior is the result of dynamic priority adjustment applied by the executive to favor I/O-bound processes and processes performing terminal I/O over those performing other types of I/O and compute-bound processes.

Normal processes run in a time-sharing environment that allocates timeslices (or quanta) to processes in turn. A normal process executes until it is preempted by a higher priority computable process (for one normal process to preempt another, the priority of the preempting process must be at least the SYSGEN parameter PRIORITY_OFFSET + 1 more than that of the preempted process), until it enters a resource of event wait state, or until it has used its current quantum (and there is another computable process at the same or higher priority).

Processes with identical current priorities are scheduled on a round-robin basis. That is, apart from the affinity and capability constraint, each process at a given priority level executes in turn before any other process at that level executes again. Most normal processes experience round-robin scheduling because, by default, the user authorization file defines the base priority for users as the value of the SYSGEN parameter DEFPRI. Its usual value is 4.

Normal processes do not generally execute at a single priority level. Rather, the priority of a normal process changes over time in a range of zero to size priority levels above the base process priority. Two mechanisms provide this priority adjustment:

- When a condition for which the process has been waiting is satisfied or a needed resource becomes available, its current priority may be increased to improve the scheduling response for the process. The size of the possible increase varies.

- Each time the process executes without the further system events, the current priority is lowered by one priority level until its base priority is reached.

Over time, compute-bound process priorities tend to remain at their base priority levels, whereas I/O-bound processes tend to have average current priorities somewhat higher than their base priorities. A normal process occasionally has its priority boosted by a mechanism called the pixscan mechanism. Temporary priority adjustment can also occur as a result of locking a mutex and through action by the $GETJPI system service.

Figure 14.2 shows some scheduling states. Primarily, there are resident and outswapped states that characterize the wait conditions. A process waiting for a local event flag is in the LEF or LEFO state, depending on its residence. Other scheduling states, such as CEF, include both resident and outswapped processes. A process in the CUR state is currently being executed. A CUR process makes a transition to the COM state when it is preempted by a higher priority process. It can also make this transition when it reaches quantum end and there is another computable process of higher or equal priority. A CUR process can make a transition to any of the resident wait states by directly or indirectly requesting a system operation that cannot complete immediately. Direct request forms like Hibernate ($HIBER) and Suspend

Mnemonic	State Name
COLPG	Collided page wait
MWAIT	Miscellaneous wait
	Mutex wait
	Resource wait
	Job quota wait
CEF	Common event flag wait
PFW	Page fault wait
LEF	Local event flag wait (resident)
LEFO	Local event flag wait (outswapped)
HIB	Hibernate wait (resident)
HIBO	Hibernate wait (outswapped)
SUSP	Suspend wait (resident)
SUSPO	Suspend wait (outswapped)
FPG	Free page wait
COM	Computable (resident)
COMO	Computable (outswapped)
CUR	Currently executing process

Figure 14.2 The concept of process states in the OpenVMS scheduler.

Process ($SUSPND) place the process in the voluntary wait states HIB and SUSP. Direct requests like $QIOW, $SYNCH, and $WAITFR place the process in the voluntary wait states LEF or CEF.

Indirect wait requests occur as a result of paging or contention for system resources. A process does not request PFW, FPG, COLPG, or MWAIT transitions. Rather, the transitions to these wait states occur because direct service requests to the system cannot be completed or satisfied at the moment.

The process's address space and PHD are accessible only while they are current. Furthermore, process deletion in the context of the process being deleted enables the use of system services, such as Deassign I/O channel ($DASSGN) and Delete Virtual Address Space ($DELTVA).

A process in the COM state is not waiting for events or resources, other than acquiring the control CPU for execution. A COM process enters the CUR state after having been selected as the next process to run. A COM process enters the COMO state when it is outswapped. A process in the COMO state is waiting for the swapper process to bring it into memory. As a COM process, it can then be scheduled for execution. Processes are created in the COMO state.

A process that is not current or computable is waiting for the availability of a system resource or the occurrence of an event. The process is in one of several distinct wait states. The wait state reflects the particular condition that must be satisfied for the process to become computable again. A process in a wait state makes the transition to COM or COMO through a system event such as the availability of a requested resource or the satisfaction of a wait condition. For most process wait states, the queuing of an AST makes a process computable even if the wait condition is not satisfied.

Three scheduling states are associated with event flag waits: LEF, LEFO, and CEF. A process enters the LEF or CEF state as a result of requesting $WAITFR, $WFLOR, $WFLAND, and $SYNCH system services directly or indirectly by the process or RMS on behalf of the process. A process enters the LEF state when it waits for local event flags or the CEF state when it waits for flags in a common event flag cluster.

An LEF process enters the LEFO state when it is outswapped. The transition from the LEF, LEFO, or CEF states to the computable (COM or COMO) states can occur as a result of an event flag being set that satisfies the wait condition, AST queuing, or process deletion.

There are separate resident and outswapped states and queues for hibernating and suspended processes. The $HIBER and $SUSPND system services cause processes to enter the HIB and SUSP wait states. Outswapping a HIB or SUSP process causes it to enter the HIBO or SUSPO state. A process makes the transition from the HIB or HIBO state to COM or COMO as a result of execution of the Wake ($WAKE) or Schedule Wakeup ($SCHDWK) system service, AST queuing, or process deletion.

The SUSP and SUSPO states are categorized by the access mode of the suspension as either supervisor mode or kernel mode. A process in supervisor mode suspension, the default, is made computable by the queuing of an AST. A process in kernel mode suspension is not made computable by the enqueuing of an AST. A process in either type of suspension is made computable when another process requests the Resume Process ($RESUME) system service for the suspended process. Process deletion, implemented with a kernel mode AST, makes any process that is being deleted computable, even one in the SUSP or SUSPO state, because the target process is resumed before the AST is queued.

Three process wait states are associated with memory management. For each there is a single queue that includes resident and outswapped processes. A process enters the page fault wait (PFW) state when code running in its context refers to a page that is not in physical memory. While the page read is in progress, the process is placed into the PFW state. Completion of the page read, AST queuing, or process deletion can cause a PFW process to become COM or COMO. If AST queuing makes the process computable before the page read completes, when the process reexecutes the instruction that caused the page fault, it is placed back into a page fault wait.

Usually a process enters the free page (FPG) wait state when it requests a physical page to be added to its working set but there are no free pages to be allocated from the free page list. In addition, a process requesting a lock through the Enqueue Lock Request ($ENQ) system service can be placed in this wait state when the lock ID table is full and a page of physical memory to extend it cannot be allocated. This state is essentially a resource wait that ends when the supply of free pages is replenished through modified page writing, working set trimming, process outswapping, or virtual address space deletion. When a physical page becomes available, all FPG processes are made COM or COMO. The first process to execute allocates the page. If the free page list is empty as a result, when the other processes execute, they are placed back into an FPG wait.

A process enters the collided page (COLPG) wait state when more than one process causes page faults on the same shared page at the same time. The initial faulting process enters the PFW state while the second and succeeding processes enter the COLPG state. All COLPG processes are made COM or COMO when the read operation completes. A process in the miscellaneous wait (MWAIT) state waits for the availability of a depleted system resource or job quota or a locked mutex.

A process may enter a resource wait if a resource it needs is not available. Common examples are the depletion of nonpaged pool or an already full mailbox. The process becomes computable when an executive routine declares the resource available. AST enqueuing makes the process computable, temporarily at least. System utilities such as SDA, MONITOR, and the DCL command SHOW SYSTEM display the state of a process in a resource wait. RWAST is a general-purpose resource wait used primarily when the wait is expected to be satisfied by the queuing or delivery of an AST to the process. The Queue I/O Request ($QIO) system service can place a process into this resource wait when the process is not allowed to issue another buffered or direct I/O request until one completes. RWAST may also indicate that the process is waiting for all the I/O requests on a channel to complete after the process has requested the $DASSGN system service or that the process which is about to be suspended or deleted is waiting for its Files-11 XQP activity to complete. A process is placed into RWMBX wait when it has the resource wait mode enabled and tries to write to a mailbox that is full or has insufficient buffer space.

A process placed into RWNPG wait when it is unsuccessful in allocating nonpaged pool. With the ability of nonpaged pool to expand, this wait is relatively rare. A process is placed into RWPAG wait when it is unsuccessful in allocating paged pool. A process in RWMPE wait is waiting for the modified page writer to signal that it has flushed the modified page list. The only process placed into this wait is one running the OPCCRASH image, which forces a flush of the modified page list prior to stopping the system. A process is placed into RWPFF wait when it faults a modified page with page file backing store out of its working set and the associated page file has not yet been initialized. A system routine that accesses data structures protected by a mutex places a process in the MWAIT state if the requested mutex ownership cannot be granted. Thus, the mutex wait state indicates a locked resource and not necessarily a depleted one. When the mutex in unlocked, each process waiting to lock that mutex is made COM or COMO to repeat its attempt to lock the mutex. AST queuing makes a mutex-waiting process computable only temporarily; the IPL at which the process is waited is 2, blocking the AST delivery interrupt. The process repeats its attempt to lock the mutex; if it is locked, the process is placed back into a wait. System utilities like MONITOR display processes waiting for a mutex as well as those waiting for a jobwide resource as MUTEX.

14.3 CAPABILITY AND AFFINITY

A capability represents a CPU attribute that a given process requires in order to execute. Generally a capability is a hardware feature. In an SMP system, a process's requirement for a particular capability may limit its execution to a subset of the available processors. For example, a process might require a capability to execute only on the primary processor.

Affinity is the requirement that a process execute on a specific processor of an SMP system. OpenVMS provides for both explicit and implicit affinity. A process must explicitly request explicit affinity and must explicitly dismiss it. Explicit affinity might allow processes to be segregated by the CPU. In contrast, a process acquires implicit affinity for a processor when there are advantages to its continuing execution on that processor. For example, a process that executed on a CPU with a large physical memory cache might have data still cached if it were placed back into execution on that CPU. Or a process placed back into execution on the same CPU as it last executed might have process-private TB entries still cached.

14.4 SCHEDULING DYNAMICS

In general, on an OpenVMS system in equilibrium, the available processors execute the highest-priority COM processes. A number of events can alter this equilibrium and require that the scheduler reschedule; that is, select another process to run and swap its context with that of the current process, taking the current process out of execution and placing the new one into execution.

The following are the principal events that require rescheduling:

- A process in the CUR state goes into a wait state.
- A process in the CUR state reaches the end of its quantum, and there is another COM process of equal or higher priority.

- A process in the CUR state requests an explicit reschedule through the Initiate Rescheduling Interrupt ($RESCHED) system service.

- A process in the CUR state changes its priority, and there is a higher-priority COM process.

- There is no longer a match between the capabilities required by a current process and the processor on which it is executing.

- A system event alters the scheduling state of a noncurrent process to COM, and its priority permits it to preempt a current process.

14.5 QUANTUM EXPIRATION

The SYSGEN parameter QUANTUM defines the size of the timeslice for the round-robin scheduling of normal processes. The quantum also determines, for most process states, the minimum amount of time a process remains after an inswap operation, but it is not an absolute guarantee of memory residence. The value of QUANTUM is the number of 10-millisecond intervals (called *soft ticks*) in the quantum. The default QUANTUM value of 20 indicates that for at least 200 milliseconds the process remains in memory after inswapping.

14.6 EVENT REPORTING

A system event potentially changes the scheduling state of a process, making it computable, memory-resident, or outswapped. Examples of system events include the setting of an event flag for which a process is waiting, AST queuing, and page fault I/O completion. An executive routine aware of a system event that may take a process out of a wait state reports it on behalf of the affected process.

14.7 PIXSCAN PRIORITY BOOSTS

The pixscan mechanism gives occasional priority boosts to normal priority COM and COMO processes. The SYSGEN parameter PIXSCAN specifies the maximum number of processes that can receive this boost each second. The priority boost prevents a high-priority, compute-intensive job from continuously blocking lower-priority processes and causing potential deadlocks. A deadlock might occur, for example, if a low-priority process acquired a volume lock on a critical disk but could not receive enough CPU time to complete its use of the lock and release it.

14.8 RESCHEDULING INTERRUPT

The IPL 3 interrupt service routine schedules processes for execution. The function of this interrupt service routine is to remove the currently executing process by saving the current process's hardware register and replacing it with that of the highest-priority computable resident process. This operation, known as *context switching,* is accompanied by modifications to the process state, current priority, and state queue of the affected processes. In some cases, a rescheduling interrupt is requested because a resident process has become computable whose priority is high enough to preempt the current process. In other cases, the current process enters a wait state, and the executive transfers into the rescheduling interrupt service routine to select another process to run. If there is no computable resident process, the interrupt service routine swaps to the hardware context called the system HWPCB. The Alpha AXP architecture was designed so that it could be extended to assist the software in performing critical, commonly performed operations, such as context switching; it provides the instruction CALL_PAL SWPCTX to swap two processes' privileged hardware contexts.

14.9 CONDITION HANDLING

Like its VAX counterpart, the OpenVMS AXP operating system defines a generalized uniform condition handling facility for the following classes of conditions:

- Conditions detected and generated by the processor, called exceptions
- Conditions detected and generated by user-mode software, called software conditions
- Conditions detected and generated by the OpenVMS executive, called special conditions

OpenVMS provides this facility for users and also uses this facility for its own purposes.

When an Alpha processor detects an anomaly or error, such as an access violation fault or a bugcheck trap, it generates an exception. The term processor as used here includes both hardware and the PALcode; hardware generates some exceptions, PALcode others. In either case, generating an exception begins with the transfer of control to an exception-handling routine. Each exception typically has its own PALcode routine; most such routines control to an exception-handling PALcode routine. Each exception typically has its own PALcode routine; most such routines converge to a common code.

When software detects an anomaly or error, it can report the error to a condition handler by simulating an exception and calling the condition dispatcher. Software simulates an exception by building exception context on the stack similar to that built as the result of an exception. Reporting processor-detected and software-detected errors in a similar manner allows user-mode software to deal with all errors using the same mechanisms.

A software-detected error reported in this fashion is called a *software condition*. User-mode software can report a software error as a software condition by calling one of two Run-Time Library procedures, LIB$SIGNAL or LIB$STOP. The OpenVMS executive reports some special conditional in a similar manner, although it uses an internal procedure rather than LIB$SIGNAL or LIB$STOP.

A condition handler is established for a specific access mode. The search for a condition handler encompasses only those handlers that were established in the access mode in which the condition occurred. A condition handler is classified as frame-based or software-vectored depending on how it is established and entered.

Based on the context of the signal array, a condition handler decides which of three actions to take:

- If the handler can fix the condition, it returns the status SS$CONTINUE to the condition dispatcher, which terminates the search and resumes the thread of execution that incurred the exception.

- If the handler cannot fix the condition, it can alter the flow of control by returning control to a previous point of execution.

- Alternatively, if the handler cannot fix the condition, it can resignal the condition. If a handler resignals, the condition dispatcher continues the search.

The VAX/VMS Run-Time Library procedure LIB$ESTABLISH is used to declare a VAX/VMS frame-based condition handler dynamically. LIB$ESTABLISH is not available in the OpenVMS AXP because the OpenVMS AXP Calling Standard only provides for static association between a procedure and its condition handler. To facilitate the porting of VAX/VMS programs, however, OpenVMS AXP compilers for certain languages, such as BLISS, DEC C, and FORTRAN, convert a call to LIB$ESTABLISH into a call to an internal procedure that provides an equivalent function through an additional level of indirection. The DEC C compiler treats a call to VAXC$ESTABLISH in the same manner. Also the translated image environment (TIE) facility provides a translated version of LIB$ESTABLISH, usable only in that environment.

The OpenVMS executive always handles:

Exceptions used in the course of normal system operations, for example page faults and CHMK exceptions.

Exceptions indicating software errors, namely bugchecks

The Alpha architecture defines two categories of exceptions, faults and traps.

A *fault* represents an error that prevents successful instruction execution. If the circumstances that led to a fault are corrected, the instruction can reexecute successfully. The most common fault is the translation-not-valid fault, usually known as a page fault. An instruction referencing a page not in memory incurs a page fault. After the page fault handler makes the page valid, the instruction can reexecute successfully.

Traps differ from faults in that they may continue to execute the code after attending to a trap service routine. Traps are varied. Some traps represent errors in instruction execution, while others are deliberately triggered. One example of an error trap is an illegal instruction trap. Change-mode-to-executive and change-mode-to-kernel traps, by contrast, are deliberately induced to request operating system services.

The TRAPB instruction allows software to guarantee that all previous arithmetic instructions will complete before any instructions following the TRAPB instruction are issued. Thus, any arithmetic traps incurred by instructions that execute before the TRAPB instruction can be handled before any instructions that follow the TRAPB instruction are issued. The TRAPB instruction enables software to request generation of more precise arithmetic exceptions. Support for this feature is available in some high-level languages. The BLISS language compiler, for example, appropriately uses instances of the TRAPB instruction in a procedure that has established a condition handler to ensure that any arithmetic traps that occur in that procedure are handled before control returns to the procedure's caller.

14.10   SOFTWARE CONDITIONS

A software condition can be considered a software-simulated exception. The mechanism used to report a software condition is similar to that used to report an exception; the only difference is that PALcode builds the exception stack frame in the case of an exception, whereas software builds the exception stack frame in the case of a software condition.

An exception is generated by the processor in response to an error or anomaly in instruction execution, whereas a software condition is generated by user-mode software in response to a software error or anomaly not necessarily related to instruction execution.

One of the choices in the design of a modular procedure is the method for reporting error conditions back to the caller. There are two common methods: returning a status in the procedure's return value (typically in R0 or F0), and signaling the error by calling one of the Run-Time Library procedures LIB$SIGNAL or LIB$STOP.

In some cases, signaling is preferable to returning status. Some procedures may return a value other than a status condition. For example, the string manipulation run-time procedure STR$POSITION returns the relative position of a substring within a source string. The procedure must therefore use the signaling mechanism to indicate an error condition—an illegal source string, for example.

This handler first checks whether the condition that occurred is SS$DEBUG. If so, it maps the debugger into P0 space (if not already mapped) and passes control to it. The condition SS$DEBUG is signaled by a Command Language Interpreter (CLI) in response to a DEBUG command. This feature allows an image that was not linked or run with debugger support to be interrupted and have a debugger invoked.

For all other errors, if the severity level of the error is warning, error, or severe (fatal) error, the handler maps the traceback facility above the end of defined P0 space and passes control to it. The traceback facility terminates the image after writing information about the exception to the process's SYS$OUTPUT device. The information resembles the following:

```
%SYSTEM-F-ACCVIO, access violation, reason mask=04, virtual
address=00000000, PC
=0002001C, PS=0000001B
%TRACE-f-TRACEBACK, symbolic stack dump follows

Image Name  Module Name  Routine Name  Line  rel PC    abs PC
ACCVIO      module1      routn1           0  0001001C  0002001C
                         routnb         230  80126F08  80126F08
                         matcom          80  7FF2432C  7FF2432C
```

If the condition is actually a successful one, and not an error condition, the traceback condition handler resignals the condition, which usually means that the condition is being reported to the catch-all condition handler.

In addition to the handlers that OpenVMS supplies for user-mode conditions, it sets up handlers for the other three access modes: kernel, executive, and supervisor modes.

14.11 INTERRUPTS

Like exceptions, interrupts are events that require the execution of software other than the current thread of execution, but asynchronously. The processor responds to such events by altering the control flow from the current thread of execution.

Most hardware interrupts are requested by signals from devices external to the processor when they need attention from the operating system. The hardware interrupt capability makes it unnecessary for the processor to poll the device to determine whether its state has changed. A few types of hardware interrupts are requested by signals from components within the processor, such as the interval timer.

A software interrupt is an interrupt requested by kernel mode rather than by an external device. The OpenVMS executive is interrupt-driven and requests software interrupts to schedule operating system functions.

To enable arbitration among concurrent interrupt requests and their servicing, each interrupt request has an associated interrupt priority level. When an interrupt is granted, processor IPL is raised to that of the interrupt. When the processor IPL is at or above that of the interrupt request, the interrupt is blocked. A processor executing a PALcode routine cannot be interrupted.

When an interrupt is requested, the processor determines whether its associated IPL permits it to interrupt:

- If the processor is running at an IPL equal to or higher than that of the interrupt request, the interrupt request is deferred until processor IPL drops below the IPL of the request.

- If the processor is running at a lower IPL than that of the interrupt request, the interrupt is granted.

To grant the interrupt, a typical Alpha processor may drain the instruction pipeline and complete any outstanding load instructions that are CPU-specific steps. It then transfers control to a PALcode routine that saves the processor state and dispatches to the interrupt's service routine through the system control block (SCB) entry associated with the interrupt.

The Alpha architecture provides 16 hardware IPLs, from IPL 31 down to IPL 16. Interrupts at the higher levels are primarily for processor errors and power failure. The middle levels are primarily for interrupts from external adapters and I/O devices. The lower levels are unused.

14.11.1 Comparison of exceptions and interrupts

The following list contrasts exceptions and interrupts:

- Normally, an interrupt occurs asynchronously to the currently executing instruction stream and is serviced between individual instructions. An exception occurs synchronously as a direct effect of the execution of an instruction. Except for imprecise arithmetic exceptions, an exception is serviced before the next instruction.

- Interrupts are generally systemwide events that cannot rely on support of a process in their service routines.

    Exceptions are generally a part of the currently executing process. Exception servicing is an extension of the instruction stream that is currently executing on behalf of that process.

- Interrupts cause an IPL change. Other than machine check exceptions, exceptions do not cause an IPL change.

- An interrupt is blocked while the processor executes at an IPL at or above the IPL associated with the interrupt.

Exceptions cannot be blocked by elevated IPLs.

14.11.2 Software interrupts

The Alpha architecture provides the capability for kernel-mode software to request interrupts at any interrupt priority level from 1 to 15. Requested by software rather than hardware, these are called software interrupts. In addition, the architecture provides four interrupts to signal AST delivery to each of the access modes.

Software interrupts are fundamental to the OpenVMS operating system. Software interrupt service routines perform many of the most important system functions of OpenVMS. These include scheduling (IPL 3), I/O postprocessing (IPL 4), servicing processes' time-dependent requests (IPL 7), and dispatching fork processes (IPLs 6 and 8 to 11).

An AST is a mechanism for signaling an asynchronous event to a process. An AST delivery interrupt signals that there is an AST for the current process to execute. An AST interrupt is always requested on behalf of the current process and must be serviced in its context.

On a VAX processor, AST delivery to all modes is initiated through an IPL 2 software interrupt and handled by a common interrupt service routine. On an Alpha processor, there are four different AST interrupts, one for each access mode. These interrupts still occur at IPL 2 but are no longer requested through the software interrupt request register (SIRR) and are not dispatched through the IPL 2 software interrupt SCB entry (see Fig. 14.3).

An AST delivery interrupt service routine delivers an AST by transferring control to the designated AST routine at the specified access mode. Some ASTs are requested by the process, for example, as notification of I/O request completion. Others are queued to the process by OpenVMS as part of normal system operations, such as automatic working set limit adjustment.

The OpenVMS executive requests a software interrupt to cause an interrupt service routine to execute and perform its designated function. It does this by executing a CALL_PAL MTPR_SIRR instruction.

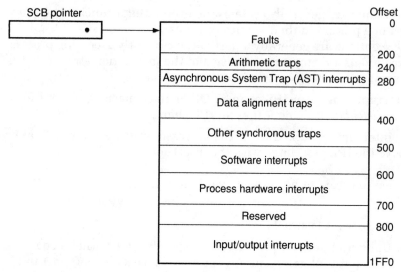

Figure 14.3 System control block.

Sometime later, when the interrupt request is granted, the initiate-exception-or-interrupt PALcode routine is dispatched.

OpenVMS uses software interrupts to schedule operating system functions. Using software interrupts is more efficient than periodically checking to see whether these functions need to be done. OpenVMS assigns IPLs to the different operating system functions, in part as an indication of their relative importance.

OpenVMS also uses specific IPLs and interrupt requests at those IPLs to synchronize access to shared data structures. OpenVMS requests the software interrupt service routines for IPLs 3, 4, 6, 7, 8, and 11 from within a hardware interrupt service routine or another software interrupt service routine. Software interrupts at 12 and 14 are requested only as the result of a person's entering a CPU console command. Although OpenVMS provides for fork dispatching at IPLs 9 and 10, OpenVMS itself makes little or no use of them. OpenVMS does not use the software interrupt vectors for IPLs 1, 2, 5, 13, and 15.

Software interrupt service routines.   There is no central monitor routine in OpenVMS that controls the sequence of operating system functions. Instead, any executive thread that identifies the need for a particular function performed within a software interrupt service routine can request the associated interrupt. Scheduling operating system functions as software interrupts eliminates any requirement for polling whether these functions need to be done. It also enables more important functions to interrupt less important ones.

In some cases, the assigned IPL only indicates the relative importance of the interrupt, and the interrupt service routine runs primarily at a higher IPL for synchronization.

OpenVMS interprets software interrupts, except the AST delivery and rescheduling interrupts, as systemwide events that are serviced independently of the context of a specific process. These higher IPL software interrupt service routines are said to run in system context.

14.12   SUMMARY

A knowledge of OpenVMS scheduling helps in efficient system management (which is the topic we discuss in the next chapter). Understanding the implication of different states that a process enters due to scheduling helps in fine-tuning the system as well as user authorization parameters like limits and quotas.

OpenVMS
System Management

15.1 INTRODUCTION

OpenVMS provides several tools to assist the functions of system management. Typical system management functions on OpenVMS include:

- Bootstrapping the operating system
- Maintaining the user account (in the user authorization file)
- Monitoring the operating system resources
- Installing new software packages and updating existing software packages
- Tuning the operating system periodically as and when the load on the operating system varies and also when new hardware is added to the configuration
- Generating accounting reports
- Performing the system and user device backups periodically

15.2 USER ACCOUNTS

User account information containing username, user identification code (UIC), quotas, privileges, and several other details is contained in two database files: the user authorization file called SYSUAF.DAT, and the rights identifier file called RIGHTSLIST.DAT. Both the databases are located in SYS$SYSTEM area.

The utility called AUTHORIZE is used to create or modify user accounts. The UIC is a pair of integers that uniquely identifies a user and the group to which the user belongs. ADD and MODIFY are the most commonly used commands of AUTHORIZE to maintain the account database. An example of the ADD command to add a new account is shown here:

```
$ set default sys$system:
$ run authorize
UAF> add btest/dir=[betatest]/dev=dua0:/uic=[100,25] –
/password=alphaxp
```

The ADD command makes a new entry of user account in the database. However, the directory corresponding to the new account must be created using the DCL command CREATE/DIRECTORY with a proper specification of the UIC. For example, for the previous account the user directory is:

```
$ create/directory dua0:[betatest]/owner_uic=[100,25]
```

The general syntax for accessing user files from another node is:

```
$ <DCL_command> nodename"username password"::file_spec file_spec
```

For example:

```
$ copy nyle"charles wtower"::sample.dat*.*
```

The preceding example shows that the username and the password have to be specified when executing certain DCL commands with reference to a remote node. The password specification in these commands defeats its purpose, i.e., the security of user accounts. In order to meet this problem of security, the concept of proxy accounts is used in OpenVMS.

By having a proxy account at a remote node one can execute DCL commands without specifying the username and password.

For example, with a proxy account defined for the user on node 'NYLE', the following command performs the copy operation sufficiently:

```
$ copy nyle::sample.dat*.*
```

The /PROXY qualifier with the ADD command is used to add the proxy account.

15.3 SECURITY OF USER ACCOUNTS

Rights identifiers are used to provide protection to files, devices, and system data structures like queues. These identifiers are a more modular way of providing security than the UIC-based protection. The identifiers are used by Access Control List (ACL) commands. The GRANT/ IDENTIFIER command adds one of the several possible rights identifiers to a specified account. The corresponding rights entries are added or updated in the rights database file RIGHTSLIST.DAT. The identifiers are assumed to be defined using ACL commands:

```
$ SET ACL file_spec/ACL-(IDENTIFIER=id_name,ACCESS-<read,write..>
```

The syntax for granting an identifier to a user is:

```
UAF> GRANT/IDENTIFIER id_name user-name
```

Some of the important fields of the user account database are listed in Fig. 15.1.

Field Name	Field Description
Username	User's name. This constitutes a kind of primary key practically used for all command level operations.
UIC	User Identification Code. The pair of numbers [n,m] uniquely identify a user associated with a group.
Default	The default device and directory at the time of login. Use /DEVICE and /DIRECTORY qualifiers with ADD or MODIFY command to define this.
LGICMD	This defines the default command procedure to execute at the time of login. Usually, this file is LOGIN.COM.
Expiration	Specifies the time when the account becomes invalid.
Pwdminimum	This field indicates the minimum length of password.
Login Fails	Indicates the number of login attempts allowed before the system disallows the user from attempting any more.
Pwdlifetime	The time allowed before the user must redefine password.
Last Login	The time-stamp of last login for interactive as well as non-interactive jobs.
Maxdetach	Maximum allowed detached processes.
Prio	Priority of processes. Normally, between 4 and 8.
CPU	Maximum CPU time allowed per process.
Film	Maximum number of files that can be opened at a time.
BIOlm	Buffer I/O limit.
DIOlm	Direct I/O limit.
ASTlm	Maximum number of ASTs allowed at any time.
Enqlm	Enqueue limit.
Bytlm	Maximum number of bytes of nonpaged dynamic memory.
WSdef	Initial working set size in pages of 512-byte length.
WSquo	Working set size the process can expand.
WSextent	The number of pages allowed beyond WSquo if there are free pages in the system.
Pgflquo	Maximum allowed pages the process can use in the system paging file.

Figure 15.1   User account database.

Normally the protection mechanism used for devices, files, and system data structures in OpenVMS is based on UIC and ACL. It provides four types of protection, read, write, execute, and delete, against four different types of users, owner, group, system, and world. However, these protections are modifiable by privileged users, especially those having SETPRV. In order to facilitate a more rigorous protection to files on OpenVMS, DEC has developed an optional tool called VMS Encryption.

The SYSGEN parameters LGI_RETRY_LIM and LGI_RETRY_TMO provide a first-level security against intruders trying to login by guessing passwords. LGI_RETRY_LIM (default value of 3 attempts) determines the number of login attempts allowed in the time limit determined by LGI_RETRY_TMO (default value of 20 seconds). These values can be modified using SYSGEN:

```
$ RUN SYS$SYSTEM :SYSGEN
SYSGEN> SET LGI_RETRY_LIM 5
SYSGEN> SET LGI_RETRY_LIM 25
SYSGEN> WRITE ACTIVE
SYSGEN> EXIT
```

Another set of SYSGEN parameters, LGI_BRK_TMO (default value of 300 seconds) and LGI_BRK_LIM (default value of 5 attempts), determines the action to be taken when a break-in attempt was repeated. The default values for these parameters dictate that only one login failure will be tolerated every 300 seconds, and a maximum of 5 such attempts will be tolerated in a time span of 25 minutes. The severity of action to be taken against break-in attempts can vary from setting a SYSGEN parameter called LGI_BRK_TERM to 0 that disables the terminal, to disabling the account by setting the login flag /DISUSER in the authorization file. The latter comes into effect if the SYSGEN parameter LGI_BRK_DISUSER is set to 1.

The AUDIT_SERVER is responsible for security auditing on OpenVMS. The security audit events are recorded in SYS$MANAGER:SECURITY_AUDIT.AUDIT$JOURNAL. The SET AUDIT command of DCL must be used to alert break-in attempts on the system resources. The ENABLE qualifier of the SET AUDIT command takes several allowed attributes which determine the class of system resources for which the auditing should be enabled. An example of declaring the audit is:

```
$ SET AUDIT/ALARM/ENABLE=(AUDIT, AUTHORIZATION, BREAKIN=ALL)
```

15.4   VMSINSTAL UTILITY

VMSINSTAL.COM, located in the area SYS$UPDATE, is used for installing new software products. It takes the product name and several options to load and install software product images. Normally, the options to be used with VMSINSTAL are given by the instruction manual describing the product installation procedure.

Many of the products need the system to remain operational, while few complex packages may require the installation to be performed as an off-line procedure, i.e., with only the system manager logged into the system. Ideally, such installations recommend taking system and user backup before beginning the installation. VMSINSTAL is programmable; the installation command procedures to install the new product can make use of this programmability to ensure a foolproof installation of the product.

15.5 SOFTWARE LICENSES

The Product Authorization Key (PAK) that is supplied with a software package defines the license to use the package. The installation of any software package is to be associated with updating the license database of OpenVMS. The license database is located in SYS$COMMON:[SYSEXE]LMF$LICENSE.LDB. A simple way to update this database when a new license is added is to execute the command procedure VMSLICENCE.COM from the SYS$UPDATE area. Or the commands LICENSE REGISTER and LICENSE LOAD can be used.

15.6 VOLUME RECOVERY

The ANALYZE utility is capable of generating file corruption or device corruption reports and on many occasions can repair the same. For example, it is possible that the file information on a disk unit can become inconsistent because of abrupt events like power failure. It is recommended to mount the volumes to be repaired as private devices. The following set of examples on using ANALYZE show how it can be used to report corruption of a disk unit and how it can be repaired:

```
$ ANALYZE/DISK_STRUCTURE DUA0:
$ ANALYZE/DISK_STRUCTURE/REPAIR/CONFIRM DUA0:
```

15.7 SYSMAN UTILITY

The SYSMAN utility can be used to issue commands on other nodes of a VAXcluster on a DECnet-based platform. The system manager can effectively use this to communicate with any node in the cluster without explicitly logging into them.

A typical use of SYSMAN first sets the node to work with and then issues commands to be executed on the selected node. The following command selects the node:

```
SYSMAN> SET ENVIRONMENT/NODE=ORION
```

Several DCL commands can be executed at the SYSMAN prompt after selecting the node. The DCL command needs to be prefixed with a DO command. For example:

```
SYSMAN> DO SHOW USERS
```

15.8   BOOTING THE OPERATING SYSTEM

The console terminal is used for privileged I/O with the operating system at the system management level. The console subsystem of OpenVMS has the prompt ">>>" that distinguishes it from the OpenVMS command prompt "$". If the console terminal is enabled, pressing <control/p> at the console terminal halts the system at any time. The BOOT command can be issued after ensuring that the system has halted. The BOOT command takes the four-letter device mnemonic (like DUA0) of the bootable device as its parameter:

```
>>> HALT
>>> BOOT DUA0
```

After loading the components of OpenVMS, the bootstrap procedure mounts the disk units, installs the printer queue manager, and performs various site-specific operations. The site-specific operations are to be specified by the system manager in the command file SYS$MANAGER:SYSTARTUP_Vn.COM. The execution of this command procedure forms the final phase of bootstrap.

15.9   QUEUES

The printer and batch job resources are treated as public resources. This is in contrast to an interactive terminal where a single user uses the terminal. Being public setups, OpenVMS ensures availability of printer and batch job resources to all users by maintaining a queue for these separately. In fact, there could be several printer queues and batch job queues. The system which maintains the queue is called the queue manager. Establishing a queue is the responsibility of system management. Printer queues are established by these steps:

■ Starting the queue manager

Example: $ START/QUEUE/MANAGER

■ Initialize one queue per device

Example: $ INITIALIZE/QUEUE/ON=LPB1: laser$pko

■ Start the queue

Example: $ START/QUEUE LASER$PKO

15.10   SHUTDOWN

SHUTDOWN.COM is an OpenVMS-supplied command procedure that performs extensive cleanup and shuts down a VMS system in a controlled fashion. SHUTDOWN is typically run from the SYSTEM account or the one similarly privileged. On a single OpenVMS system, SHUTDOWN performs the following tasks:

- Optionally saving AUTOGEN feedback information to the file SYS$SYSTEM:AGEN$FEEDBACK.DAT
- Disabling interactive logins
- Shutting down DECnet
- Stopping the job controller's queue operations
- Stopping user processes
- Dismounting mounted volumes
- Stopping secondary processors on a multiprocessing system
- Removing installed images
- Invoking the site-specific shutdown procedure SYSSHUTDOWN.COM
- Closing the operator's log file
- Stopping the AUDIT_SERVER and ERRFMT processes
- Recalibrating the system time from the time-of-year clock and recording the change in the base image

The shutdown command procedure SYS$SYSTEM:SHUTDOWN.COM is executed by the system manager to shut down the operating system. The OPER privilege is required to execute this command procedure. Any site-specific shutdown requirement for a given configuration needs to be specified in another command procedure, SYS$MANAGER:SYSHUTDWN.COM.

SHUTDOWN runs the OPCCRASH program to actually shut down the system. It passes parameters to OPCCRASH via logical names. SHUTDOWN uses the following logical names:

SHUTDOWN$MINIMUM_MINUTES

SHUTDOWN$TIME

SHUTDOWN$INFORM_NODES

OPCCRASH performs the minimal tasks required to shut down an OpenVMS system. Typically, it is executed as the final step of the SHUTDOWN.COM procedure, described in the previous section, but it can be executed directly in an emergency.

15.11   MEMORY MANAGEMENT FILES

The size of the page file called PAGEFILE.SYS located in SYS$SYS-TEM determines the total number of pages that can be outswapped at any given time on a running OpenVMS system. Parameters like the size of physical memory and the number of allowed users determine an appropriate size as default. The default size is used when the operating installation procedure creates the page file. The size, however, can be changed by the system manager as and when the situation demands it. SYSGEN commands called CREATE and INSTALL can be used to create additional page files. Or the utility called AUTOGEN can be executed periodically to revise the existing size of the page files. AUTOGEN takes the SYSGEN parameters that are concerned with paging for its input to calculate the size of the page files.

15.12   BACKUP UTILITY

Periodically taken backups of the system and user files are most important for a smooth operation of the operating environment. Mainly, backup operations are of two types: image backup, i.e., the backup of the entire volume of a disk, tape, or other devices, and save set backup (using a file select qualifier) that contains a set of specified files. These mechanisms can save users' and systems' files in a compressed form. These days, the backup philosophy in computer operations is standard, and several advanced tools are available from DEC to automate this important aspect of system management.

The BACKUP utility of OpenVMS is widely used for taking backups, and it is supplied in the standard distribution.

The image backup is used to take backup of the entire volume, say, a disk image to a tape. This example takes the image backup of disk DUA0: to tape MTA0:

```
$DISMOUNT/NOUNLOAD DUA0:
$MOUNT DUA0: SYSTEM
$INITIALIZE MTA0: SYSBCK
$MOUNT/FOREIGN MTA0:
$BACKUP/IMAGE DUA0: MTA0:
```

The /SELECT qualifier is responsible for taking backup of specified files. The directory tree structure is retained on the target device. An example of using the /SELECT qualifier is shown below:

```
$ BACKUP MTA0:SYSBCK/SAVE_SET/SELECT=(*.DAT;*, *.PAR;*)
DUA0:[SYSMGR...]
```

The directory of saved files from a backup device can be seen with the /LIST qualifier. The /REWIND qualifier ensures the list begins with the first save set:

```
$ BACKUP/REWIND/LIST MTAO:
```

In addition to the timeshared BACKUP utility just described, there is a standalone BACKUP utility also. The standalone version is mainly used for loading the operating system. It can also be used like its time-shared version.

15.13   SYSBOOT AND SYSGEN UTILITIES

On OpenVMS VAX, SYSGEN also provides device driver loading, device database creation, and device auto-configuration support. In OpenVMS AXP, this functionality has been removed from SYSGEN; IOGEN provides it.

When SYSGEN executes, it maintains a private table of working parameters. It is manipulated by the following SYSGEN commands:

- Displayed by SHOW parameter-name commands
- Altered by SET parameter-name value commands
- Overwritten in memory by a USE command
- Written to the file VAXVMSSYS.PAR by the SYSGEN WRITE CURRENT command
- Dynamic parameters are written to the memory image of the OpenVMS base system by the SYSGEN WRITE ACTIVE command

To adjust the system parameters one can use a conversational standalone boot:

```
>>>B/E0000001 DUAO
SYSBOOT>
```

or set the corresponding SYSGEN parameters by running SYSGEN:

```
$ RUN SYS$SYSTEM:SYSGEN
SYSGEN> USE SYS$DEVICE:[SYS.SYSEXE]VAXVMSSYS.PAR
SYSGEN ...
SYSGEN> WRITE SYS$SYSDEVICE:[SYSE.SYSEXE]VAXVMSSYS.PAR
```

15.14   AUTOGEN UTILITY

The AUTOGEN utility acts as a supplement to the SYSGEN utility by performing some of the system tuning automatically. The SYS-GEN parameters play a crucial role in AUTOGEN's functions. Whenever the configuration of hardware is updated (like memory enhancement), it is recommended to run AUTOGEN to keep the system updated globally.

AUTOGEN also needs to be run whenever some SYSGEN parameters are modified. The file SYS$SYSTEM:MODPARAMS.DAT must be used to enter new values for SYSGEN parameters. The new parameters can be brought into effect by running AUTOGEN:

```
$ @SYS$UPDATE:AUTOGEN SAVEPARAMS REBOOT
```

The AUTOGEN utility goes through several phases before building an update VAXVMSSYS.PAR file. The modified parameters specified in MODPARAMS.DAT are used in conjunction with those from VMSPARAMS.DAT.

15.15   ERROR HANDLING

Systemwide error-reporting mechanisms include:

- The error logging subsystem, by which device drivers and other system components record errors and other events for later inclusion in an error log report
- The bugcheck mechanism, by which OpenVMS shuts down the system and records its state when internal inconsistencies or other unrecoverable errors are detected
- Servicing of machine checks, by which the processor indicates that it has detected hardware errors

The error logging subsystem records device errors, CPU-detected errors, and other noteworthy events, such as volume mounts, system startups, system shutdowns, and bugchecks.

When appropriate, the ERRFMT process is awakened to copy completed error messages to the error log file, SYS$ERRORLOG: ERRLOG.SYS. Subsequently, the system manager can run the Error Log utility to analyze the contents of the error log file and produce a formatted report.

If the system is shut down or crashes, the error log allocation buffers are copied to the dump file to prevent the loss of valid error messages that have not yet been copied to ERRLOG.SYS. If the system crashes, an error log message is formed and also saved in the dump file. On the next system boot, the SYSINIT process copies the error log allocation buffers and the crash error log message that had been saved in the dump file to a piece of nonpaged pool. When ERRFMT runs, it scans the nonpaged pool copies for valid messages to write to the error log file. In this way, no error log information is lost across a system crash or shutdown.

When VMS detects an internal inconsistency, such as a corrupted data structure or an unexpected exception, it generates a bugcheck. If the inconsistency is not severe enough to prevent continued system operation, the bugcheck generated is nonfatal and merely results in an error log entry.

If the error is serious enough to jeopardize system operation and data integrity, OpenVMS generates a fatal bugcheck. This generally results in aborting normal system operation, recording the contents of memory to a dump file for later analysis, and rebooting the system.

System initialization code locates and opens a dump file for dumping crash and bugcheck information. The dump file must be in the directory SYS$SPECIFIC:[SYSEXE] on the system disk. By default, the dump file is SYSDUMP.DMP. In its absence, OpenVMS instead writes a dump to PAGEFILE.SYS, if it exists. Subsequent analysis of a dump written to the page file requires that the SYSGEN parameter SAVEDUMP be 1.

On OpenVMS VAX, the code that performs fatal bugcheck processing and its data are not referenced during system operation. When needed, they are read into memory, overlaying nonpaged read-only executive code. This implementation saves memory during normal operations but results in added complexity when a fatal bugcheck occurs.

In contrast, all OpenVMS AXP fatal bugcheck code and most of the associated data are permanently resident. As a result of the Alpha instruction set and addressing modes, moving a piece of code to a different virtual address requires that its address references be relocated. Rather than overlay other code with the fatal bugcheck code and then have to relocate the fatal bugcheck code, OpenVMS AXP makes the code and data resident, except for the ASCII bugcheck messages.

15.16 MONITOR UTILITY

The MONITOR command can be used to view system behavior. It sends output to a file or displays it to your terminal, updating the information at regular intervals of 3 seconds. The qualifiers for this command are:

TOPCPU	lists the processes which are consuming the most CPU time.
TOPDIO	displays processes performing the most I/O, mainly to disks and tapes.
TOPBIO	displays processes performing the most I/O, mainly to terminals, printers, and over the network to other nodes.

15.17 SUMMARY

The system management on OpenVMS is a relatively easy task compared to that in other operating systems like Unix. Many other tools, such as the Performance Analyzer, can be used to tune the OpenVMS system periodically for better efficiency.

Migration from OpenVMS VAX to OpenVMS AXP

16

Alpha AXP
Architecture

16.1 INTRODUCTION

The Alpha project of DEC designed the AXP architecture with the goals of high performance, longevity, and easy migration from VAX architecture. Alpha architects have set an ambitious goal of keeping the architecture relevant for another 15–25 years. Digital was able to come up with an optimal design avoiding as much limitation as possible. In VAX architecture, a 32-bit memory address is the primary limitation. So, Alpha architects employed a 64-bit architecture. The design also provides the VAX compatibility by providing a subset of 32-bit memory operations. It is hoped that by combining suitable factors like the multiprocessing capability of Alpha architectures, raw clock speed of 200 MHz, and providing multiple instruction execution possibilities for a given quantum of time, the new processor can deliver several times faster response over the existing architecture of VAX.

AXP-based computers are now supporting the three major operating systems in the market today: OpenVMS, Unix, and Microsoft Windows NT. In order to be ready for these operating systems, Alpha is designed to provide interrupt delivery, interrupt return, exceptions (also known as conditions), context switching, memory management, and error handling. These functions are treated as privileged and are provided in a set of subroutines called *PALcode*. These subroutines have access to real hardware registers. Also, they can run with interrupts disabled and entry points controlled. By selecting a PALcode set per operating system, the configuration is simplified and interface matches are made easy.

A binary translator called the VAX Executable Software Translator (VEST) can convert a VAX image to an image that is claimed to run on an AXP platform without any change. This is largely true, especially for applications using a high-level language. But, assembly programs, time- and space-critical applications like real-time applications, data acquisition systems, etc., need to be cautious about the programming implications of the fundamental difference between VAX and AXP architectures (this is discussed in Chap. 18). The VAX data types for integer and floating point are supported in AXP. There are no other compatibility issues planned in the AXP design.

The Alpha AXP is based on reduced instruction set computing (RISC). In a typical RISC design, memory access is through a set of simple *load and store instructions,* i.e., all data items are moved to registers and memory locations without any computation. All computations are performed in the registers. Both *little-endian* and *big-endian* byte addressing and VAX/IEEE floating point are carried over from the VAX architecture bases. The architecture uses a linear 64-bit virtual address space. Registers, addresses, floating-point numbers, integers, and character strings are all operated on as full 64-bit quantities without any address segmentation. Thus, for example, by processing 8 bytes at a time, string manipulation on Alpha can be up to 8 times faster.

In Alpha AXP architecture there is no way of precisely handling the exceptions, i.e., to stop executing instructions subsequent to the one causing the overflow or underflow. This is because incorporating these precisions in the design is time-consuming and affects the performance of the processor. In this design the emphasis is more on the performance of normal operations. But there are secondary instructions provided, like Trap Barrier (TRAPB), which can be used by the software to make the exception reporting as precise as possible. On the other hand, the memory management exceptions like page fault are reported precisely to avoid relatively more expensive software development time.

Unlike other RISC designs, the Alpha AXP architecture design incorporates shared-memory multiprocessing. The RISC instructions used here provide a reliable synchronization and byte addressing. There is no strict read-write ordering possible in Alpha. In a strict read-write ordering, the sequence of reads and writes issued by one processor in a multiprocessor configuration is delivered to all other processors in exactly the same sequence as received. In Alpha, this has to be achieved by using explicit Memory Barrier instruction.

For both VAX and AXP systems, I/O devices at local and remote sites form a part of any typical configuration. The speed of AXP also has thrown a challenge to build I/O systems that can cope with the CPU speed. The processor and memory are of course two other important components of a configuration (see Fig. 16.1).

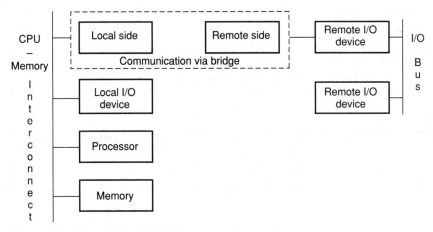

Figure 16.1 Alpha AXP and VAX system components.

16.2 ALPHA AXP DATA STRUCTURES AND PROCESSOR STATE

In the Alpha architecture a 32-bit data is always viewed in 64-bit registers or memory locations as a basic unit of data, a quadword (64-bit datum). Basically, there are three data types in Alpha: integer, IEEE floating point, and VAX floating point. All these are available in both 32- and 64-bit forms. VAX floating-point values in memory have 16-bit words swapped to provide compatibility with VAX and PDP-11 formats. The VAX floating-point load and store instructions do word swapping to make the result compatible with representation in registers. The 32-bit load instructions expand values to 64-bit form, and the 32-bit store instructions shrink the 64-bit representation back to 32. So whether it is an integer or floating-point data, operations with reference to registers are done on full 64-bit. When representing a 32-bit data in a 64-bit register, Alpha pads the higher 32 bits with the contents of bit 31, making all 33 bits equal to bit 31. This helps signed integer values to be used directly in 64-bit arithmetic and branches. Figure 16.2*a* shows a summary of characteristics of the Alpha instruction set.

The floating-point data of 32 bits in a quadword had the 8-bit exponent field expanded to 11 bits, and the 23-bit mantissa field expanded to 52 bits. Except for IEEE denormals, this allows single-precision floating-point values to be used directly in double-precision arithmetic and branches. Figure 16.2*b* shows the main features of the Alpha data format.

Bytes and words which are represented in 16-bit memory on PDP-11 and 32-bit memory on VAX are not basic data types on AXP. However, byte-addressing instructions are made available when referencing registers.

All instructions are 32 bits long.

There are 32 integer registers: R0 through R31, each 64 bits in length. R31 reads as zero, and writes to R31 are ignored.

There are 32 floating-point registers (F0 through F31), each 64 bits wide. F31 reads as zero, and writes to F31 are ignored.

All memory references are done using load/store instruction combinations between registers and memory.

There are no branch condition codes. Branch instructions test register values that may be the result of a previous compare.

Integer and logical instructions operate on quadwords.

A subset of VAX compatibility instructions is included.

(a)

All operations are done between 64-bit registers.
There are 32 integer registers and 32 floating-point registers.
Longword (32-bit) and quadword (64-bit) integers are supported.
Four floating-point types are supported:
        – VAX F_floating (32-bit)
        – VAX G_floating (64-bit)
        – IEEE single (32-bit)
        – IEEE double (64-bit)

(b)

Figure 16.2 (*a*) Characteristics of Alpha instruction set; (*b*) Alpha data format.

There are 32 registers, R0–R31, of 64-bit length. R31 is always zero. Also, there are 32 floating-point registers of 64-bit length, F0–F31, with F32 always zero. Writes to R31 and F31 are ignored.

The program counter (PC) is a 64-bit quadword with a virtual byte address whose low 2 bits are always zero to make it longword-aligned. The VAX keeps the PC in general register R15 where it is directly used for PC-relative memory addressing.

In addition to these state registers, the privileged architecture library routines for the various operating systems implement an additional state. This state typically includes a processor status (PS) word, kernel and user stack pointers, a process control block (PCB) base for context switching, a process-unique value for threads, and a processor number for multiprocessor dispatching. Additional PALcode states may include a floating-point enable bit, interrupt priority level, and translation lookaside buffers for mapping instruction-stream and data-stream virtual addresses. All these states can optionally be provided by the implementer for a particular operating system. In a multiprocessor implementation, the states are duplicated for each processor.

AXP retains the VAX byte-addressing mechanism of using the lowest-numbered byte of a given data. The longwords and quadwords need to be aligned, i.e., their addresses need to be multiples of 4 and 8, respectively. If they are not aligned in this sense, an alignment trap is generated to be processed by the PALcode. This PALcode can either access the data from two aligned locations or generate a fatal error. It depends on the version of the operating system where the PALcode is resident. The addressing in Alpha supports both big-endian and little-endian wherein byte 0 is the high byte of an integer and the low byte, respectively. But the big-endian approach has a slight bias of an extra instruction.

For virtual addresses Alpha can use the 64-bit structure. But, in many Alpha systems a smaller size is used. Fixed-size pages are used to map virtual addresses to physical addresses using per-page memory protection. Any mapping errors such as memory protection violation, page faults, etc., are treated as traps and processed in PALcode. Read, write, or instruction-fetch for each page can be made to provide a trap service routine in the PALcode.

Many numbers of separated address spaces can be marked with address space numbers in the virtual addresses. The mapping from virtual to physical address space is done per-page and the page size can be 8KB, 16KB, 32KB, or 64KB, and many virtual spaces can map to a single physical address space, allowing many-to-one correspondence.

Longword granularity (see Glossary) is maintained, i.e., two processors may simultaneously access adjacent longwords without mutual interference. The load-locked/store-conditional sequence discussed previously can be used to have byte granularity also (see Chap. 18).

The Alpha data representation and preprocessor state are summarized in Figs. 16.3 and 16.4, respectively.

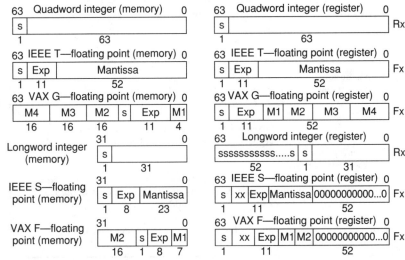

Figure 16.3 Data representation in Alpha.

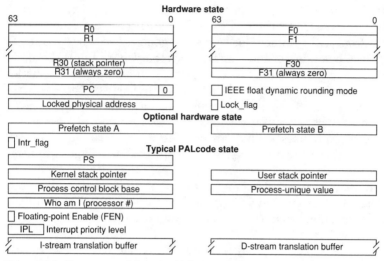

Figure 16.4 Preprocessor states in Alpha.

16.3 ALPHA INSTRUCTIONS

There are four types of Alpha instructions: PALcode, conditional branches, and load/store and operate instructions.

The PALcode instructions specify one of the many available PALcode library functions. Conditional branch instructions are used to test register Ra and to specify a signed 21-bit PC-relative longword target displacement. Subroutine calls put the return address in register Ra. Load and store instructions are used to move either quadwords or longwords between register Ra and memory. The operate instructions are used for integer and floating-point operations.

Figure 16.5 shows a summary of Alpha instructions.

PALcode instructions:
   These instructions specify, in the function code field, one of the several Privileged Architecture Library's operations.
Conditional branch instructions:
   These branch instructions are used to test register Ra and specify a signed 21-bit PC-relative longword target displacement. Subroutine calls put the return address in register Ra.
Load and store instructions:
   These are typical RISC instructions. Load and store instructions are used to move longwords or quadwords between register Ra and memory, using Rb plus a signed 16-bit displacement at the memory address.
Operate instructions:
   Operate instructions are used for floating-point and integer operations, as shown in Fig. 16.3.

Figure 16.5 Types of Alpha instructions.

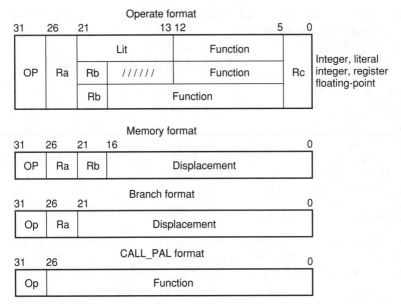

Figure 16.6 Alpha instruction formats.

There are four fundamental instruction formats as shown in Fig. 16.6: Operate, Memory, Branch, and CALL_PAL. All instructions are 32 bits wide and reside in memory at aligned longword addresses. Each instruction contains a 6-bit opcode field and zero to three 5-bit register number fields, Ra, Rb, and Rc. The remaining bits contain functions of the opcode, literal, or displacement fields. Rb is never written and Rc is never read.

Loads and stores are 2-operand instructions, having a register Ra and a base-displacement virtual byte address. The effective address calculation sign extends the 16-bit displacement to 64 bits and adds the 64-bit Rb base register. This ignores any overflow condition. The virtual byte address thus calculated is mapped to a physical address. Other miscellaneous instructions make use of Ra, Rb, and displacement fields differently.

All the operate instructions are 3-operand register-to-register, i.e., calculations of the type:

$$Rc = Ra \ OP \ Rb$$

In integer operate instructions, the opcode and a 7-bit function field specify the exact operation. Integer operates may have an 8-bit literal instead of Rb. The literal must be zero-extended. In floating-point operates, the opcode and an 11-bit function field specify the exact operation. There are no floating-point literals.

Branch format instructions use a single-register Ra and a signed PC-relative longword displacement. The calculation for specifying the branch target shifts the 21-bit displacement left by 2 bits to make it a longword displacement instead of a byte displacement. Then it sign-extends to displace the longword before adding it to the updated PC. Conditional branch instructions test register Ra, and unconditional branches write the updated PC to Ra for subroutine linkage. The large longword displacement allows a range of ±4MB. This significantly reduces the need for branches around or to other branches.

The CALL_PAL instruction has only a 6-bit opcode and a 26-bit function field. The function field is a small integer specifying one of a few dozen privileged architecture library subroutines to invoke.

16.3.1 Load/store instructions

The load and store instructions do not apply any interpretation to the data. They only move data and therefore never take any data-dependent traps. This scheme allows moving completely arbitrary bit patterns in and out of registers, and allows completely transparent saving/restoring of registers.

Load and Store Quadword Unaligned (LDQ_U, STQ_U) integer instructions ignore the low three bits of the byte address and always transfer an aligned quadword (see Fig. 16.7 for an example of using LDQ_U and STQ_U instructions). These are used with the in-register byte-manipulation instructions to operate on byte, word, and unaligned data via short sequences of RISC instructions.

Example 1: Load Byte (unsigned)

7	6	5	4	3	2	1	0	

LDQ_U R2, 0(R1) | Byte | R2

EXTBL R2, R1, R2 | 0 | Byte | R2

Example 2: Store Byte

7	6	5	4	3	2	1	0	

LDQ_U R2, 0(R1) | Old | R2

INSBL R0, R1, R3 | New | R2

MSKBL R2, R1, R2 | | R2

OR R2, R3, R2 | New | R2

STQ_U R2, 0(R1) | New | 0(R1)

Example 3: Explicit Load Quadword

7	6	5	4	3	2	1	0	

LDQ_U R2, 0(R1) | Low part | R2

| 15 | 14 | 13 | 12 | 11 | 10 | 9 | 8 | |

LDQ_U R3, 7(R1) | High part | R3

| 7 | 6 | 5 | 4 | 3 | 2 | 1 | 0 | |

EXTBL R2, R1, R2 | Low part | R2

EXTQH R3, R1, R3 | High part | R3

OR R2, R3, R2 | High part | Low part | R2

Figure 16.7 Examples of using load/store instructions in Alpha.

Load-locked and store-conditional (LDQ_I, LDI_I, STQ_C, DTL_C) integer instructions are included in the architecture to facilitate atomic updates of microprocessor shared data. As described previously, they can be used in short sequences of RISC instructions to do atomic read-modify-writes. Note that changing the LDQ_U/STQ_U in example 2 to AND/LDQ_I/STQ_C/BEQ gives a byte/store sequence that is safe in a multiprocessor environment.

There are two related load address instructions, LA calculates the effective address and writes it into Rc. LDAH first shifts the displacement left 16 bits, then calculates the effective address and writes it into Rc. LDAH is included to give a simple way of creating most 32-bit constants in a pair of instructions. 64-bit constants are loaded with LDQ instructions.

16.3.2 Operate instructions

The register-to-register operate instructions are classified into five groups: integer arithmetic, logical, byte-manipulation, floating-point, and miscellaneous. All instructions operate on 64-bit quadwords unless otherwise specified.

The integer arithmetic instructions are add, subtract, multiply, and compare. Add, subtract, and multiply have variants that enable arithmetic overflow traps. They also have longword variants that check for 32-bit overflow (instead of 64) and force all the high 33 bits of the result equal to bit 31. Add and subtract also have scaled variants that shift the first operand left by 2 or 3 bits (with no overflow checking) to speed up the arithmetic involved in simple subscripted addresses. The UMULH instruction gives the high 64 bits of an unsigned 128-bit product, and may be used for dividing by a constant. There is no integer divide instruction; instead, a subroutine is used to divide by a nonconstant. The compares are signed or unsigned and write a Boolean result (0 to 1) to the target register.

The logical instructions are AND, OR, and XOR, with the second operand optionally complemented (ANDNOT, ORNOT, XORNOT). The shifts are shift left logical, shift right logical, and shift right arithmetic. The 6-bit shift count is given by Rb or a literal. The conditional move instructions test Ra (same tests as the branching instructions) and conditionally move Rb to Rc. These can be used to eliminate branches in short sequences such as MIN(a,b).

The byte-manipulation instructions are used with the Load and Store Unaligned instructions to manipulate short unaligned strings of bytes. Long strings should be manipulated in groups of eight (aligned quadwords) whenever possible. The byte-manipulation instructions are fundamentally masked shifts. They differ from normal shifts by having a byte count (0...7) instead of a bit count (0...63), and by zeroing some bytes of the result, based on the data size given in the function field.

The extract (EXTxx) instructions extract part of a 1-, 2-, 4-, or 8-byte field from a quadword and place the resulting bytes in a field of zeros. A single EXTxL instruction can perform byte or word loads, pulling the datum out of a quadword and placing it in the low end of a register with high-order zeros. A pair of EXTxL/EXTxH instructions can perform unaligned loads, pulling the two parts of an unaligned datum out of two quadwords and placing the parts in result registers, where they are ready for combining into the full datum by a simple OR.

The insert (INSxx) and mask (MSKxx) instructions position new data and zero out of old data in registers for storing bytes, word, and unaligned data.

The compare-byte instruction allows character-string search-and-compare to be done eight bytes at a time. The ZAP instructions allow zeroing or arbitrary patterns of bytes in a register. These instructions allow very fast implementations of the C language string routines, among other uses.

The floating-point arithmetic instructions are add, subtract, multiply, divide, compare, and convert. The first four have variants for IEEE and VAX, single and double. They also have variants that enable combinations of arithmetic traps, and that specify the rounding mode. The single-precision instructions write 64-bit results, but do exponent checking and rounding to single-precision ranges. The compare instructions write a Boolean result (zero or nonzero) to the target register. The converts transfer between single and double, floating-point and integer, and two forms of VAX double (D-float and G-float). A combination of hardware and software provides full IEEE arithmetic. Operations on VAX-reserved operands, dirty zeros, IEEE denormals, infinities, and non-a-numbers are done in software.

There are also a few floating-point instructions that move data without applying any interpretation to it. These include a complete set of conditional move instructions, similar to the integer conditional moves.

The miscellaneous instructions include memory prefetching instructions to help decrease memory *latency* (see Glossary), a Read Cycle Counter instruction for performance measurement, a Trap Barrier instruction for forcing precise arithmetic traps, and Memory Barrier instructions for forcing multiprocessor read-write ordering.

Examples in Fig. 16.7 show the usage of some of the operate instructions.

16.3.3 Branching instructions

The branching instructions in Alpha include conditional branches, unconditional branches, and calculated jumps. Also, the architecture contains improvements over conditional moves to achieve an efficient branching performance.

Register Ra is tested by the integer conditional branch instructions for an opcode-specified condition (>0 >=0 =0 !=0 <=0 <0 even odd) and either branches to the target address or falls through to the updated PC address. The floating-point conditional branches are the same, except they do not include even/odd tests. Arbitrary testing and faulting on VAX or IEEE nonfinite values can be done by sequences of compare instructions and branch instructions. Logical or arithmetic instructions can combine compare results without using branches.

Also, register Ra receives the updated PC from unconditional branch instructions for subroutine linkage and branch to the target address. Register Ra, which will have the same values as those in R31, may be used if no linkage is needed. Calculated jumps write the updated PC to Ra for subroutine linkage and branch to the target address in Rb. Calculated jumps are used for subroutine call, return, CASE (SWITCH) statements, and coroutine linkage.

Alpha provides three types of branching hints for a better arithmetic performance. The first one is an architected static branch prediction rule which means forward conditional branches are predicted as not-taken, and backwards as taken. The architects claim that to the extent that this rule is followed, programs can run faster with little hardware cost. Nevertheless, one has to perform dynamic branch prediction, perhaps less frequently. The second hint is related to computed jump targets.

In order to provide instruction offset information within a page, 14-instruction bits are provided. These are often enough to start a fastest-level instruction cache fetch many cycles before the actual target value is known. Instruction bits which are otherwise unused are defined to give the low bits of the most likely target, using the same target calculation as unconditional branches.

The third hint is for subroutine and coroutine returns. By marking each branch and jump as 'call', 'return', or 'neither', the architecture provides on implementation enough information to maintain a small stack of likely subroutine return addresses. This implementation can be used to prefetch subroutine returns quickly. These provisions together with the conditional move instructions speed up the branching sequences and eliminate some unnecessary branches.

Only 43 bits of virtual address are used in the initial implementations of AXP. But, all these AXP systems check the remaining 21 bits. This is done in order to support later implementations which will use all 64 bits. Also, initial implementations use only 34 bits of physical address while the page-size parameters and Page Table Entry (PTE) formats allow growth to 48 bits and pages are of size 8KB (the design supports a size of up to 64KB). In fact, the hint provided by the architecture allows groups of 8, 64, or 512 pages to be treated as a single large page, thus effectively extending the page-size range by a factor of 1000 or more. Each PTE format also has one bit reserved for future expansion. Many PALcode registers like the PS or ASN are designed to be 64 bits in length with future expansion in mind.

All traps, interrupts, exceptions, and machine checks are handled by PALcode routines. PALcode establishes the initial state of the machine before execution of the first software instruction. The support for any standard operating system is done by PALcode routines for a given operating system and they are flexible. They handle all access to physical hardware resources, including physical main memory and memory-mapped I/O device registers. Implementers are given the opportunity to design their own set of PALcode routines meant for special applications like real-time systems in addition to supporting the basic operating system functions.

One hurdle that would hinder the performance of AXP is exception handling. The PALcode routines can deliver exception-handling routines with room for a gradual improvement. Generally, the PALcode routines working as a supplement provide the opportunity to study the present design and performance of the Alpha architecture and modify later on, if needed, like removing unnecessary instructions.

16.3.4 PALcode library

A privileged architecture library (PALcode) is a set of subroutines that are specific to a particular Alpha operating system implementation. These subroutines provide context switching, interrupts, exceptions, and memory management. PALcode is similar to the BIOS libraries that are provided in personal computers. It is written in standard machine mode with some implementation-specific extensions to provide access to low-level hardware. One version of PALcode allows AXP implementations to run the full OpenVMS operating system by reflecting many of the OpenVMS VAX features. The OpenVMS PALcode instructions let Alpha run OpenVMS with little more hardware than that found on a conventional RISC machine: the PAL mode bit itself, plus 4 extra protection bits in each translation buffer entry. Similarly, other versions of PALcode can be developed for special applications like real-time, data, and system security. Figure 16.8 shows a summary of OpenVMS PALcode routines.

Alpha does not contain a subroutine call instruction that moves a register window by a fixed amount. Thus, Alpha is a good match for programming languages with many parameters as well as those with no parameters. Also, Alpha does not contain a global integer overflow enable bit. Such a bit would need to be changed at every subroutine boundary when a FORTRAN program calls a C program.

Mnemonic	Name	Function
AMOVRM	Atomic move Register/Memory	Provide a multiprocessor interlocked store of a byte, word, longword or quadword from a source register to a byte-addressable memory location and provide a memory-to-memory transfer of up to 63 aligned longwords. This routine may be used only by translated VAX programs and will be eliminated from the architecture in a future implementation.
AMOVRR	Atomic move Register/Memory	Provide a multiprocessor interlocked store of a byte, word, longword or quadword from up to two source registers to up to two byte-addressable memory locations. This routine may be used only by translated images.
CRFLUSH	Cache flush	Flush one physical page from current processor's cache.
CHME	Change mode to Executive	Save context and change to Executive mode.
CHMK	Change mode to Kernel	Save context and change to Kernel mode.
CHMS	Change mode to Supervisor	Save context and change to Supervisor mode.
CHMU	Change mode to User	Save context and change to User mode.
INSQxxx	Insert entry in queue	Routines to insert entry at the head or tail of a longword or quadword queue. Variations also exist for interlocked queue access among multiple processors.
LDQP	Load quadword	Return value of a quadword-aligned physical memory location.
MFPR	Move from processor register	Return internal processor register value.
MTPR	Move to processor register	Store a value in an internal processor register.
PROBER	Probe read access	Check read accessibility of specified address range.
PROBEW	Probe write access	Check write accessibility of specified address range.
RD_PS	Read processor status	Return processor status.
READ_UNQ	Read unique context	Read hardware process context value previously written by WRITE_UNQ.
REI	Return from interrupt or exception	Restore context from current stack.
REMQxxx	Remove entry from queue	Routines to remove entry from the head or tail of a longword or quadword queue. Variations also exist for interlocked queue access among multiple processors and for access to queues known to be entirely memory-resident.
RSCC	Read system cycle counter	Return system cycle counter.

Figure 16.8 OpenVMS PALcode routines.

These data types available in VAX are not supported on AXP hardware: Octaword, H_floating, D_floating (load/store and convert from/to G_floating is allowed), Variable-Length Bit Field, Character String, Trailing Numeric String, Leading Separate Numeric String, and Packed Decimal String.

In Alpha, a floating-point trap can occur if one of the following events is encountered:

- Invalid operation

- Division by zero

- Overflow

- Underflow

- Inexact result

- Integer overflow

(Note that the trap support for the last three conditions may be eliminated in future versions of AXP systems.)

Some miscellaneous instructions in Alpha are:

CALL_PAL	Call Privileged Architecture Library Routine
FETCH	Prefetch Data
FETCH_M	Prefetch Data, Modification Anticipated
MB	Memory Barrier
RPCC	Read Process Cycle Counter
TRAPB	Trap Barrier

The VAX compatibility instructions are:

RC	Read and Clear
RS	Read and Set

These are provided only for VEST; they should not be used in native Alpha code because it may be discontinued sometime in the future.

PALcode is used to implement the following functions:

- Instructions that require complex sequencing as an atomic operation

- Instructions that require VAX-style interlocked memory access

- Privileged instructions

- Memory management control, including translation buffer (TB management)

- Context swapping

- Interrupt and exception dispatching

- Power-up initialization and booting
- Console functions
- Emulation of instructions with no hardware support

The PALcode environment differs from the normal environment in the following ways:

- Complete control of the machine state
- Interrupts are disabled
- Implementation-specific hardware functions are enabled
- Some memory management traps are prevented

PALcode uses the Alpha instruction set for most of its operations. A small number of additional functions are needed to implement the PALcode. There are five opcodes reserved to implement PALcode functions: PALRES0, PALRES1, PALRES2, PALRES3, and PALRES4. These instructions produce an illegal Instruction Trap if executed outside the PALcode environment.

Because PALcode is resident in main memory and holds privileged data structures in main memory, the operating system code that allocates physical memory cannot use all of the physical memory. But this would be negligible, as PALcode occupies a small chunk of memory. Some PALcode instructions are:

BPT	Breakpoint trap
BUGCHK	Bugcheck trap
GENTRAP	Generate trap
RDUNIQUE	Read unique value
WRUNIQUE	Write unique value
DRAINA	Drain aborts
HALT	Halt processor

OpenVMS VAX has been a very successful product for DEC. As was expected, the Alpha designers have provided support to already installed bases of OpenVMS VAX users although limitations of VAX are becoming visible after the advent of AXP. The VAX was designed in the late 1970s and the architecture was totally specific to running VMS, whereas Alpha AXP was planned to be more open and flexible. In fact, it was designed to be so flexible to support not only OpenVMS but also Unix and Microsoft Windows NT and, strictly speaking, any operating system. Also, the compatibility issues were carefully studied and no permanent support for any backward compatibility is considered for Alpha, which would be a significant constraint in the future. Any hardware fixes or support, keeping only OpenVMS in mind, would mean compromising performance when considered from the viewpoint of supporting any other operating system. On the other hand, OpenVMS AXP, originally written for VAX, needed to keep the majority of VAX features to avoid any software rewriting and to be able to deliver total solutions to customers in the near future.

Alpha designers have come up with the concept of the privileged architecture library as a software extension of the hardware. It resembles BIOS on personal computers and microcode instructions on VAX. It is more like an interface of the hardware to the operating system. Hardware features required by a given operating system or even a special application in principle can be provided in PALcode. A separate set of PALcode routines can be crafted and loaded for each operating system.

In CISC architectures like VAX, hardwired microcode is used to provide complex instructions which cannot be directly supported in the CPU chip. On Alpha AXP, the designers chose to use PALcode for these functions as a more modest way to provide a flexible interface that could span many operating systems. Examples of such a PAL function are hardware exception delivery, translation buffer, and acknowledging an interrupt. In order to support atomicity of instructions like the CISC architecture does for VAX, PALcode routines can merge several instructions into a single operation. This makes it possible to execute such widely used VAX instructions as insert entry in queue (INSQ) and remove entry from queue (REMQUE). OpenVMS-specific PALcode routines also provide backward compatibility for VAX applications.

PALcode routines use standard instructions provided by the Alpha AXP architecture. In fact, a special environment for PALcode is made possible in the architecture, which gives an efficient way for PALcode to perform its functions and use specially available RISC instructions. This special environment is called *PALmode*. It has three main characteristics. First, all interrupts are disabled, allowing PALcode to provide atomic operations. Most of the PALcode instruction stream is guaranteed to execute to completion. Second, the PALcode routines have privileged access to the internal hardware register and physical memory. These processor control registers are available in PALmode only. Third, I-stream virtual memory mapping is disabled. In PALmode, virtual addresses directly correspond to physical memory addresses. Translation-table management, page-fault exception handling, and other similar memory management functions of PALcode need this feature. Using CALL_PAL instruction or via a hardware event, the PALcode routines can be invoked. Doing so will trigger the following sequence of events:

- The instruction pipeline is drained. No further instructions can start until the current ones complete.
- The specific PALcode routine is then entered by dispatching through a table of PALcode return entry points.
- Virtual memory mapping and interrupts are disabled by the CPU.
- PALcode routine instructions are executed.
- Upon completion of the PALcode routine, the memory mapping and interrupts are enabled.
- The instruction execution before entering the PALmode is resumed.

Many VAX-like instructions in the PALcode make it easier to port applications. Because these instructions are noninterruptable, they execute as atomic instructions as on VAX. Some examples of PALcode instructions are change mode to kernel, issue a breakpoint, and insert or remove an entry from queue. A list of PALcode routines for OpenVMS is shown in Fig. 16.8.

16.4 SUMMARY

A pragmatic outlook into the future of open systems has been carefully considered in the design of Alpha architecture. The PALcode library and RISC architecture supplement a unique 64-bit design to provide a hardware platform on which powerful operating systems like OpenVMS, Windows NT, and OSF are being developed.

17

Binary Translator

In AXP systems, the binary translator reproduces the behavior of programs developed on VAX systems by generating a sequence of AXP instructions. Typically, much of the state information of the old machine is kept in registers in the new machine. Translated code reproduces faithfully the calling standard, implicit state, instruction side effects, branching flow, and other artifacts of the old machine. Translated programs can be much faster than interpreters or emulators, but certainly slower than the natively compiled programs. The binary translator of OpenVMS AXP ensures the following key issues for VAX compatibility:

1. Translated code on Alpha AXP computers for programs developed on VAX systems to meet or exceed the performance of the original code on VAX architecture.

2. Translation of almost all user-mode applications from the Open-VMS VAX system to the OpenVMS AXP system.

3. If translation is not possible, generation of explicit messages that give reasons and specify what source changes are necessary.

The translator also provides optional source analysis information and reproduction of subtle old-architectural details at the cost of run-time performance, for example, complex instruction set computer (CISC) instruction atomicity for multithreaded applications and exact arithmetic traps for sophisticated error handlers.

17.1 VEST: VAX IMAGE TRANSLATOR

The VAX Executable Software Translator (VEST) translates VAX images to run on AXP computers. The function of VEST involves two steps: analyzing VAX code and generating Alpha AXP code. The translated images produced are OpenVMS AXP images and may be run just like native images. Translated images run with the assistance of the translated image environment (TIE), which also will be discussed in this chapter (see Fig. 17.1). The VEST binary translator is written in C++ and runs on VAX and Alpha AXP computers. TIE is written in BLISS, the OpenVMS system programming language and Alpha AXP assembler.

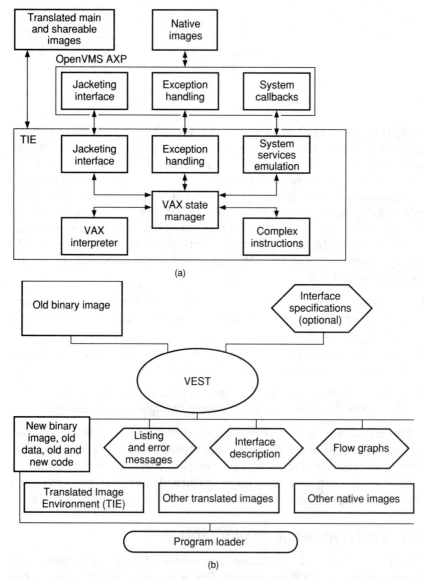

Figure 17.1 (a) Run-time environment of VEST and TIE; (b) Binary translation in Alpha AXP systems.

VEST locates VAX code by disassembling the code at known entry points and tracing the program's flow of control recursively. Main and global routines, debug symbol table entries, and optional information files (including run-time feedback from the TIE) provide the necessary entry points. Context information includes condition code usage, register contents, stack depth, and other information that allows VEST to generate optimized code. VEST builds a flow graph that consists of basic blocks, annotated with information derived from parsing instructions. VEST analysis of the so-generated flow graph results in propagating context information to each basic block and eliminating unnecessary operations. This analysis helps achieve good performance.

VEST analysis of the code can detect many problems, including some that indicate latent bugs in the source image. For example, VEST can detect uninitialized variables, improperly formed VAX CASE instructions, stack depth mismatches along two different paths to the same code (the program expects data to be at a certain stack depth), improperly formed returns from subroutines, and modifications to a VAX call frame. A latent bug in the source image should be fixed, since the translated image may demonstrate incorrect behavior due to that bug.

Also, analysis detects the use of unsupported OpenVMS features including unsupported system services. The analysis report indicates that the source image must be modified to remove the use of these features.

For example, in the Alpha architecture there are no condition codes. Without analysis it would be required to compute condition codes for each VAX instruction even if the codes were not used. Furthermore, several forms of analysis were invented to allow correct translation. For example, VEST automatically finds out if a subroutine does a normal return.

17.1.1 Code generation

VEST converts each VAX instruction into zero or more Alpha AXP instructions. VAX-to-AXP instruction mapping is relatively easy because there are more Alpha AXP registers than VAX registers. VAX architecture has only 15 registers, which are used for both floating-point and integer operations.

Alpha AXP architecture has separate integer and floating-point registers. VAX registers R0 through R14 are mapped to Alpha AXP R0 through R14 for all operations except floating point. Registers R12, R13, and R14 retain their VAX designations as argument pointer, frame pointer, and stack pointer, and R15 is used to resolve PC-relative references. Floating-point operations are mapped to F0 through F14.

VAX architecture has condition codes that may be referenced explicitly. In translated images, condition codes are mapped into R22 and R23. R23 is used as a fast condition code register for positive/negative/zero results. R22 contains all four condition code bits, which are calculated only when necessary. All remaining Alpha AXP registers are used as scratch registers or for OpenVMS AXP standard calls.

17.1.2 Translated images

The translated image environment contains the run-time VAX interpreter. The interpreter needs the original VAX instructions as a fallback. Therefore, in addition to generating a translated image that has the same format as an OpenVMS AXP image, VEST also outputs and retains the original OpenVMS VAX image as well as the Alpha AXP instructions that were generated for the VAX code. Also, some error handlers look up the call stack for pointers to specific VAX instructions. The addresses of statically allocated data in the translated image are identical to their VAX addresses. The image contains a VAX-to-Alpha AXP address-mapping table for use during lookups and may contain an instruction atomicity table.

Native images in OpenVMS AXP use different conventions than the OpenVMS VAX calling standard. Automatic jacketing services are provided in the TIE to convert calls using one set of conventions into the other. In many cases, jacketing services permit substitution of a native shareable image without modification. However, a jacket routine is sometimes required. For example, on OpenVMS AXP systems, the translated FORTRAN Run-Time Library, FORRTL_TV, invokes the native Alpha AXP library DEC$FORRTL for I/O-related subroutine calls. DEC$FORRTL has a different interface than FORRTL has on an OpenVMS VAX system. For these calls, FORRTL_TV contains handwritten jacket routines.

17.2 TRANSLATED IMAGE ENVIRONMENT (TIE)

The translated image environment (TIE, see Fig. 17.2) is a run-time feature in OpenVMS AXP. TIE acts as a supplement to VEST and helps in executing translated OpenVMS VAX images under the OpenVMS AXP operating system. Failure to find all code during translation, VAX instruction guarantees, instruction atomicity, memory update, and preserving VAX exceptions are some complications that may occur when a translated OpenVMS VAX image is run under the OpenVMS AXP operating system.

VEST generates code to call one of the TIE lookup routines whenever it encounters a branch or subroutine call to an unknown destination. The lookup routines map a VAX instruction address to a translated Alpha AXP code address. If an address mapping exists, then a transfer to the translated code is performed. Otherwise, the VAX interpreter

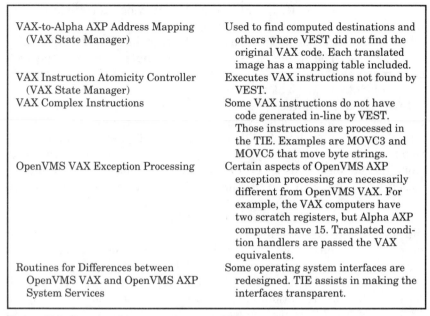

VAX-to-Alpha AXP Address Mapping (VAX State Manager)	Used to find computed destinations and others where VEST did not find the original VAX code. Each translated image has a mapping table included.
VAX Instruction Atomicity Controller (VAX State Manager)	Executes VAX instructions not found by VEST.
VAX Complex Instructions	Some VAX instructions do not have code generated in-line by VEST. Those instructions are processed in the TIE. Examples are MOVC3 and MOVC5 that move byte strings.
OpenVMS VAX Exception Processing	Certain aspects of OpenVMS AXP exception processing are necessarily different from OpenVMS VAX. For example, the VAX computers have two scratch registers, but Alpha AXP computers have 15. Translated condition handlers are passed the VAX equivalents.
Routines for Differences between OpenVMS VAX and OpenVMS AXP System Services	Some operating system interfaces are redesigned. TIE assists in making the interfaces transparent.

Figure 17.2   Translated image environment (TIE).

executes the destination code. When the VAX interpreter encounters a flow-of-control change, it checks for returns to translated code. If the target of the flow change is translated code, the interpreter exits to this code. Otherwise the interpreter continues to interpret the target.

Lookup operations that transfer control to the interpreter record the starting VAX code address in a hand-edited information file (HIF) entry. The VAX image can be retranslated then with the HIF information, resulting in an image that runs faster.

Lookup routines are also used to call native Alpha AXP (nontranslated) routines. The TIE supplies the required special autojacketing processing that allows interoperation between translated and native routines, with no manual intervention. At load time, each translated image identifies itself to the TIE and supplies a mapping table used by the lookup routines. The TIE maintains a cache of translations to speed up the actual lookup processing.

Every translated image contains both the original VAX code and the corresponding Alpha AXP code. When a translated image identifies itself, the TIE marks its original VAX addresses with the page protection called *fault on execute* (FOE). An Alpha AXP processor that attempts to execute an instruction on one of these pages generates an access violation fault, which is processed by a TIE condition handler to convert the FOE fault into an appropriate destination address lookup operation. For example, the FOE might occur when a translated routine returns to its caller. If the caller was interpreted, then its return address is a VAX code address instead of a translated VAX (Alpha AXP code) address. The Alpha AXP processor attempts to execute the VAX code and generates an FOE condition. The TIE condition handler converts this into a JMP lookup operation.

Instruction guarantees, characteristics of a computer architecture, are inherent to instructions executed on that architecture. For example, on a VAX computer, if instruction 1 writes data to memory and instruction 2 writes data to memory, a second processor must not see the write from instruction 1. This property is called *strict read-write ordering.*

The VEST/TIE pair can provide the illusion that a single CISC instruction is executed in its entirety, even though the underlying translation is a series of RISC instructions. VEST/TIE can also provide the illusion of two processors updating adjacent memory bytes without interference, even though the underlying RISC instructions manipulate four or eight bytes at a time. Finally, VEST/TIE can provide exact memory read-write ordering and arithmetic exceptions, e.g., overflow. All these provisions are optional and require extra execution time. Figure 17.3 shows the differences between various instruction guarantees in VAX and Alpha AXP systems as well as for translated VAX programs.

Some optional files such as image information files (IIFs), symbol information files (SIFs), and hand-edited information files are generated by the VEST/TIE pair in addition to the translated image.

VEST-created IIFs automatically provide information about shareable image interfaces. The information includes the addresses of entry points, names of routines, and resource utilization.

Topic	VAX	Translated VAX	Native Alpha AXP
Instruction Atomicity	An entire VAX instruction	An entire translated VAX instruction with /PRESERVE= INSTRUCTION _ATOMICITY and TIE's instruction atomicity controller, else a single Alpha AXP instruction	A single Alpha AXP instruction
Byte Granularity	Yes, hardware ensures this	Yes, with /PRESERVE= MEMORY_ATOMICITY	Yes, via LDx_L, merge, STx_C sequence
Interlocked Update	Yes, for aligned datum using interlock instructions	Yes, for aligned datum using VAX interlock instructions	Yes, via LDx_L, modify, STx_C sequence

Figure 17.3 Instruction guarantees in OpenVMS.

VEST generates SIFs automatically to control the global symbol table in a translated shared library, facilitating interoperation between translated and native images.

TIE generates HIF automatically, which may be hand-edited to supply information that VEST cannot deduce. HIFs contain directives to tell VEST about undetected entry points, to force it to change specific assumptions about an image during translation, and to provide known interface properties to be prepaged into an IIF.

17.3 PERFORMANCE OF VEST

In VEST, users can select several architectural assumptions and optimizations, including alignment, instruction atomicity, memory granularity, and D-float precision.

Unaligned memory operations cause alignment faults, which are handled transparently by software at significant run-time expense. The user may direct VEST to assume that data references are unaligned whenever alignment information is not available. Alpha instructions support only naturally aligned longword (32-bit) and quadword (64-bit) memory operations.

Multitasking and multiprocessing programs may depend upon instruction atomicity and memory operation characteristics similar to those of the VAX architecture. VEST uses special code sequences to produce exact VAX memory characteristics. VEST and the TIE coordinate to ensure VAX instruction atomicity when instructed to do so.

D-float precision with only 53-bit mantissas is supported on Alpha architecture, whereas the VAX architecture provides 56-bit mantissas. The user may select translation with either 53-bit hardware support, which is faster, or 56-bit software support, which is slower.

17.4 UNTRANSLATABLE IMAGES

Some characteristics make OpenVMS VAX images untranslatable, including exception handling, direct reference to undocumented system services, exact memory management requirements, and image format.

Images that depend on examining the VAX processor status longword (PSL) during exception handling must be modified, because the VAX PSL is not available within exception handlers. Some software contains references to unsupported and undocumented system services, such as an internal-to-VMS service, which parses image symbol tables. VEST highlights these references. Programs that use images as data are not able to read OpenVMS AXP images without modifications, because the image formats are different.

17.5   INSTRUCTION ATOMICITY

The VAX requires that interrupted instructions complete or appear never to have started.

Since translation is a process of converting one VAX instruction to potentially many Alpha AXP instructions, run-time processing must achieve this guarantee of instruction atomicity. Hence, a VAX instruction atomicity controller (IAC) was created to manipulate the Alpha AXP state to an equivalent VAX state. When a translated asynchronous event-processing routine is called, the IAC is invoked. The IAC examines the Alpha AXP instruction stream and either (1) backs up the interrupted program counter to restart at the equivalent VAX instruction boundary or (2) executes the remaining instructions to the next boundary. Many VAX programs do not require this guarantee to operate correctly, so VEST emits code that is VAX instruction-atomic only if the qualifier

```
/PRESERVE=INSTRUCTION_ATOMICITY
```

is specified when translating an image.

VEST-generated code consists of four sections that are detected by the IAC. These sections have the following functions:

- Get operands to temporary registers
- Operate on these temporary registers
- Atomically update VAX results that could generate side effects, i.e., cause an exception or interlocked access
- Perform any updates that cannot generate side effects, for example, register updates

The VAX interpreter achieves VAX instruction atomicity by using the atomic-move register to memory (AMOVRM) instruction, which is implemented in privileged architecture library (PAL) subroutines. At the beginning of each interpreted VAX instruction, a read-and-set-flag (RS) instruction sets a flag that is cleared when an interrupt occurs on the processor. AMOVRM tests the flag and, if set, performs the update and returns a success indication. If the flag is clear, the AMOVRM instruction indicates failure, and the interpreter reprocesses the interrupted instruction.

VAX instruction atomicity ensures that an arithmetic instruction does not have any partially updated memory locations, as viewed from the processor on which that instruction is executed. In a multiprocessing environment, inspection from another processor could result in a perception of partial results.

Since an Alpha AXP processor accesses memory only in aligned long-words or quadwords, it is therefore not byte-granular. To achieve byte granularity, VEST generates a load-locked/store-conditional code sequence, which ensures that a memory location is updated as if it were byte-granular. This sequence is used also to ensure interlocked access to shared memory. Longword-size updates to aligned locations are performed using normal load/store instructions to ensure longword granularity.

Many multiprocessing VAX programs depend on byte granularity for memory update. VEST generates byte-granular code if the qualifier

```
/PRESERVE=MEMORY_ATOMICITY
```

is specified when translating an image. In addition, VEST generates strict read-write ordering code if the qualifier

```
/PRESERVE=READ_WRITE_ORDERING
```

is specified when translating an image.

17.6   VAX EXCEPTIONS

Alpha AXP instructions do not have the same exception characteristics as VAX instructions. For instance, an arithmetic fault is imprecise, i.e., not synchronous with the instruction that caused it. The Alpha AXP hardware generates an arithmetic fault that is mapped into an OpenVMS AXP high-performance arithmetic (HPARITH) exception to retain compatibility with the VAX condition handler. Most VAX languages do not require precise exceptions. For those that do, such as BASIC, VEST generates the necessary Trap Barrier (TRAPB) instructions if

```
/PRESERVE=FLOATING_EXCEPTIONS
```

is specified when translating an image.

17.7   OPENVMS DIFFERENCES

We can identify three main differences between OpenVMS VAX and OpenVMS AXP: functional differences, issues related to exception handling, and complex instructions.

Most OpenVMS AXP system services are identical to their OpenVMS VAX counterparts. Services that depend on a VAX-specific mechanism are changed for the Alpha AXP architecture. The TIE intervenes in such system services to ensure the translated code sees the old interface.

For example, the declare change mode handler ($DCLCMH) system service establishes a handler for VAX change mode to user (CHMU) instructions. The handler is invoked as if it were an interrupt service routine, required to use the VAX return from interrupt or exception (REI) instruction to return to the invoker's context. On OpenVMS AXP systems, the handler is called as a normal procedure. To ensure compatibility, the TIE inserts its own handler when calling OpenVMS AXP $DCLCMH. When a CHMU is invoked on Alpha AXP computers, the TIE handler calls the handler of the translated image, using the same VAX-specific mechanisms that the handler expects.

OpenVMS AXP exception processing is almost identical to that performed in the OpenVMS VAX system. The major difference is that the VAX mechanism array needs only to hold the value of two temporary registers, R0 and R1, whereas the Alpha AXP mechanism array needs to hold the value of 15 temporary registers, R0, R1, and R16 through R28.

Translating some VAX instructions would require many Alpha AXP instructions. Instead, VEST generates code that calls a TIE subroutine. Subroutines are implemented in two ways: (1) handwritten native emulation routines, e.g., MOVC5, and (2) VEST-translated VAX emulation routines, e.g., POLYH.

17.8 SUMMARY

Together, VEST and TIE can translate and run most existing user-mode VAX binary images. From the performance viewpoint, it is obvi-

Program SPECmark89	VAX Time on VAX 6610 (83.3 MHz)	VEST Translated Time on DEC 7000 AXP (167 MHz)	Native Time on DEC 7000 AXP (167 MHz)
gcc	1.9	–data not available–	—
expresso	3.1	2.7	1.0
spice2g6	2.8	1.8	1.0
doduc	2.9	3.0	1.0
nasa7	4.4	6.2	1.0
li	2.7	4.2	1.0
eqntott	3.3	2.2	1.0
matrix300	8.8	4.2	1.0
fpppp	3.8	2.7	1.0
tomcatv	5.3	2.9	1.0
Geometic Mean (without Gcc)	3.8	3.1	1.0

Figure 17.4 Translated VAX performance.

ous that CISC designs have certain disadvantages over the RISC designs. Some benchmark results (SPECmark89) are shown in Fig. 17.4. Note that performance depends on the frequency of use of VAX features that are not present in Alpha AXP computers. In order to exploit the performance of Alpha, OpenVMS is tactically ported from its VAX version, avoiding much coding in order to deliver the product in time. The issue of supporting existing applications and users of VAX on AXP-based platforms is taken as another important goal by Digital when they worked on porting OpenVMS VAX to OpenVMS AXP. Therefore, many VAX flavors are incorporated into the Alpha AXP architecture to help migration of applications from VAX to AXP with the least impact on the performance degradation, essentially meeting the requirement that the application should run faster on AXP platforms.

18

VAX-to-AXP Migration

18.1 INTRODUCTION

Fast CPU, available technology for a matching memory interface, and Digital's effort to smooth the migration from VAX to AXP have together made the Alpha series of computers one of the most attractive data crunchers today. For this reason, many industries are keen to migrate their applications from the VAX platform to the AXP platform. Recognizing users' typical requirements for such a migration, DEC has made suitable additions to Alpha architecture as well as OpenVMS AXP architecture. The privileged architecture library (PAL) routine library and VEST Binary Translation are two notable supplements.

Memory alignment problems and synchronization are two of the major issues to be considered for VAX-AXP migration.

VAX provides such basic instructions as read-modify-write, whereas AXP, being a RISC design, provides only the load-and-store type of memory operation. This is how RISC machines can be faster. In VAX a read-modify-write operation is an atomic operation, i.e., no interrupt is possible before the complete instruction is executed. On the other hand, the same read, modify, and write sequence tends to have multiple RISC instructions and hence be interruptable.

Alignment is an attribute of a data item that refers to its placement in memory. A data item is naturally aligned when its address is an integral multiple of the size of the data in bytes. For example,

A byte is aligned at any address.

A word is aligned at any address that is a multiple of 2.

A longword is aligned at any address that is a multiple of 4.

A quadword is aligned at any address that is a multiple of 8.

Data that is not aligned is referred to as unaligned.

18.2 SYNCHRONIZATION PROBLEMS

By synchronization, we mean the technique of maintaining sequential order for handling events of a typical process. This is a problem in AXP because no update as a part of a single atomic instruction is possible on AXP. While VAX can do read, modify, and write as a single unit function, AXP requires three instructions to do the same. There is a likelihood of some event interrupting the AXP's sequence of three instructions and accessing the same memory location, causing a false data to be read.

A *thread* is a piece or group of instructions accessing a memory location. Multiple threads meant to occur asynchronously, like asynchronous system trap (AST) routines, can also address the same memory location. In such cases, the synchronization needs to be handled manually by the AXP programmer. This involves identifying shared data and locating those portions of the threads that access the shared data. Normally, this is not an issue for a majority of the programs because the system library routines, kernel, and the optimizations performed by compilers handle the synchronization to a satisfying extent. So, a high-level language programmer does not normally feel the need for manual handling of coordination of events, but for an application involving simultaneous execution of multiple threads the synchronization problem tends to be critical.

For example, consider an image-processing application interfaced to a real-time data acquisition system. Here, threads spread over different modules of the image processor may empty the data from the buffer and perform data reduction. The real-time module, usually being faster, can then use the same buffer to dump the collected data. In this example, we can see a need for each of the distributed threads of the image processor to know which buffer is empty and in what sequence the buffer was emptied. Otherwise, a given thread may read the same data set over and over again or read a data set which is distorted by another thread. Typically, the memory subsystem of a complex instruction set computer like VAX can carry extra instructions than that provided by the hardware in order to solve problems like this by protecting shared data. A reduced instruction set computer like Alpha cannot afford to do this because of significant overhead that such an extra instruction set imposes on the overall performance. An RISC computer expects the software to handle such problems by using the basic functions that it provides in its architecture.

ASTs, exception handlers, DECthreads, and those threads used by the system services referred to in the process can constitute a group of threads in addition to the mainline code of a given process. These threads could eventually result in accessing faulty data due to the lack of synchronization. Here, ASTs are routines that interrupt the mainline code within the current process, exception handlers execute as a result of some exception like integer overflow, and DECthreads are used to create and control multiple concurrent threads within a process. If you wish to migrate your OpenVMS VAX application to an OpenVMS AXP platform, then you need to exercise caution for the integrity of shared data. Otherwise the program may give unpredictable results due to an inconsistent data occurrence in the shared data region. Two threads competing for the same memory location may not resolve properly the point of time to access the data.

Explicit synchronization mechanisms such as locks, mutual exclusive semaphores, and interlocked instructions to protect shared data are provided by OpenVMS VAX applications running on multiprocessor systems. However, on uniprocessor systems, many OpenVMS applications have depended on the synchronization guarantees provided by the VAX architecture to implicitly protect shared data used by multiple threads. The VAX architecture provides the capability of performing a read-modify-write operation as a single, noninterruptable sequence. This is called an *atomic update operation,* from the viewpoint of multiple application threads executing on a single processor. For example, applications that use a mutual exclusion semaphore variable to synchronize access to a critical region of code by multiple threads might depend on the semaphore's being incremented atomically from the viewpoint of those threads. On VAX systems, the architecture included many atomic instructions that provided this behavior, such as INCL (increment long instruction). RISC systems like Alpha can do only a single memory load or store in any one instruction, but not both; there is no possibility of an atomic update operation. Therefore, Alpha AXP architecture does not provide the same synchronization guarantees as the VAX architecture. On OpenVMS AXP systems, access to a semaphore variable or any data that can be accessed by multiple threads of execution must be explicitly synchronized.

18.3   ATOMICITY OF INSTRUCTION

Alpha AXP architecture does not contain any read-modify-write memory operations in its instruction set. Instead it provides a mechanism for determining if a sequence of instructions was interrupted or not, through a pair of instructions: load-locked (LDx_I) and store-conditional (STx_C). These instructions are used to solve the problem of a read-modify-write sequence's requiring three RISC instructions and thus being inherently interruptable, i.e., not atomic.

These instructions do not provide atomicity by blocking access to data, shared by competing threads, as interlocked instructions do on the VAX. Instead, the load-locked instruction sets a lock flag in addition to loading the requested data into a register. Before data is stored using the store-conditional instruction, the lock flag is checked. If the lock flag is set, the store-conditional will succeed. Otherwise, the store-conditional fails and the applications must retry the instruction sequence from the load-locked operations.

After the lock flag is set by the load-locked instruction, it can be cleared before the store-conditional instruction is executed, for any of the following reasons:

- Access was requested to a memory location in addition to the one accessed in the load-locked and store-conditional sequence.

- The current thread was interrupted by an exception or interrupt, e.g., hardware clock interrupt service routine.

- An interfering write from another processor was issued to the same memory location on multiprocessor systems.

- A PALcode call was issued during the sequence.

It is also important to note that these instructions can be used only for aligned longword and aligned quadword data.

Consider a situation where a process A loads data from memory into a register. Then, the operating system context switches to process B. Process B modifies the same data in memory that process A is using. Then, the operating system context switches back to process A and process A continues execution with stale data in its register, eventually storing a new value back to memory, overwriting the data that process B wrote.

In this example, if process A had used the load-locked instruction to load the data into the register, when it reached the store-conditional instruction in step 5 of the update sequence above, the store would not be done; instead, an interrupted sequence state would be reported to the process. Compilers can generate code that checks for this explicit failure and causes the entire sequence to be repeated, starting with the load-locked instruction. When the sequence executes without interruption, the store-conditional instruction succeeds, hence completing the operation as an atomic, or uninterrupted, update.

18.4 MEMORY GRANULARITY

Another difference between the VAX and Alpha AXP architectures is the memory granularity. The term *granularity* refers to the size of the smallest datum that can be read or written in a single memory operation, i.e., a grain of memory is the size of datum that can be read or written as a single unit. Note that a grain can include more than one datum. For example, consider a record called NAME containing first name, last name, and middle initial as fields. Now, you could think of two systems, one in which the whole record has to be read as a single unit and later the first name, etc., to be decoded, and another system which gives you an additional facility (of course, with some overhead for this function) of reading any fields in the record.

The VAX architecture requires hardware implementations to provide byte granularity. This means that process A writing byte "b1" does not interfere with process B writing byte "b2". Under all circumstances, both bytes are correctly written to memory without any synchronization being requested by the programmer. In VAX systems, this functionality is provided by the memory hardware subsystem that fetches, shifts, and merges multiple bytes of data as necessary to do the requested read, write, or update operation. Many VAX hardware implementations actually provide byte granularity through microcode in the memory subsystem, while the hardware itself does only longword operations, i.e., longword granularity in order to provide good memory performance.

This complexity in VAX memory subsystems, while desirable from the software viewpoint, is costly from the hardware viewpoint. Because it requires more complex hardware, the design, debug, and test of this complexity take longer during the development of a new VAX system than if this complexity was handled by the software. There is also an additional cost, in performance, for every memory operation, because there are many different memory reference cases to test for and handle. The VAX has to do this every time it accesses memory, but the problem occurs only rarely.

Therefore, when the Alpha AXP architecture was designed, the architects chose not to require byte granularity, but only quadword granularity from the hardware. This means that a quadword of memory is read, written, or updated for each memory reference. So when a programmer requests that a single byte of data from the middle of a quadword be loaded into a register, the code generated by the compiler:

1. Loads a quadword of data into the register, using an unaligned quadword load instruction (LDQ_U)

2. Computes through load (LDA) instruction the number of bits to shift left

3. Shifts the data in the register left (EXTQH) until the desired byte is in the lower-most byte of the register, thus getting rid of the unrequested bytes of data at higher addresses

4. Shifts the data in the register right (SRA) until the desire byte is in the lower-most byte of the register, thus getting rid of the unrequested bytes of data at higher addresses

Depending on which byte(s) are actually requested, various other code sequences can be generated, but the effect is the same. It is up to the software to extract the data actually requested from the quadword fetched. This is exactly what the VAX implementations were doing in hardware, usually through microcode in the memory subsystem.

There are several longword instructions included in the Alpha AXP architecture that provide longword granularity for memory access, but it is usually more optimal for compilers to make quadword memory references, as several data accesses can frequently be satisfied with one memory reference for fields that are contained within one aligned quadword. That is, shift the quadword data into one register in one direction to get the first field, and shift the quadword data differently into another register to get another field. Note that register-to-register operations, such as shifts or masks, are faster than memory references.

18.5   DATA ALIGNMENT

On Alpha AXP systems, software is responsible for the prevention of interference between processes for data that fall within an aligned quadword. The application programmer must understand the effects of quadword granularity and specify the data that must be handled specially for granularity reasons at compile time. With this information, the compilers can use a combination of quadword, longword, and load-locked and store-conditional sequences to provide byte granularity where it is required in an application.

In addition to being a performance consideration, data alignment is an important issue when you synchronize access to memory locations. Unaligned data references can require multiple memory operations to read the data, whereas aligned data can be read with a single memory operation. For example, if a compiler knows that a longword falls within an aligned quadword of memory, then it can issue a single quadword load instruction. However, if the longword might cross an aligned quadword boundary, then the compiler must either issue two aligned quadword load instructions or risk taking an alignment exception on a single load, which costs about 100 times as much in performance as the two quadword loads.

Just as in granularity, the Alpha AXP and VAX architectures differ in what they require to be done by hardware for unaligned data. The Alpha AXP architecture was designed to enable streamlining the memory reference paths in the memory hardware to provide the fastest possible memory for Alpha AXP systems. The VAX architecture requires that the memory subsystem handle unaligned data references transparently to software.

The Alpha AXP architecture places the burden for handling unaligned data references on software. When the hardware detects an unaligned data reference, it generates an exception that is delivered to software.

The OpenVMS AXP operating system implemented an exception handler that transparently does the required number of quadword fetches, shifts, and so on, to get the requested data and provide it to the requestor without any action on his or her part. Note that to provide better performance, this handler has been incorporated into the privileged architecture library (PALcode), which optionally reports any unaligned data exceptions to the operating system as it handles them.

Programmers need to understand that unaligned data references cause the same kind of synchronization problems that quadword granularity causes. In both cases, other data fields contained in the same quadword(s) can be read and rewritten. Only if multiple streams of execution are accessing data in the same quadword(s) is there a synchronization window that must be managed by the programmer.

18.6 READ-WRITE ORDERING

Another difference between the VAX and Alpha AXP architectures deals with the buffering of memory write operations by the memory subsystem. Better performance is achieved when a memory subsystem can delay writing cached data back to main memory at its discretion. For example, optimizations might include waiting for a spare memory bus cycle or combining two writes' adjacent data into a one write operation. One aspect of the VAX architecture caused many memory optimizations to be prohibited—the requirement that the memory subsystem preserve the order in which memory reads and writes are issued by software.

The design of memory caches plays a key role. A cache provides fast, temporary storage for memory data. The cache is loaded with data that the system expects a program to reference next. For example, when a program references a quadword of data, the memory hardware can load one or more additional quadwords into its cache for sequential addresses following the referenced quadword.

On a single CPU system, there is no other path to main memory except through the cache. Therefore, the hardware resolves all memory references first by checking for the data in the cache, which is the fastest access, and second by going all the way to main memory for data that is not in the cache. Data that is written can be placed in the cache by the hardware and not written immediately back to main memory as part of the performance optimizations in the memory subsystem. However, any references to that data will be resolved first from the cache, so the references never see stale data but always the latest value written.

However, on a multiprocessor system with multiple CPUs, each CPU has a unique path to main memory and its own cache along that path.

Data that is waiting in one CPU's cache cannot be seen by the other CPUs, since they have no path to the other caches, only to main memory. Every computer architecture must provide some way to make sure that data moves from cache to memory when requested, so that software can ensure there is no data waiting. For example, on VAX systems, the interlocked instructions cause any cached data to be flushed to memory and other memory references to wait until the data operation being synchronized is complete. Now let's consider what happens when the CPU decides it is time to write cached data back to main memory.

The VAX architecture requires that each CPU maintain the order of memory reads and writes, i.e., preserve read-write ordering. This means that if data field A is written first and then data field B, then all CPUs that see the new data in B will also see the new data in A. A program can never see new data in B and stale data in A. Thus, most VAX multiprocessor systems have complicated memory subsystems that can do some memory optimizations and also preserve read-write ordering.

RISC systems need extremely fast memory access time in order to keep the CPU fed with data and instructions. This means that you need a lean, mean memory subsystem, as fast as you can possibly make it. So, the Alpha AXP architects decided to allow reordering of memory reads and writes. In other words, Alpha AXP systems are not required to preserve read-write ordering.

Some programs can have hidden dependencies on read-write ordering. Take, for example, the image processing application. The processes belonging to the data collection module empty the data buffers and may do something like this:

1. Test the buffer's full flag.

2. If clear, go to 5.

3. If set, empty buffer.

4. After buffer is empty, clear the full flag.

5. Point to next buffer.

6. Go to 1.

The other half of the synchronization mechanism is in the data collection process that always fills the buffer with new data and then sets the full flag. Read-write ordering guaranteed that the processes emptying the buffers would always see good data in the buffer, if they saw the full flag set. This is called a hidden dependency on read-write ordering, as it is not explicitly coded anywhere into the algorithm through a mutual exclusive semaphore variable, interlocked instruction, or other mechanism. Such dependencies are broken on Alpha AXP multiprocessing systems, where the CPU can decide to flush the flag back to main memory before the data buffer.

Note that a dependency on read-write ordering is possible on multi-processing systems, not on single CPU systems. This is true because the cache is the coherency point on a single CPU system, while main memory is the coherency point on a multiprocessing system.

Identifying assumed synchronization of an OpenVMS application, you must first identify the data shared among multiple threads of execution and then examine each access to the data from the viewpoint of each thread.

To locate the threads of execution in your application, look for:

Use of parallel processing library routines (PPLRTL)

Condition handlers

User-written AST routines

Asynchronous system service usage, which can cause the system to generate AST threads on behalf of the process; $GETJPI, $QIO, and other system services use ASTs to copy data to the process's buffers

After determining the code threads that can potentially share data, examine the code carefully to determine what data each thread reads or writes. Global sections, in particular, indicate that data is being shared; therefore, code that issues $CRMPSC or $MGBLSC system services uses a global section that should be carefully examined.

Next, examine the code carefully to determine if another thread could view the data in an intermediate state and, if so, if that is important to the application or not. Note that in some cases, the exact value of the shared data may not be important if the application depends only on the relative value of the variable; a thread of execution may not care if it sees the data in an intermediate state, but only cares if the data is nonzero.

To determine if the threads of execution need synchronizing, ask the following questions:

- Is the operation performed on the shared data atomic from the viewpoint of other threads of execution?

- Is it possible to perform an atomic operation to the data type involved?

During the process of determining which threads of execution share data, remember to include unintentionally shared data because of its proximity to data that is accessed by other threads of execution. Also note that unintentionally shared data can result from ASTs generated by the OpenVMS operating system as a result of system services such as $QIO, $ENQ, or $GETJPI.

Because the OpenVMS AXP compilers use quadword granularity by default, all data items located within the same quadword as a data item updated by an asynchronous thread of execution can become unintentionally shared. For example, the OpenVMS compilers use quadword load instructions to access data items that are not aligned on natural boundaries by default.

Unaligned data is another cause of unintentionally shared data. For example, a compiler can issue two quadword loads to read an unaligned quadword. The VAX Executable Software Translator (VEST) is one tool for locating unaligned data; the Performance Coverage Analyzer (PCA) is another. Note that you cannot synchronize unaligned data, except by using some sort of semaphore for the quadwords containing it.

Solutions for synchronization issues are possible through VEST. Through the use of command qualifiers, VEST allows the translated versions of VAX applications to run on OpenVMS AXP systems with the same guarantee of atomicity that is provided on OpenVMS VAX systems. The /PRESERVE qualifier can be used to preserve three types of VAX architectural synchronization dependencies in translated VAX images: INSTRUCTION_ATOMICITY, MEMORY_ATOMICITY, and READ_WRITE_ORDERING.

The /PRESERVE=(INSTRUCTION_ATOMICITY) qualifier will ensure that an operation that can be performed atomically in a translated image runs on an OpenVMS AXP system.

The /PRESERVE=(MEMORY_ATOMICITY) qualifier will ensure that simultaneous updates to adjacent bytes within a longword or quadword can be accomplished without interfering with each other.

The /PRESERVE=(READ_WRITE_ORDERING) qualifier will ensure that read-write operations appear in the order you specify them. If you are migrating applications by recompiling for Alpha AXP systems, you may need to examine some of the following options:

- Align data on natural boundaries, sometimes moving separate fields into different aligned quadwords. If you cannot align the data in your OpenVMS application where multiple threads of execution share the same quadword, it may be necessary to redesign the application to use $ENQ and $DEQ system services or to create a mutex to protect the shared data.

- Redesign an application to use the interlocked instruction routines available in the LIB$ Run-Time Library facility to protect shared data.

- Use explicit synchronization primitives provided by some of the OpenVMS AXP compilers—e.g., language semantics or switches—in the application code wherever needed. For example, the DEC C compiler for OpenVMS AXP systems has enhanced the language semantics to implement the Memory Barrier (MB) instruction as a built-in function for an application that may need to force strict read-write ordering.

The Alpha AXP architecture applies atomicity constraints, and orders memory reads and writes, only when necessary to achieve fast performance. Therefore, you must use explicit synchronization rather than rely on assumptions of atomicity when migrating applications from OpenVMS VAX systems to OpenVMS AXP systems.

Applications that have multiple threads executing in parallel, and that contain various VAX architectural memory behavior dependencies, can require some modification to execute correctly on OpenVMS AXP systems. Depending on the application, it may be necessary to employ a few of the following techniques:

- Redesign the application to use the $ENQ and $DEQ system services to protect data shared by multiple threads of execution.

- Redesign the application to use the interlocked instruction routines available in the LIB$ Run-Time Library facility to protect shared data.

- Use explicit synchronization primitives provided by some of the OpenVMS AXP compilers, e.g., language semantics or switches.

- Use VEST to provide additional VAX architectural compatibility, such as for byte granularity, read-write ordering, or instruction atomicity.

- Align data on natural boundaries, sometimes moving separate fields into different aligned quadwords.

18.7   MACRO-32 ASSEMBLY LANGUAGE

OpenVMS kernel is written in the assembly language MACRO-32. The OpenVMS VAX MACRO-32 uses a precompiler on OpenVMS AXP to generate the native MACRO-32 code on OpenVMS AXP.

To a large extent, MACRO-32 on OpenVMS AXP precompiles the VAX MACRO-32 code remaining transparent to the user. But, when certain AXP dependencies occur in the code, the precompiler informs the user about a change that is required in the code. For example, consider Jump to Subroutine and return commands of VAX: JSB/RSB. On VAX, JSB keeps the return address on the top of the stack. RSB refers to this to return. System subroutines also often refer to and modify this address. This level of stack control is not possible from the precompiler. Also, the assembler that is ported from VAX to AXP conforms to the OpenVMS Calling Standard on Alpha AXP.

In VAX MACRO-32, a routine refers to its argument by an argument pointer register (AP) which points to an argument list built by the calling routine. On Alpha AXP, up to six routines are passed to the called routine in registers. Other additional arguments are passed in stack locations. Normally, the VAX MACRO-32 compiler transparently converts AP-based references to their correct Alpha AXP locations and converts the code which builds the list to initialize the arguments correctly. In some cases, the compiler cannot convert all references to their new locations, so an emulated arguments list must be constructed from the arguments received in the registers. This is required if the routine contains indexed references into the argument list or stores or passes the address of an argument list element to another routine.

The flow analysis of the MACRO-32 compiler on AXP behaves very similarly to any high-level language compiler. It notes the coding practices involving the argument list reference and optimizes them. It builds a flow graph for each routine and tracks stack depth through all paths in routine flow. This information is required to build correct and optimized code.

The VAX MACRO-32 compiler on AXP also supports both a subset of Alpha AXP instructions and PALcode calls and access to the 16-integer registers other than those mapped to the VAX register set. The instruction set of the compiler corresponds to those where an equivalent VAX instruction cannot be found or those which execute efficiently in the OpenVMS AXP environment. These constructs were required as OpenVMS AXP users' full 64-bit page table entries. The compiler includes some other optimizations which are important from the AXP architecture viewpoint. For example, a reference to an external symbol on Alpha AXP requires a load from a data region to obtain the symbol's address prior to loading the symbol's value (on VAX it is not so). Where possible, MACRO-32 reduces multiple loads of this address from the data region to a single load, or moves the load out of a loop to reduce memory references. Elimination of memory reads on multiple page references, register-based memory references, redundant register save/restore removal, and local code generation are some more examples of optimization. Peephole optimization of local code sequences and low-level instruction scheduling are performed by the compiler's back end. But, the compiler refrains from making certain optimization the high-level language compilers can afford to do. For example, in the assembly language the assumptions made by the programmer regarding the order of memory reads may not be manipulated by the compiler.

18.8 IMPORTANT ARCHITECTURAL DIFFERENCES IN THE OPENVMS KERNEL

Apart from synchronization, memory management, and I/O following architectural differences between VAX and Alpha AXP, memory reference are worth noting:

- Load/store architecture rather than atomic modify instructions
- Longword and quadword writes with no byte writes

- Read/write ordering not guaranteed
- Details of process context switching
- Alpha AXP does not have an architectural division between shared and process-private address space
- Alpha AXP's three-level page table structure allows the sharing of arbitrary subtrees of the page table structure and the efficient creation of large, sparse address spaces. (There is also the possibility of larger page sizes on future Alpha AXP processors.)

Although the smallest allowed page size of 8 KB results in an 8-gigabyte (GB) region for each level-2 page table. OpenVMS VAX emulation on OpenVMS AXP uses only 2 GB of each to keep within the OpenVMS VAX's 4-GB, 32-bit limit. Therefore each process will have a 2-GB process-private address region (VAX P0 and P1) and a 2-GB shared address region (VAX S0 and S1). This is done by giving each process a private level-1 page table (L1PT), which contains two entries for level-2 page tables (L2PTs). These two entries of L2PT are the shared and process-private entries for the shared system region and process-private address region, respectively. The L2PTs are selected to place the base address of the shared system region at

```
FFFFFFFF80000000 (hex)
```

which is the same as the sign-extended address of the top half of the VAX architecture's 32-bit address space.

The OpenVMS concept of mapping process page tables as a single array implementation in shared system space is retained in its emulation on AXP although it complicates the paging and address space creation mechanism. Unprivileged code is not affected by the memory management changes unless it is sensitive to the new page size. Also, privileged code is affected only if it has knowledge of the length or format of page table entries.

18.9   TRANSLATION BUFFER AND GRANULARITY HINT

The translation buffer (TB) is a CPU component that caches the result of recent successful virtual address translation of valid pages. Each TB entry caches one translation: a virtual page number—and a portion of its corresponding Page Frame Number (PFN), address space match, and protection bits. A TB is more like a cache memory to assist CPU access more quickly than physical memory.

An Alpha AXP TB supports what are called granularity hints by which a single TB entry can represent a group of pages that are virtually and physically contiguous. During system initialization, Open-VMS reserves physical memory and system address space for granularity hint regions for each of the following purposes:

- Base and executive images' nonpaged code
- Base and executive images' nonpaged data
- PFN-like database that is nonpaged dynamically allocated system data

The OpenVMS AXP kernel is made up of many separate images, each of which contains several regions of memory with varying protections. For example, there is read-only code, read-only data, and read-write data. Usually, a kernel image is loaded virtually contiguously and relocated so that it can execute at any address.

To take advantage of granularity hints, kernel code and data are loaded in pieces and relocated to execute from discontiguous regions of memory. OpenVMS AXP also uses the code region for user images and libraries. This covers customer applications and layered products in addition to OpenVMS-supplied images. This dramatically improves the performance on OpenVMS AXP.

On VAX systems, accessing control and status registers (CSRs) corresponding to I/O devices is done just like any other memory reference, but with few restrictions. Whereas Alpha presents a variety of CSR access models, the OpenVMS AXP operating system provides a number of routines that allow drivers to be coded as if CSRs were accessed by a mailbox, like several QIO system services are. Systems without a supporting mailbox concept are provided an emulation of CSR access. These routines provide independence from hardware implementation details at the cost of performance. But it makes drivers reusable on a number of systems.

The drivers provided an OpenVMS AXP solve AXP's lack of read-write ordering by inserting memory barriers where appropriate in order to force the ordering of read-writes.

Another important difference between VAX and AXP is that on AXP there is no interrupt stack. On VAX, it is a separate stack for system context. But, on AXP any system code must use the kernel stack of the current process. Hence, a process kernel stack must be large enough for the process and for any nested system activity. Relatively, this is an extra burden on OpenVMS AXP. Another problem is that the VAX I/O subsystem depends on absolute stack control to implement threads. As a result, most of the I/O code is in MACRO-32, which is a compiler language on the OpenVMS AXP system and does not provide absolute stack control. To solve this problem of stack control, OpenVMS AXP provides a kernel-threading package for system code at elevated IPLs.

SPEC Benchmark Name and Number	DEC 7000 Model 610 (182 MHz) SPECratio	VAX 7000 Model 610 (91 MHz) SPECratio	Relative Performance
001.gcc	67.5	34.9	1.93
008.espresso	94.7	28.8	3.29
013.spice 2g6	87.7	30.9	2.84
015.doduc	126.3	42.1	3.00
020.nasa7	293.0	67.2	4.36
022.li	100.2	34.7	2.89
023.eqntott	127.6	38.4	3.32
030.matrix300	1219.7	138.8	8.79
042.fpppp	193.8	48.8	3.97
047.tomcatv	276.5	61.6	4.49
SPECint89	95.1	34.0	2.80
SPECfp89	244.2	57.6	4.24
SPECmark89	167.4	46.6	3.59

Figure 18.1   SPEC benchmark results (Release 1).

OpenVMS System Service	CPU Time of AXP Relative to VAX CPU
Memory Management Services	
Create Virtual Address Space	0.97
Delete Virtual Address Space	0.69
Expand Address Region	0.63
Page Fault without I/O (Soft Page Fault)	0.95
Logical Name Services	
Translate a Logical Name	0.57
Event Flag Services	
Set an Event Flag	0.69
Clear an Event Flag	0.74
Process Control Services	
Create a Process and Activate an Image	0.85
File System Services (File on a RAM disk)	
File Open	0.75
File Close	0.83
File Create	0.81
File Delete	0.76
Record Management Services (RMS) (File on RAM disk)	
Get record from a Sequential File	1.02
Put record into a Sequential File	1.04

Figure 18.2   Performance of OpenVMS system services.

This package, known as *kernel processes,* provides a simple set of routines that support a private stack for any given thread. The routines include support for starting, terminating, suspending, and resuming a thread of execution. The private stack removes the requirements for absolute stack control and thus facilitates high-level language support in the I/O system. The stack is managed and preserved across the suspension with no overhead on the part of the execution thread.

18.10 SUMMARY

An understanding of byte addressability, synchronization, and memory alignment in Alpha AXP systems will help in designing applications that need to make good use of the RISC architecture.

The results of benchmark tests to compare VAX and AXP have been generally encouraging. (SPEC benchmark results are shown in Fig. 18.1. Test results on the performance of OpenVMS system services are shown in Fig. 18.2.) For example, the SPECmark89 shows that OpenVMS AXP Version 1.0 outplays OpenVMS VAX Version 5.2 by a factor of 3.59. For specific applications, this improvement in speed can be far better.

Glossary

Access modes The four modes of access in OpenVMS are the kernel, executive, system, and user modes. The user mode is least privileged and the kernel mode is most privileged.

Affinity The requirement that a process execute on a specific processor of a Symmetric Multiprocessor (SMP) system.

Alignment A datum of size 2^n bytes is said to be aligned if its byte address has n low-order zeros. Otherwise, the datum is unaligned.

Alpha AXP A 64-bit RISC architecture from Digital Equipment Corporation.

Asynchronous system trap (AST) A scheme during which the OpenVMS system can interrupt a program and transfer the control to a predefined subroutine to service the AST. After executing the AST subroutine, the control is returned to the interrupted program.

Atomicity A program instruction is said to be atomic if it cannot be interrupted when the execution of the instruction is in progress, i.e., no partial execution of the instruction is observed.

Balance set Processes resident in memory. This is in contrast to the processes that are swapped out of the memory.

Big-endian memory addressing A view of memory in which byte 0 of an operand contains the most significant (sign) bit of an integer.

Binary translation A software technique to change an executable program written for one architecture/operating-system pair into an equivalent program for a different architecture/operating-system pair.

Bucket An area in memory used as a buffer for storing data from an open relative or index file. This is used by RMS and its size can be a maximum of 63 blocks.

Buffered I/O I/O that uses a buffer (usually from a system pool buffer). This is in contrast with direct I/O.

Byte An 8-bit datum.

Byte granularity The appearance that two processors can update adjacent bytes in memory without interfering with each other.

Capability Represents a CPU attribute that a given process requires in order to execute. Generally a capability is a hardware feature. In an SMP system, a process's requirement for a particular capability may limit its execution to a subset of the available processors. For example, a process might require a capability to execute only on the primary processor.

CICS Complex instruction set computer, characterized by variable-length instructions, a wide variety of memory addressing modes, and instructions that combine one or more memory references with arithmetic. CISC designs express computation as a few complex steps.

Command file A file containing a set of DCL commands that is invoked using the @ command.

Command Line Interpreter (CLI) The interface between the user and the operating system. It accepts user commands, parses them, and passes the resultant command to the appropriate OpenVMS task for interpretation.

Console terminal The terminal which communicates with the CPU even when OpenVMS is not running. The console terminal is a privileged terminal from which the system manager can boot, shut down, and execute many other privileged commands.

Context switching The act of CPU switching from one process to another. It involves setting up CPU registers and performing some housekeeping operations.

DECnet Networking component of OpenVMS.

DECwindows DEC's implementation of the windowing system X-windows.

Demand zero paging A page initialized to zero when allocated during a page fault. The page is not written to the disk paging file during a write operation if the page has not been modified. This way, disk space is conserved and page faults are serviced faster.

Detached process A process that is created using either the RUN/DETACH command or the $CREPRC system service.

Event flag A bit used for achieving synchronization between two events.

Exceptions Interruptions like a fault or a trap that occur within the context of the executing process.

Exit handler A procedure that is executed prior to exiting from a program for performing some housekeeping operations.

Faults Interrupts that occur while executing an instruction. An example of a fault is an attempt to access nonexistent memory. The execution halts when a fault condition occurs.

Granularity On multiprocessor systems, the memory is said to be granular if independent write operations to adjacent aligned data produce consistent results. Byte, word, longword, quadword, and octaword granularity refer to writing 1-, 2-, 4-, 8-, and 16-byte adjacent data.

IEEE denormalized number (denormal) A floating-point number with magnitude between zero and the smallest representable normalized number. Numbers in this range are typically not representative in other floating-point arithmetic systems; such systems might signal an underflow exception or force a result to zero instead.

IEEE double-extended format A loosely specified floating-point format with at least 64 significant bits of precision and at least 15 bits of exponent width; typically implemented using a total of 80 or 128 bits.

IEEE dynamic rounding mode One of four different rounding rules.

IEEE floating point A form of computer arithmetic specified by IEEE standard 754. IEEE arithmetic includes rules for denormalized numbers, infinities, and not-a-numbers. It also specifies four different modes for rounding results.

IEEE infinity   An operand with an arbitrary, large magnitude.

IEEE not-a-number (NaN)   A symbolic entity encoded in a floating-point format. The IEEE standard specifies some exceptional results (like 0/0) to be NaNs.

Interlocked update   The property of memory update operations (sequences such as read-write-modify) on multiprocessor systems such that simultaneous independent updates to the same aligned datum will be consistent. This property causes serialization of the independent read-modify-write sequences and is not guaranteed for an unaligned datum.

Interrupt priority level (IPL)   One of the levels in which CPU can be executing. An IPL can range from 1 to 31. High-priority levels (toward IPL 31) can interrupt low-priority levels. The high-priority range (16 through 31) is reserved for hardware interrupts while the low-priority range (1 through 15) is used by software interrupts.

Latency   The number of cycles a program must wait to use the result of a previous instruction.

Lexical functions   A set of functions which can be called from DCL at a terminal or from DCL command files. They are used for finding information about processes, system, and files, and also to perform string operations.

License   Every product which is installed on OpenVMS has to be registered or made known to OpenVMS. This is done by the license that comes with the product authorizing the validity of the product.

Linear addressing   A memory addressing technique in which all addresses form a single range, from 0 to the largest possible address. Subscript calculations can create any address in the entire range.

Little-endian memory addressing   A view of memory in which byte 0 of an operand contains the least significant bit of an integer. From the religious wars of the Lilliputians as narrated in *Gulliver's Travels*.

Lock   One of the mechanisms used for synchronizing the events occurring at system resources.

Logical names   Symbolic names to identify devices, data structures, and other system resources. Some default logical names already exist in OpenVMS. New logical names can be defined.

Login directory   The directory defined by the logical name SYS$LOGIN. When logged in, the user's working directory will be this login directory by default.

Longword   A 32-bit datum.

Mailbox   Two or more processes communicate together using mailbox as a common area for information storage.

Multiple instruction issue   A high-performance computer implementation technique of starting more than one instruction at once. An implementation that starts (up to) two instructions at once is called dual-issue; four instructions, quad-issue or 4-way issue; and so on.

Octaword   A 128-bit datum.

Options file   OpenVMS linker options can be specified in a separate file called the options file.

P0 space   An area in the virtual address space where the program code and data of a given process reside.

P1 space   Stack, DCL tables, logical names, etc., reside in P1 space of the virtual address space.

Priority   OpenVMS assigns priorities to processes. The priority may range between 0 and 31. The priorities are used for scheduling processes.

Privileges   Parameters that permit and limit OpenVMS users to perform certain actions. For example, an operator would have the OPER privilege.

Procedure calling standard   A standard used in OpenVMS to allow programs written in one programming language to call routines written in another language. This standard also defines parameter types, parameter passing standard, and the scheme for returning status information from the routines.

Process   A unique environment defined by OpenVMS to distinguish between different users as well as program executions.

Process identification (PID)   A unique identification number defined for each process. It is a hexadecimal code with a length of 8 digits.

Processor status longword (PSL)   A 32-bit register used to show the CPU status.

Proxy account   Using the proxy account, one can access another node without specifying the passwords.

Quadword   A 64-bit datum.

Record Management Services (RMS)   A set of data structures and callable system functions used for efficient file processing in OpenVMS.

Rights identifier   The file SYS$SYSTEM:RIGHTSLIST.DAT contains the rights identifier for each user. It is used as a means of protecting software resources.

RISC   Reduced instruction set computer, characterized by fixed-length instructions, simple memory addressing modes, and a strict decoupling of load/store memory access instructions from register-to-register arithmetic instructions. RISC designs express computation as many simple steps.

Run-Time Library (RTL)   A set of callable programs that are interpreted at the run time.

Save set   The BACKUP utility makes use of save sets, which are files containing a set of RMS files.

Segmented addressing   A memory addressing technique in which addresses are broken into two or more segments. Subscript calculations can only be done within a single segment, and elaborate software techniques are needed to extend addressing beyond a single segment.

Spawn   A parent process can spawn a subprocess that shares the resources allocated to the parent process.

Spinlock   A lock shared by multiple CPUs in a multiprocessor system. It can be information associated with a single bit. A CPU waiting to acquire the lock that is used by another CPU will loop until the lock is released.

System services   A set of callable OpenVMS subroutines.

Thread   A piece or group of instructions accessing a memory location.

Trap   An interrupt within a program. The program, unlike a fault, can continue execution after the trap.

User authorization file (UAF)   The file SYS$SYSTEM:SYSUAF.DAT containing user accounts and other information for each user. It is used by the AUTHORIZE utility.

User identification code (UIC)   A pair of numbers associated with each user account. The first number indicates the actual user identification number, while the second number indicates the group to which the user belongs.

VAX dirty zero   A zero value represented with a nonzero fraction; must be converted to a true zero result.

VAX floating point   A form of computer arithmetic specified by the VAX architecture manual. VAX arithmetic includes rules for reserved operands and dirty zeros.

VAX reserved operand   A non-number that signals an exception when used as an operand in VAX floating-point arithmetic.

VAX word swapping   The rearrangement needed for the 16-bit pieces of a VAX floating-point number to put the fields in a more usual order; this is an artifact of the PDP-11 16-bit architecture.

Word   A 16-bit datum.

Word tearing   An aligned memory write operation on a multiprocessor system is said to have the property of word tearing if a read operation independent of the write operation can see partial results of the write operation.

Working set   The number of pages used by a process.

Bibliography

Anagnostopoulos, Paul C., *VAX/VMS. Writing Real Programs in DCL,* Digital Press, Bedford, Mass., 1989.

Brunner, R., ed., *VAX Architecture Reference Manual,* Digital Press, Bedford, Mass., 1991.

Bynon, D.W., and T.C. Shannon, *Introduction to VAX/VMS, 2d ed.,* Professional Press, Spring House, Pa., 1987.

Goldenberg, Ruth E., et al., *VAX/VMS Internals and Data Structures,* Digital Press, Bedford, Mass., 1991.

Goldenberg, Ruth E., and Saro Saravannan, *VMS for Alpha Platforms, Internals and Data Structures,* Digital Press, Bedford, Mass., 1992.

Malamud, Carl, *DEC Networks and Architectures,* McGraw-Hill, New York, 1989.

McCoy, Kirby, *VMS File Systems Internals,* Digital Press, Bedford, Mass., 1991.

Miller, David, *VAX/VMS Operating System Concepts,* Digital Press, Bedford, Mass., 1992.

OpenVMS Calling Standard, Digital Equipment Corporation, Maynard, Mass., 1992.

OpenVMS manuals and guides on programming languages, DCL, RMS, System Services, System Management, and Run-Time Library.

Peters, James F., and Patrick J. Holmay, *The VMS User's Guide,* Digital Press, Bedford, Mass., 1990.

Sawey, Ronald M., and Troy T. Stokes, *A Beginner's Guide to VAX/VMS Utilities and Applications,* Digital Press, Bedford, Mass., 1992.

Shaw, Jay, *VAX/VMS Concepts and Facilities,* McGraw-Hill, New York, 1990.

Sites, R., "Alpha AXP Architecture," *Communications of the ACM,* 36, 2, 1993.

Sites, R., et al., "Binary Translation," *Communications of the ACM,* 36, 2 (Feb. 1993).

Sites, R.L., ed., *Alpha Architecture Reference Manual,* Digital Press, Bedford, Mass., 1992.

Index

:= (assignment symbol), 46
! (comment symbol), 45
$ (DCL prompt), 45
$STATUS (global symbol), 62,63
<control-t> key, 14,15
<control-y> key, 14
@ (command), 46
Accessing symbols, 114
ACP, 151–152
Affinity, 184
Alignment, 239
Alpha:
   data format, 212
   data representation, 213
   data structures, 211–212
   instruction formats, 215
   instruction set, 212
   instruction types, 214
   processor state, 211–214
   virtual address components, 170
   virtual addresses, 171
ALTPRI, 179
ANALYZE/DISK, 199
ANALYZE/FDL, 128
AP register, 249
Appending records, 60
Architectural differences, 250–251
ASSIGN/TABLE command, 69
AST, 146,161–163
AST arguments, 162
Atomicity, 164
Atomic update, 241
AUDIT_SERVER, 198
AUTHORIZE Utility, 195

BACKUP, 201
Balance set, 21, 143

Batch process, 9
Battery-backed watch, 156
Binary overlays, 47
Binary translation, 228
Branching hints, 219
Branching instructions, 218–220
Bucket, 123
Byte-addressing mechanism, 212

CALL command, 46
CALL_PAL, 224
Capability, 184
CASE like structures in DCL, 49,
   52–53
CCB, 151
ccs_fab prototype, 121
ccs_rab prototype, 121
CDU Built-in-types, 97–98
CDU programming, 94
CEB, 149, 177
CEF, 148, 177
CHANGEABLE key, 125
Channel, 153
Cleanup actions, 144
Code generation, 229
COLPG state, 183
Command interpretation, 46
Command line editing, 15
Command procedure, 28
Command tables, 93–94
Common Link errors, 87–88
COMO state, 143
Compilation 80–83
   errors, 82
   information, 83
   warnings, 83
Compiler message format, 82

Compiler options, 81–82
    SHOW command, 82
Condition handling, 5
Conditions, 5, 188–189
Context switching, 186
CONVERT, 128
COPY command, 17
CREATE command, 24
CREATE/DIRECTORY, 196
CREATE/FDL, 127
CSR, 150
CTRL/Y interrupts, 63,64
CUR state, 180

Data alignment, 244–245
DCL commands, 25
Debugger:
    breakpoints, 104
    CANCEL BREAK, 105
    keypad functions, 102
    keypad mode, 103
    modes, 101
    rules, 114
    SET TRACE command, 105
    SHOW BREAK, 105
    STEP command, 103
    STEP command qualifiers, 104
    TRACE commands, 106
    watchpoints, 104
Debug options, 102
Debug SET MODE, 102
DEFINE/KEY, 113
DEFINE SYNTAX, 96
DEFINE/TRANSLATION, 70
DEFINE VERB command, 94
DELETE command, 18
DEPOSIT, 106
Detached process, 9
Device driver, 150
Device specification, 20
Device types, 20
DIRECTORY command, 15
DIRECTORY/FOLDERS, 133
DISALLOW clause, 98–99
Disk cluster, 122
DISMOUNT, 201
Display control, 111
DMA, 150
DO command (in SYSMAN), 200
DUMP format, 136
DUMP/RECORD, 137
Duplicate key, 125

EDIT/FDL, 127
Error handling, 61
Error messages, 19
EVALUATE, 106–107
EVE:
    buffers, 33
    editor features, 29–30, 32
    help, 39
    keypad functions, 34
    LEARN command, 37
    line commands, 33
    on VT200 terminals, 30
    place markers, 37
    procedures in, 38
    screen mode, 30
    spawning process in, 37
    TWO WINDOWS command, 36
    windows, 36
Event flags, 147
EXAMINE, 106–110
Examining arrays, 115
Exceptions, 5
EXTRACT, 131

Fatal bugcheck, 205
Fatal error in compilation, 82
Fault, 188
FDL, 126
FDT, 151
File protection, 24, 125
File specification, 21
Fill factor, 126
Floating-point arithmetic, 218
Floating-point trap, 222
FOE, 231
Folders, 133
FOR loop, 114
FPG state, 182, 175

Global symbols, 147
GRANT/IDENTIFIER, 197
Granularity, 242
Granularity hint, 172, 251–254
Granularity hint regions, 172

Hardware context, 7, 178
Hardware interface register, 150
HIF, 232

IAC, 234
IF-ELSE condition, 113
If-then-else in DCL, 48,49

IIF, 232
Image activator, 166
Indexed files, 125
INITIALIZE, 201
Initializing, 108
Input/Output:
    errors, 60,61
    post processing, 153
    processing, 153–154
    space, 150
    system services, 152
Instruction atomicity, 234
Instruction guarantees, 232
Interactive process, 9
Interface register, 150
Interrupts, 189–190
Interval timer, 156
IPL, 178
IRP, 150
ITB_ENTRIES, 172
Iterations, 64

JIB, 143

Keypad input, 113

Latency, 218
Layers of executive, 166
LEF state, 180
Lexical functions, 72–77
    for file information, 74
    for process information, 74,75
    for string manipulation, 76,77
    for system information, 75,76
LIB$FREE_EF, 148
LIB$GET_EF, 148
Limits, 8
Link command format, 84
Linkage section, 160
Linker:
    /BRIEF qualifier, 86
    /CROSS_REFERENCE qualifier, 86
    defaults, 85
    /FULL qualifier, 86
    /LIBRARY option, 86
    map information, 87
    /MAP qualifier, 86
    options, 84
Linking, 83–88
Load and Store, 210,216
LOAD_SYS_IMAGES, 172
Local event flag, 180

Lock management, 146
Logical name:
    commands, 73
    group level, 68
    job level, 68
    process level, 67,68
    system level, 68
    tables, 68–72
Login procedure, 5

Macro-32, 249
Mail characteristics, 131–133
MAIL:
    command line, 130
    commands, 132
Mailbox, 154
MBDRIVER, 154
Memory barrier instruction, 210
Memory barriers, 164
MERGE/KEY, 135
MOUNT/EXTENSION qualifier, 122
Mutex, 165

NETACP, 151
Network process, 9
Nonspanning records, 124–125
/NOOPTIMIZE qualifier, 107
NOTES information classes, 138

ON command, 61,62
Onion layer structure, 4
OPEN/APPEND command, 56
OPEN command in DCL, 53–56
OPEN/READ command, 54
OPEN/WRITE command, 54–56
OpenVMS differences, 235–236
Operate instructions, 217
/OPTIMIZE qualifier, 107
OPTIMIZER, 107
Owner count value, 165

P0, 7, 173, 176
P1, 7, 173, 176
Page, 10
Page fault, 10
Page sizes in Alpha, 172
Page table structure, 171
Paging, 10, 174
PAK, 199
PALcode, 209,222
    library, 220–225
    routines, 221

PALmode, 224
Parameter passing, 91–92
  by descriptor, 91–92
  by reference, 91
  by value, 91
Password, 13
PC, 212
PCB, 6, 143, 149, 212
PFN, 176
PFW state, 174, 182
PHD, 149, 175
PHONE commands, 135
Pixscan mechanism, 180,185
Preprocessor states, 214
/PRESERVE=FLOATING_
  EXCEPTIONS, 235
/PRESERVE=INSTRUCTION_
  ATOMICITY, 234
/PRESERVE=MEMORY_ATOMICITY,
  235
/PRESERVE=READ_WRITE_
  ORDERING, 235
PRINT command, 18
Priority, 7
Priority adjustment, 180
PRIORITY_OFFSET, 180
Privileges, 7
Procedure descriptor, 160
Process:
  creation, 144
  priority, 178
Process control services, 145
Process private space, 169
Program:
  locations, 115
  variables, 106
PSW, 212
PTEs, 170
PURGE command, 18

QIO, 150
Quantum, 9
Quotas, 8

RAB, 121
READ command, 56,57
Read-write ordering, 245–249
RECALL/ALL command, 26
Record formats, 118–119
Record locking, 125
Recursion, 65
RENAME command, 17
Rescheduling events, 184

Resolving references, 116
Rights identifiers, 196
RIGHTSLIST.DAT, 195
RISC architecture, 210
RMS data structures, 119–121
RMS functions, 119–120
RS instruction, 234
RTL, 90–92
RUN command, 88
Run-time symbol, 114
RWMBX, 183

SAVEDUMP, 205
SCB, 192
Screen mode commands, 112
SEARCH, 111, 131
SEARCH qualifiers, 137
SEND, 130
Sequential files, 117
SET AUDIT, 198
SET COMMAND, 94
SET commands, 24
SET COMMAND/TABLE option, 96
SET COPY_SELF, 132
SET EDITOR, 130
SET ENVIRONMENT, 200
SET MESSAGE command, 83
SET PERSONAL_NAME, 131
SET PROCESS/NAME, 160
SET PROCESS/PRIORITY, 179
SET PROMPT command, 23
SET SCOPE, 110
SET TIME, 155
SET TIME command, 18
SHARE privilege, 153
Sharing the file I/O, 56
SHOW commands, 22
SHOW/LOGICAL command, 69
SHOW SYSTEM, 183
Shutdown tasks, 201
SIF, 232
SIRR, 191
Soft tick, 156
Software condition, 187
Software context, 7
Software devices, 20
Software interrupts, 191
Software ISRs, 192–193
SORT/KEY, 135
Sort key data types, 136
Spanning records, 124–125
Spawning DCL commands, 113
SPEC benchmark results, 253

Spinlock, 164
  acquiring, 164
  releasing, 165
Standard logical name tables, 69
Stream I/O, 155
Strict read-write ordering, 232
Subprocedures in DCL, 49,52
Subprocess, 9
Subroutines in DCL, 49,52
Substring overlays in DCL, 47
Swapper, 174
Swapping, 11, 174
Symbol substitution, 46
Synchronization problems, 240
Synchronization techniques, 163
SYS$COMMAND, 68
SYS$ERROR, 68
SYS$INPUT, 68
SYS$OUTPUT, 68
SYSPARAM module, 167
System components, 211
System service performance, 253
System services:
  $ASSIGN, 151,153
  $CANTIM, 157
  $CANWAK, 157
  $CREMBX, 154
  $DASSGN, 153
  $DASSGN, 181
  $DCLAST, 162
  $ENQ, 3, 18, 162
  $GETJPI, 179
  $GETTIM, 155
  $HIBER, 180
  $IMGACT, 166
  $QIOW, 153
  $RESUME, 182
  $SCHDWK, 156, 157
  $SETACL, 197
  $SETAST, 162
  $SETEF, 149
  $SETIME, 155
  $SETIMR, 156, 157
  $SETPRI, 179
  $SETPRN, 160

System services (Cont.):
  $SUSPND, 181
  $WAITFR, 149
System space, 169
System tuning, 203
SYSUAF.DAT, 195

Terminal server, 14
Thread, 240
TIE, 228, 230–233
Time keeping, 156
Timer support, 155
Traceback information, 81
Translated images, 230
Translation attributes, 71
Translation buffer (TB), 170, 172,
  251–254
Translator performance, 236
Traps, 188
Type-ahead buffer, 26

UAF, 143
UCB, 152
UIC, 195
Untranslatable images, 233
Updating records in DCL, 58, 59
User account, 6, 13
User account database, 197

VAX compatibility, 227
  instructions, 222
VCB, 152
VEST, 209, 210, 227–230
VEST performance, 233
Virtual address space, 7, 172
VIRTUALPAGECNT, 173

WHILE-DO loop, 114
Wildcard, 16
Working set, 10
Working set dynamics, 175
WRITE command, 57,58
WSLE, 176
WSQUOTA, 176

XQP, 179

ABOUT THE AUTHOR

Raj Bhargava has over 15 years of software engineering and application development experience. His association with VMS began in 1984. He studied at MIT and the universities of Bangalore and Mysore. He has a masters degree in computational mathematics. He has worked as a computer scientist in India's Raman Research Institute, and as a consultant with Digital Equipment Corporation, Corning Labs, Hoechst, and other industries.